The

GUSTAV MAHLER
The Conductors' Interviews

edited by
Wolfgang Schaufler

GUSTAV MAHLER
The Conductors' Interviews

UE 26311
ISMN 979-0-008-08493-5
UPC 8-03452-06873-0
ISBN 978-3-7024-7162-0

© Copyright 2013 by Universal Edition A.G., Wien

Interviews: Wolfgang Schaufler
Cover Design: Stefan Fallmann
Illustrations: Peter M. Hoffmann
Photo Gustav Mahler: Moritz Währ
Layout: www.vielseitig.co.at
Proofread by Clare Clarke and Grant Chorley

Content

7	Foreword
9	Reinhold Kubik
	"The company does its work in grand style" –
	Gustav Mahler and Universal Edition
14	Claudio Abbado
	"Mahler is the bridge to the modern era"
20	Daniel Barenboim
	"I began to conduct Mahler out of spite"
30	Herbert Blomstedt
	"Mahler must have been a great man"
38	Pierre Boulez
	"One cannot refer to the biography to explain the music"
48	Riccardo Chailly
	"Mahler's *First* was the great emotion of my youth"
56	Christoph von Dohnányi
	"Mahler composed inwardly"
64	Gustavo Dudamel
	"Wow, Mahler!"
70	Christoph Eschenbach
	"Mahler is certainly the greatest symphonist ever"
78	Daniele Gatti
	"Mahler should be performed simply and humbly"
84	Valery Gergiev
	"Mahler's *Seventh* made me sleepless"
92	Michael Gielen
	"Bernstein turned Mahler into kitsch"
100	Alan Gilbert
	"In New York he was kind of giving up"
108	Bernard Haitink
	"I always found Mahler alarming"
116	Manfred Honeck
	"The rubato is essential when conducting Mahler"
124	Mariss Jansons
	"With Mahler you have to give everything"

132	Lorin Maazel
	"I would never have asked him anything"
140	Zubin Mehta
	"I would love to ask him a thousand questions"
150	Ingo Metzmacher
	"Mahler is my point of reference"
158	Kent Nagano
	"Mahler was a pioneer – not only a radical"
166	Andris Nelsons
	"Mahler wanted to show the world: I have a problem!"
174	Jonathan Nott
	"Frozen for eternity in death"
180	Sakari Oramo
	"Mahler controls chaos"
188	Sir Antonio Pappano
	"Mahler wanted to live, that's the whole point!"
194	Josep Pons
	"Mahler is more contemporary now than in 1910"
202	Sir Simon Rattle
	"Mahler is the reason why I'm a conductor today"
212	Esa-Pekka Salonen
	"Mahler embraced everything that exists"
220	Michael Tilson Thomas
	"Jump! Cut! Bang!"
228	Franz Welser-Möst
	"Mahler was like an earthquake for me"
234	David Zinman
	"Mahler is a universe in itself"
241	Conductors' biographies
247	Gustav Mahler – short biography
249	Index of names

Foreword

In 1960, public interest in the 100th anniversary of Mahler's birth was at best *moderato*. There were performances, but Mahler was still a marginal figure in the repertoire. "One forgets how off-centre Mahler was at the time", recalls Simon Rattle. Musicians struggled with Mahler rather than play his music gladly. Alfred Einstein (1880–1952) exemplifies the situation: " … out of emotion grew more and more exhibition: at the end of the century, exhibition as strong as with Tchaikovsky or Gustav Mahler."

Mahler was relegated to a period of decay; even the post-war avant-gardists found no approach to him for a long time. At an earlier date, Pierre Boulez numbered Mahler among those "minding the shop of passé Romanticism … adipose and degenerate", ripe for "apoplexy due to excess expressive pressure". Zubin Mehta recalls how even students of musicians who had played under Mahler told him when he was a young student in Vienna that Mahler had merely copied from others – epigone art, not worth talking about.

But now, more than 50 years later, things are fundamentally different; esteemed as a seismograph of the century, Mahler developed into a virtual cult. He became acceptable to the masses, the number of performances of his music vying with those of Beethoven. There are some who wish to defend Beethoven against Mahler, recalling how uninterruptedly revolutionary he was in pondering the *conditio humana*, the circumstances of the individual and of society.

So what happened? This book attempts to find answers based on interviews with the great Mahler conductors of the present day. Originally, the intention was to ask all conductors the same five questions – but the topic of Mahler soon turned out to be an emotionally charged one and a wealth of stories and experiences emerged that are worth keeping for the record. Questions were deliberately repeated in order to make room for comparisons: When did the conductors hear Mahler for the first time? Was his world immediately accessible to them? When did they begin to conduct Mahler?

Issues such as subjective *espressivo* versus objective structure, Romantic tradition and utopian vision loom larger with Mahler than with any other composer; how do they rehearse Mahler? Where do they place the main focus – and why? Which positioning of the players is most advantageous? Are there particularities in terms of practical performance? How did the Mahler renaissance develop in different countries? Unease, feverishness, inner conflict shortly before World War I broke out: Are the Mahler clichés aiming into empty space or did he in fact anticipate the catastrophes of the 20th century, as Leonard Bernstein believed? This question elicited exceedingly contradictory responses. Which role did anti-Semitism play?

Does Mahler touch a nerve in people today with his loneliness and deracination, his search for meaning and yearning for a long-gone paradise? Does Mahler provide a release for *Weltschmerz* and the feeling that life is fractured? Is that what Mahler wanted? Is that why he is so hugely successful today? And what about his sense of irony?

Mahler's scores are densely strewn with agogic markings and other performance instructions. Did he burst open the door to the 20th century in composing that way? How much influence did he have on Schönberg and his circle? – and, conversely, how much did Wagner and Bruckner influence Mahler? Finally: Who was this "foreign confidant" exactly? Is his music an aural biography? What would the conductors have asked Mahler?

Such questions can of course never be exhaustively answered. The intensity of some of the interviews was astonishing though, as were some of the contradictions, which will hopefully prove illuminating to the reader.

One thing has become clear during the conductors' imaginary discussion: Mahler will continue to occupy us well into the 21st century.

I am deeply indebted to the conductors for being so generous with their time and for offering an unadulterated view of their work.

Wolfgang Schaufler

"The company does its work in grand style" – Gustav Mahler and UE

By Reinhold Kubik

> *Dear friend,*
> *A company here is taking over the publishing of my three symphonies – they're also printing the entire (!) orchestra material. What about the plates of the C minor Symphony? I was so bold as to declare them my own. Just now, the publisher told me to cause the plates to be delivered to Röder. And it occurred to me that I would still have to ask my two patrons about it. Therefore, dear friend, would you be so kind as to take the necessary steps with friend Berkan and Röder? – and, incidentally, what do you say to all of this? […] Yours, Gustav Mahler*

This letter, which Mahler sent to his friend Hermann Behn from Vienna on 13 January 1898, is the oldest known record of his collaboration with the Vienna publishing industry. It requests the engraver's plates of the *2nd Symphony*, stored at the Röder company in Leipzig and paid for by Mahler's friends Hermann Behn and Wilhelm Berkan in Hamburg. Of course, "a company here" does not refer to Universal Edition (which was founded in 1901); the firm in question is the music engraver Eberle & Co. [Vienna] VII, Seidengasse 3, about which Mahler writes in a letter dated 21 January:

> *The company does its work in grand style; they have already printed all of Bruckner, they are going to print all of my stuff and even have piano reductions made and engrave the orchestra parts.*
>
> *Eberle & Co. are just an engraving firm à la Röder, with colossal operating capital (stock corporation for improving Austrian publishing), which chooses its own publishers.*
>
> *Döblinger [sic] will probably get my works.*
>
> *Propagation is being done in grand style.*

However, the *2nd Symphony* was published by Weinberger, not Doblinger. Josef Weinberger had founded a publishing house in 1890; Mahler had already signed a contract with them on 27 September 1897 for the *Lieder eines fahrenden Gesellen* [*Songs of a Wayfarer*], followed by an agreement dated 12 August 1898, on which basis Weinberger presented *Symphonies 1, 2* and *3*, as well as *Das klagende Lied* [The Song of Lamentation] as of 1899; Doblinger initially received only the *4th Symphony* (1902).

In 1976, Alfred Schlee sketched the founding of Universal Edition this way:
Universal Edition was born into the 20th century as a true child of the German industrial boom of the 1870s. Specialists in the music-printing business considered it the nation's duty to wrest classical music born and bred during the Imperial and Royal Monarchy period from foreign publishers. It was not until a few years later, when the prematurely anticipated success had not yet materialised and the founders had passed the enterprise on to a young, enthusiastic layman, that UE gained the profile now known throughout the world.

The "specialists in the music-printing business" included publishers who had released Mahler's early works: Waldheim (Josef Stritzko), Weingartner and Doblinger (Bernhard Herzmansky Sr), all of whom were founding members of UE; all of them ceded rights, engraver's plates and printed inventory to the new publisher (including Mahler's first four symphonies and *Das klagende Lied*). Thus, UE was able to amalgamate Mahler as part of its catalogue at a time when actual collaboration between the publisher and the Court Opera director had not yet begun.

The ultimate cooperation was thanks to a "young, enthusiastic layman" named Emil Hertzka (1869–1932), who was elected to UE's Supervisory Board in 1907 and named its director in 1909. In June of that year, Hertzka signed an initial contract with Mahler, acquiring the rights to his 8th Symphony; the publisher acquired the 9th Symphony and *Das Lied von der Erde* [*The Song of the Earth*] the following year. Thus, UE initially handled Mahler's early works from other publishers and, as of 1909, the late pieces which UE acquired through Hertzka's initiative.

In the meantime, Mahler was obliged to look around for other publishers; the 5th Symphony went to Peters and the 6th and some important Lieder to Kahnt (both in Leipzig), the 7th to Bote & Bock in Berlin – apparently UE was not interested in acquiring new Mahler works between 1906 and 1909. But that changed when Hertzka arrived, resulting in respectful, close and even amicable contact between publisher and composer; that is the only explanation for the riders which UE agreed to add to the publishing contract with Mahler regarding the revisions which exclusively concerned the composer's artistic wishes (not the publisher's commercial interests):

[...] regarding my aforementioned four symphonies, you have agreed to undertake to enter the changes which I have made to them since they were published, at your expense, into all plates of the full score[s] and orchestra parts, and to align the inventory material destined for sale or

hire with the now definitively established full score[s]. However, these changes may not be invoiced as new manufacturing costs.

Yet contrary to this contractual negotiation, UE continued to deliver outdated materials for those works for years, entailing many misunderstandings because the labelling (title, copyright notices, etc.) did not correspond to the actual content. In 1955, Erwin Ratz began a complete critical edition in an attempt to clarify and organise the facts, meanwhile struggling with the still predominating reservations against Mahler. It was only the New Complete Critical Edition, begun in 1992, which succeeded in applying the general philological and editorial standards to Mahler as well.

Mahler's most important contact person at UE was probably Josef Venantius von Wöss (1863–1943), a composer and the publisher's lector, who had done highly satisfactory work for Mahler at Weinberger, where he had prepared the piano reduction of *Das klagende Lied*. While working as a proofer at Eberle he had supervised UE's takeovers of *Symphonies 1–4* and made the piano reduction of the 4th, before switching to UE in 1908, where he prepared the piano reduction of the 8th.

Hertzka even tried – without success – to bring Mahler back to Vienna from America; the composer's early death put an end to their promising collaboration. Up until then, updating his works had been Mahler's great concern. (After resigning from his post at the Court Opera, he revised his 1st, 2nd and 4th *Symphonies*, largely in connection with performances of each.) Around 1910 he provided the publisher with full scores which he had revised over the years, to be used for new editions, typically labelling them "the only corrected and authentic one" (the 2nd) and "corrected and approved for reprinting" (the 1st).

One of Mahler's last letters arrived at the publisher's on 21 February 1911 from New York, the day on which he conducted the final concert of his life. Writing to "Dear Mr Director" Hertzka about a revised edition of his 4th, he said, "Dear friend, please carefully ensure that my symphonies are only published in their retouched form. The [amendments] I've made to the 4th have proved to be terrific here [...] The mistakes in the [orchestra] parts of the 4th are unbelievable – I am convinced that a new impression is indispensable."

UE published *Das Lied von der Erde* and the 9th *Symphony* after Mahler died, as well as a facsimile edition of the draft full score of the 9th; UE also took part in various attempts to evaluate the sketches of the 10th. Thereafter, the years up to 1938 were relatively good ones for Mahler's music, with UE doing its part in marketing it.

Thus, as part of the Corona Collection series, a three-volume set of "Mahler Symphonies – Famous Movements" was published, arranged for piano two hands by Ernst Rudolph, the edition remarkably numbering 6,000 copies per volume. Mahler's widow Alma also profited from this marketing, of course; she was able to acquire a small palazzo in Venice, Casa Mahler (even if it took financial support from her new paramour Franz Werfel) as well as the house in Breitenstein in Austria's Semmering area. For years and years, she bombarded UE with letters, both critical and demanding, but, although their relationship was not without friction, it carried on in a due and proper manner until Alma's death.

UE also played a major role in the foundation of the International Gustav Mahler Society; to this day, the two are jointly active in furthering Mahler's art by issuing scholarly, reworked publications (the New Critical Edition) of his music. The fact that Mahler's works have now become commercially as well as artistically successful is an indication of how positively his reception has developed, certainly due not least to the publisher's efforts on his behalf.

Reinhold Kubik is Vice President of the International Gustav Mahler Society; from 1992 to 2012 he directed the Complete Critical Edition of Mahler's works.

Claudio Abbado

"Mahler is the bridge to the modern era"

Do you remember the first time you heard Mahler's music?

Abbado: Yes, certainly. It was the 4th *Symphony*, with Bruno Walter, and I believe Kathleen Ferrier was the soloist. I also remember Mahler concerts with Leonard Bernstein and Dimitri Mitropoulos. Their interpretations differed greatly; each of them had a strong personality.

Did you ever have a chance to talk with Bruno Walter about Mahler?

Abbado: No. I only sang under him in the chorus, together with Zubin Mehta – and it was the Mozart *Requiem*, not Mahler. Walter was quite old at the time; we were always waiting for the interval, so that we could perhaps talk with him briefly. Most of the time he sat there quietly, a smile on his face – so I didn't want to disturb him.

Did Mahler figure in your studies in Italy?

Abbado: Everything happened later in Italy. For instance, I gave the first performances of Bruckner symphonies there. Let's not forget that Mahler and Mendelssohn were forbidden during Fascism. Of course, I was studying the music and listening to it during that time.

Toscanini never conducted Mahler.

Abbado: No, and what a shame. He would certainly have conducted Mahler intriguingly. But unfortunately, he and Mahler had that confrontation in New York about conducting *Tristan*.

You are the first great Italian conductor to take on Mahler.

Abbado: No. Don't forget Carlo Maria Giulini – he was terrific.

When Herbert von Karajan invited you to the Salzburg Festival for the first time in 1965, you said at once that you wanted to conduct Mahler's 2nd. You had just turned 32 then. Do you remember that?

Abbado: Yes. He extended the invitation to me in Berlin. I had just conducted the Radio Symphony Orchestra. He wanted me to do the Cherubini *Requiem* in Salzburg. I said that it was wonderful music, but how would it be if I did a Mahler symphony? He thought about it for all of two seconds before saying, "Excellent idea."

I didn't yet know at the time that Karajan was being criticised in Salzburg for not conducting any Mahler. So for him, it was a good thing for a young conductor to perform Mahler.

He didn't begin to conduct Mahler until later – much later, actually. I think it was the *5th Symphony* he performed first.

Did Karajan come to your concert?

Abbado: He was at the dress rehearsal.

In fact, you were taking a big risk with that concert – not everyone has the courage to make his Salzburg debut with Mahler's 2nd.

Abbado: Yes, that's true. But you know, I had already studied it when I was Bernstein's assistant in New York and I also rehearsed it for Lenny. I led the offstage orchestra and I was used to doing it by memory. He asked me why I was conducting by memory, and I replied, "Do you really think I would come to the New York Philharmonic without being prepared?" If I conduct something and I haven't memorised it, that means I don't know the score well enough.

How many rehearsals did you have in Salzburg? Mahler was still nowhere to be seen in the Vienna Philharmonic's repertoire.

Abbado: I told Karajan at the outset that I would need more than three rehearsals. I think there were five in all.

What did Bernstein say to you about Mahler?

Abbado: He thought he was Mahler, his reincarnation. That's understandable.

How much did your conducting professor Hans Swarowsky influence you with regard to Mahler?

Abbado: He was a truly great teacher. We learned how to coordinate our hands independently. He gave us an excellent technique for analysing and expressing musical architecture. He insisted that we use our gestures sparingly. It was quite amusing when Zubin and I saw him conduct at the opera because his gestures were huge. The important thing we learned was to shape large arcs without forgetting the details. You need that all the time in music, not just with Mahler.

You once talked about how important it was for your understanding of Mahler to see a funeral procession on the street in Vienna.

Abbado: Yes, that was a very significant experience. It was on Rennweg, the street leading to the cemetery. A funeral procession was passing by; there was a band, the people dressed in mourning black, a catafalque – everything happened very slowly. It was like Mahler – a funeral cortège. It was in the 1950s; I think the practice stopped in the 60s.

Mahler lived on Rennweg for over 10 years. He must have known those funeral processions.

Abbado: He certainly did. He lived at the top of the street. There was a restaurant with cheap student fare close by. We ate there – not much and not well. But it was our regular haunt.

Bernstein said that we wouldn't really understand Mahler until after the disasters of the 20th century. Do you agree?

Abbado: Yes, certainly. Mahler sensed what was to come. He was very perceptive. But you can say that about Alban Berg as well. Take his *Three Pieces for Orchestra*, the last movement; that's music for or about a catastrophe. It's more dramatic than Mahler's 6th.

How do you view Mahler's personality?

Abbado: He knew everything about love and death. He had an incredibly large soul, a huge empathetic heart.

Mahler lost a brother, a victim of suicide.

Abbado: That event was crucial; I'm sure of it. It was the first stroke of fate. I don't think many people realise how calamitously his brother's death affected him.

What is the most important advice you would give to a young Mahler conductor?

Abbado: Study, keep studying, immerse yourself, and bring your own experiences, your own personality into the music. Everyone confronts love and death in life. Besides, there's always something new to be discovered in musical scores; we can never know exactly what Mahler really wanted.

You have conducted the 9th more often than any other Mahler symphony.

Abbado: I didn't know that. Maybe that's because we often played it on tour. It's easier to realise. It's a monument, of course.

Does Mahler open the door to a new aesthetic at the end of the 9th?

Abbado: Yes, but not only there. He is the bridge to the modern era – Schönberg wrote that. Mahler opened the door to modern music. I see the final pages of the 9th as Mahler's death. He disappears.

In Lucerne, you conducted the Scherzo of the 4th without a baton. I had never seen you do that before. Have you found a new approach to some movements over the years?

Abbado: I have no idea; it wasn't a conscious decision. Of course, I hope I'm still discovering new things as the years pass. Mahler very often writes in the style of chamber music; we mustn't overlook that. I recall Mitropoulos saying, "Look into my eyes." He didn't conduct with his hands; now and then he gave a cue, but he conducted the rest with his eyes. The most important thing is to create an atmosphere for the musicians – and you can do that with your eyes.

What would you have asked Mahler?

Abbado: [*long pause*] I would have tried to listen to what he said.

Are there questions about his scores you would like to have answered?

Abbado: Of course. He was always rearranging everything, and he didn't manage to do that with other works. I'm sure he would have changed some things yet again. It was always his principle to hear his works first and then to improve them – but with the 9th, for instance, that was not possible.

Like Mahler, you were director of the Vienna State Opera. Did you occasionally have the feeling that history was repeating itself in Vienna?

Abbado: Vienna is a wonderful city – ideal, in fact. Great concert halls, superlative orchestras. But they are sometimes conservative – Mahler knew very well that it would take time for his music to be accepted here.

(Vienna, 01/10/2011)

Daniel Barenboim

"I began to conduct Mahler out of spite"

Do you remember the first time you heard Mahler's music?

Barenboim: Not exactly. I remember playing the songs with Dietrich Fischer-Dieskau in the early 70s, when we did the *Wunderhorn-Lieder, Lieder eines fahrenden Gesellen* [*Songs of a Wayfarer*] and the *Rückert-Lieder*: all except the *Kindertotenlieder* [*Songs on the Death of Children*] because they were not originally written for piano. The first Mahler symphony I conducted was the 5th, in 1973. I came quite late to Mahler.

Do you remember a concert that opened your ears to Mahler's world?

Barenboim: No, rather the opposite. I remember many concerts that made me dislike it even more because I found, in the Mahler concerts I had heard, two extremes of realisation. One was overemotional, in the sense that the music was used as an excuse for self-expression on the part of the conductor, even if it was sometimes done at a very high level. The other withdrew from any kind of emotional content, making it rather dry.

I was 'allergic' to what I found at that time to be artificialities in the music. I also disliked – I'm deliberately being very negative here – the fact that Mahler was, and still is, the only composer to be discussed mostly in non-musical terms. Whenever somebody says "I don't like Mahler" or "I love Mahler", it usually has to do with a psychoanalytical take on his music: Sigmund Freud and all that. And I think it's terrible. You would never think or talk about Beethoven like that, about his deafness or anything else, or about Chopin's tuberculosis. In other words, a composer's life and musical diary – and the oeuvres of all great composers are musical diaries – are not really related. Beethoven wrote some of the most positive music at a time of complete distress, and vice versa.

How did your opinion change?

Barenboim: Little by little – even when I thought I didn't like it – I became interested in so many details of his orchestration, his keen attention to dynamics.

Mahler was probably the first composer who consistently wrote specific dynamics for every instrument.

Very often, he wrote the same music, the same notes, for different groups of instruments, with opposing dynamics.

Barenboim: Absolutely. You have the same notes, but you have, for instance, the clarinets starting fortissimo and making a diminuendo, and at the same time in unison, the violas starting pianissimo and making a crescendo to fortissimo. So you have the line more or less sustained on one level of volume, but with a complete change of colour. Rather than being artifice, which is what I had initially thought, this aspect, I realised then, was in fact indicative of his complexity.

And that was what drew me more and more to Mahler – although I must mention my involvement with Wagner. His influence on Mahler is very often ignored. One only talks about Mahler's Jewish origins, Klezmer music and psychoanalysis, etc., but basically, without Wagner there would have been no Mahler. And the most interesting thing about Mahler is that he really had one foot in the past and one in the future, one foot in Wagner's world and the other in Schönberg's, and as such was a great transitional figure.

He wrote with a historical modernism, which I would say is almost unique because it was linked to a very old-fashioned sense of form. The Mahler symphonies are old-fashioned in that they started with Haydn and Mozart, then evolved through Beethoven, Schumann, Brahms and Bruckner. And you find yourself with this strange combination of an enlarged 18th-century structure with a 20th-century content and a 19th-century musical idiom. So in effect, Mahler's complexity and its greatest appeal to me is that it is, in a way, the culmination of three centuries of musical thinking.

The Mahler renaissance did not begin until the late 60s ...

Barenboim: ... with Bernstein in America and Barbirolli in Europe. One must not underestimate Barbirolli's importance as a Mahler conductor. He was less famous than Bernstein, and had less appeal to the general public, but he was the conductor who brought Mahler to the Berlin Philharmonic at a time when Mahler was unknown and never played. It was only after he created a furore with a recording of the *9th Symphony* that Karajan himself became interested and conducted Mahler. Furtwängler conducted quite a lot of Mahler, much more than one realises, in the early 30s and the 20s – the *3rd Symphony* and other works.

But Mahler was one of those composers who inspired – and in a way still does – a sort of specialisation. Therefore, if you were not a Mahler expert, and you were an expert in other areas, you didn't touch Mahler. But as early as the 20s there were two approaches: Bruno Walter's on the one hand, and Klemperer's on the other. And I remember I heard most of the Mahler symphonies – not all, certainly not the 8th and not the 1st – under Klemperer in London, and it was a completely different world from Bruno Walter's. And then, of course, came Bernstein with his unique exuberance and personal involvement, which was the antipode.

Bernstein said: "We are now ready to understand Mahler after the catastrophes of the 20th century."

Barenboim: I don't believe in talking about music in those terms. I really don't believe that the world is more ready or less ready. With older composers, you see that there is a different zeitgeist that led to performances of works, and some composers inspire, if you will, a certain way of dealing with their music very quickly, and others more slowly. Take Beethoven; there were different schools of thought about Beethoven in the piano world: with Schnabel, Backhaus, Edwin Fischer and Kempff – I'm talking about the older generation – there were four different worlds. Different, if you like, 'styles of interpretation', although I don't like the word interpretation. On the other hand, even today, the interest in Schubert, who died only one year after Beethoven, has not yet brought different schools of thought, not to mention composers who came later, like Debussy. In the piano world there were Michelangeli, Gieseking and Claudio Arrau, but it hasn't really been followed as such. I have a lot of admiration for Bernstein – I heard him and I played with him, and I heard so many wonderful concerts of his – but I don't like speaking about music in those terms.

So Mahler's biography did not affect his music?

Barenboim: I don't think you can find the reason for anything artistic in his biography. Some people are more articulate than others. Christoph Schlingensief, who is a fantastically talented stage director, creator, artist, and does so many different things, suffered terribly in the last couple of years from an absolutely devastating lung cancer, about which he has written a whole book. He felt the need to do so, and I'm sure that book, which I'm reading now, will help a lot of cancer patients, and people who suffer from other illnesses, to learn about the necessity to talk about it. But does it make me understand Schlingensief the artist better? No. It's a completely separate entity. And Mahler talked about his neuroses and things, and Beethoven didn't. I'm sure he had his own; we all do.

Otto Klemperer and Bruno Walter knew Mahler. Did you ever talk with them about that?

Barenboim: I never met Bruno Walter, but I knew Klemperer – I played quite a lot with him, and I recorded all the Beethoven concertos with him in the 60s – and he repeated to me what he said on television. They asked him: "You are a great Mahler conductor, you knew Mahler, and there was another conductor, Bruno Walter, who also knew Mahler. What is the difference between the two of you?" And he said, "Bruno Walter was a moralist, and I'm an immoralist."

There were other people who gave terrific Mahler concerts, but who are not considered in the mainstream. I recall hearing Rafael Kubelík once, most wonderfully conducting the *1st* with the Bavarian Radio Symphony Orchestra in London, where suddenly I saw the connection between Mahler and Dvořák – not because Kubelík was Czech, but because there was something so natural about it in that symphony. Jascha Horenstein and Paul Kletzki were also great Mahler conductors. They don't mean so much today, but it wasn't that Mahler was not played; he was just not played by the 'big names' as it were. All of this was in the 50s, before Bernstein and Barbirolli became interested in Mahler. But the development of how his music is seen is one thing, and the development of its popularity is another.

You started in '73 with the 5th.

Barenboim: I conducted the *5th* because I was a very stubborn child, and then a stubborn young man. I went to a concert of Mahler's *7th Symphony* in London, conducted by Klemperer. I hated the piece, and I told him, "I can't stand it." It happened to be Yom Kippur, the Day of Atonement, and Klemperer said to me, "You terrible man – you prefer Mahler's *7th Symphony* to going to a synagogue." And then he gave me a whole lecture, saying: "You are so limited; this is the Furtwängler influence [on you]." Furtwängler didn't like Mahler because he was Jewish, [said Klemperer], adding all sorts of exaggerated, unnecessary remarks. And he said to me, basically, "the only Mahler symphony that is not good is the *5th*." So of course that was the one I conducted – out of spite.*[laughs]*

And which came later?

Barenboim: I didn't conduct another Mahler symphony for over 20 years. It was Fischer-Dieskau who taught me a lot about Mahler, particularly about the nervousness, the disquieting atmosphere in his music. There is always something behind it that creates a certain nervousness, including the sound he looked for. And I remember playing an all-Mahler recital with him – it must have been in the 70s – and I thought, "My God, this is really quite extraordinary." And then I conducted many of the Lieder, and then *Das Lied von der Erde* [*The Song of the Earth*]. I cannot give you an exact date, but it wasn't until the mid 90s that I conducted more Mahler symphonies: the 7th, the 9th, and then the 1st. And I conducted the Adagio of the 10th two months ago for the first time, so I'm anything but a Mahler specialist.

You've conducted the 9th. It's the only one of his that he never heard, and he never revised it. Do you think he would have revised some parts, or is the balance perfect?

Barenboim: You know, the Mahler revisions are a very complex subject. If you take the 5th, and the first version and the revised version, there are some things which have obviously been changed with a clear idea of what he wanted to achieve. But there are other changes which I feel were a result of the insufficiency of the technical capabilities of the orchestras at the time. There are doublings in the 5th of the violas and the 2nd violins, but he felt the violas would not be able to play some passages, and so he deleted them – and there are many other such instances. That is why, to this day, the 5th as I conduct it is a mixture of the revised versions, which I have to say, nobody who has heard the symphony – and I have conducted the 5th many, many times – has ever noticed, including critics from all over the world. So I think this is very much a theoretical subject; it's not something that is obvious to the ear.

I don't know whether he would have made some technical changes in the 9th. Except for a few passages, it's not as difficult as the 5th, the 6th and the 7th.

Rather than being technical, the difficulties lie elsewhere. I think the most wonderful thing about the Mahler symphonies – and this is why Pierre Boulez and I decided to do the entire cycle in one go – is that it's as if Mahler looked for and found a different idiom for each symphony. Very few composers did that, apart from Beethoven. If you don't know much about music and you hear Beethoven's *5th Symphony*, and then the *Pastoral*, you might think they're by different composers, which you cannot say about Brahms, Bruckner, or Schumann; but you can certainly say it about Mahler. Yes, there are the early symphonies,

1-4; and then you have *5, 6, 7* and *8*; and then the end. But basically, in each symphony, even between the *2nd* and *3rd* and the *3rd* and *4th*, they seem to be by a different creator, a different composer. And this is the most fascinating thing. When we did the complete cycle for the first time two years ago, it was a fascinating experience for us both, as conductors, because we both heard each other's concerts, so we lived the cycle in chronological order.

Is there any Mahler work you feel especially close to, one that means more to you than all the others?

Barenboim: No. I only conduct the symphonies I feel, in the moment I'm conducting them, are my favourite pieces. But I say that not only about Mahler; I say that about every composer. I don't conduct any music in the line of duty. I don't conduct contemporary music because I ought to; I conduct the *Notations* of Pierre Boulez, and countless pieces by Elliott Carter and Harrison Birtwistle, because I like the music, and I like to delve further and further into it. I have been conducting Pierre Boulez' *Notations* since the world premiere in 1980, 30 years ago – and each time I find something new in them, in the same way that I always find something new in the *Eroica*. And I get that same strong feeling every time I conduct the symphonies of Mahler, too.

What's the most important thing a conductor has to avoid when conducting this music? Can it be conducted too emotionally?

Barenboim: I don't believe music is either emotional or rational. As I've said, all this terminology only speaks about our reaction to it. If there's only emotion, you cannot really make music because music is a combination of things; music is larger than all of this. And the difficulty in talking about music is that music definitely has a very strong content, but that content can only be expressed in sound. If you try to express it in words, you only reduce it. The greatness of music is precisely that it can laugh and cry at the same time, that it can be mathematical and sensual at the same time, that it can be all extremes and opposites put together. Music, in that sense, is a whole creation, a creation of a world where everything is expressed through sound. And therefore whatever you say about it is not a description of the thing itself, but a description of your perception of it at that moment. Therefore you are not speaking about Mahler, and if I say to you, yes, you can conduct Mahler's *2nd* emotionally, it doesn't say anything about the music. I think that in Mahler you need a combination of everything, like in all music, like in Mozart, though it's a completely different style. Or, like you would need in the works of Pierre Boulez, although again it's a completely different style. You need the structure; you need to fill the structure with emotional content and give the emotional content a structure because music happens in time. You play so many bars, and after so much time you go into another area, and in order to do that, the time has passed, and you really need that. And when you talk about music being emotional or rational, you take each section individually, and you lose the fluidity of it.

To come back to Mahler's Jewish background, you said that it didn't influence his music, even though he was confronted with anti-Semitism all his life.

Barenboim: No, I didn't say that. I said that Leonard Bernstein, in his very beautiful and very poetic essay, *The Little Drummer Boy*, talks about this, and he gives the explanation that Mahler's sense of guilt came from having been Jewish.

It's very lovely and it's very poetic, but it doesn't help to understand the music one bit, in my view. I remember the most wonderful performance of Mahler's 9th with Giulini, but then people were saying: "Oh yes, Giulini is a fervent Catholic, and you feel this redemption, and you feel this as being one with God", and so on. In the end, I'm reminded of a reply by Toscanini, when he was asked about the *Eroica*: "Maestro, what do you think? Some people say that Beethoven wrote the *Eroica* against Napoleon." "Bah!" he said, "I know, they say it is against Napoleon, and then they say it is against Mussolini and against Hitler. For me, the *Eroica* of Beethoven is allegro con brio."

In other words, it is very dangerous to try to verbalise music because in the end, we don't speak about the music, we speak about our reaction to it. And frankly, I am not interested in Leonard Bernstein's reaction to the music, what he says; I am interested in how he conducted the music, and for that I don't need words. I know that sounds very radical, but it's not an unimportant point.

But I will tell you another Klemperer story, which will show you exactly what I mean. I met Klemperer in '65 or '64, shortly before I met my future wife, Jacqueline du Pré. Jacqueline came from a perfectly, purely English background, from the English countryside. She had a unique musical talent. She once said, perhaps naively, "You know, there is something so beautiful and wonderful about Jewish players' string tone, Heifetz, and so many other Jewish musicians." They had this very vibrant sound, and because of that – it sounds like a great exaggeration but it isn't – she said, "If we get married, I want to convert." And it was then that Klemperer also met her, and we told him that. "Oh", he said, "then we must go to the synagogue together." So we went to a synagogue in London together: Jacqueline, who had not converted yet, Klemperer, who had converted from Judaism to Christianity and back, and I, who was born a Jew. And after the service in the synagogue, I asked Klemperer, "Why did you convert? Was it because of the fear of anti-Semitism?" And he said, "No. When I was 23 years old I wanted to conduct the *St Matthew Passion* of Bach, and in my stupidity I thought that in order to conduct and understand the *St Matthew Passion*, one had to be Christian. So I converted to Christianity." And I said, "Why did you convert back?" (He was already quite old when he converted back to Judaism.) And he said, "Because I realised that it was not necessary."

Now while I don't know so much about Mahler's feelings in that regard, i.e. his guilt or lack of guilt, etc., I am sure that the anti-Semitism under which he suffered so desperately was very strong and very real, no question about that. Did he feel the necessity because of that to write some parts which sound Jewish? Maybe. Probably, yes.

Did Mahler discover new dimensions of orchestral power?

Barenboim: No. But in the harmonic world, in the use of compositional techniques and dynamics, in the orchestration, in the complexity of it all, he discovered new worlds. But in what you would call the emotional content of the music, no. I think the emotional content of the music, the relation of the music to the human being, with the condition of being human, is already in Bach. It went through so many transformations and complexities and new techniques, and new instruments of course. But I think that the problems facing people today, in the most intimate and personal sense, are the same problems they have been confronting for millennia.

Now it is quicker, the tempo of life is different; now we can fly in aeroplanes when we once took horses, we can cook with microwaves and so on; there has been technological development, the development of understanding in so many realms, the acceptance of social development. In 1957, when I was 15, I went to a golf club in Miami; there was a sign that read: "No Jews, No Negroes, and No Dogs Allowed". And now, 62 years later, we have a black president in America. This is progress because people have learned from their past mistakes – although I don't think that the human condition, existential human problems, have changed.

You can imagine anything; you can imagine that huge fortissimo in the *9th Symphony* of Beethoven in the last movement, "Und der Cherub steht vor Gott"[And the Cherub stands before God], where there is a fantastic, terrifying modulation – you feel the whole world is coming to an end. And somebody will tell you that this is already a premonition of Auschwitz. Sure, you can imagine all those things, and very often these images are very helpful to many people in the way they perceive the music – but the music is always larger than that.

You mentioned Auschwitz. It's very likely that Hitler attended a performance of Lohengrin *at the opera in Vienna which Mahler conducted.*

Barenboim: I didn't know that.

Is there a meaning behind it?

Barenboim: Probably not. No. But how can you explain it? Hitler went to many performances of *Lohengrin*, and he is supposed to have gone to a performance of *Lohengrin* in Bayreuth in 1936, conducted by Furtwängler, which I am sure was wonderful, and it moved him to tears. How do you reconcile the fact that you can be moved to tears by music and then murder millions of people? Or take Stalin, whose favourite piece of music was the *D minor Piano Concerto* of Mozart; it probably moved him to tears, too, and yet he murdered 20 million people. You cannot relate these things.

Music is like a complete world, a world you can talk about; you can talk about nature, you can talk about lakes, you can talk about mountains, you can talk about cities, and you can talk about the desert. But the whole world always includes a lot more. And when you talk about Mahler's neuroses and his fear of anti-Semitism and all that, it's as if you are talking about the world, [yet that is] only one element in it. And they are all things that were inside him, and like all great musicians, what he gave us is not only an exercise in counterpoint, melody and rhythm, but what he felt as the innermost content of his being.

Mahler said: a mystery remains.

Barenboim: That's right.

(Vienna, 27/04/2009)

Herbert Blomstedt

"Mahler must have been a great man"

Do you remember the first time you heard Mahler's music?

Blomstedt: I think so. It was the *1ˢᵗ Symphony* and I didn't like it particularly. I was 14 or 15 and I thought it was vulgar. It was in Gothenburg. I am sure Issay Dobrowen conducted it very well, but I was right in the Bach-Beethoven-late-quartets-phase of my development, so anything that diverged too much from that I felt was not really worth my attention [*laughs*]. It took quite a few years before I realised that Mahler was great music.

Did Mahler figure in your musical education?

Blomstedt: Not really … what I know about Mahler I taught myself at a later age, when I was 30 or 40. I was not interested in Mahler when I was young. It was challenging enough trying to find my way to Mozart, Haydn, Beethoven and Brahms – Bruckner was very close to me from the beginning. I really only started to become fascinated by Mahler's music when I was in Dresden, when I was 50 years old. I conducted my first Mahler symphony in Dresden with the Staatskapelle. It was the *2ⁿᵈ* – I loved it, and I was disappointed that the orchestra didn't like it. This was maybe in 1975 or 1978, I don't remember exactly. The orchestra played wonderfully and the choir was also wonderful – I think it was a very good performance. But I noted that the orchestra felt "Hmm, yes, not bad, but not really great."

Were the difficulties only the 'exotic' materials or were there other reasons why you didn't like Mahler at first?

Blomstedt: No, that was my main objection. Of course, when I studied the scores more closely, I realised what great compositions they were and how clever he was as a musician and as a composer. These so-called 'vulgar' quotations were part of his world and he wanted to bring that whole world into his music, sort of like confessions.

But how utterly different that was from other big symphonies written at the same time – by Jean Sibelius, for example, who never would have written something like that and still wrote symphonies with enormous integrity. But Sibelius never quoted folk melodies; there is something similar in his work, and his music is, of course, strongly influenced by his Finnish background – but as personal as his symphonies are, they are objective truths. They are not just outpourings of his sentiments. His music is no less personal than Mahler's music, but it is personal on a different level.

Sibelius and Mahler met, as you know, in 1907. They had some common ground, but of course they had completely different views. I think they respected each other very much as great musicians. Sibelius created an ideal world of his own, which was far removed from the streets of Helsinki or Vienna, while in Mahler's music you can hear very well what is going on in the street, in the pubs, as well as in the Musikverein and in the churches. He takes it all in, it's all there. It is extremely emotional, which is why I think it appeals so much to today's audiences.

Is there a risk of overpowering Mahler? Bernstein has been blamed for that.

Blomstedt: Well, I am not the one to judge this, but I think Mahler can easily be misused if one is ultra-emotional. Certainly, Bernstein was an artist who was enormously emotional and he had a right to be like that: that was Mr Bernstein! I knew him pretty well, personally. He was not a showman, but a naturally theatrical person. He didn't try to create an effect, he *was* like that. He was completely genuine. And in this respect, I think he was the ideal Mahler interpreter.

I think that Mahler's own way of conducting was not like that. Of course the young Mahler was different from the mature Mahler, but the mature Mahler was an extremely well-controlled conductor. No gymnastics, no histrionics on the stage; he was calm, but with an enormous methodology – he asked for the orchestra to completely give themselves over to the music and to his demands as a conductor. And it was natural for him to get exactly what he wanted because of his grandeur, not only as a fascinating performer, but as a person. He must have simply been a great man.

Certainly, Mahler must be played with complete understanding, with great personal involvement and emotion. Yet in order to have control and maintain the relationship between the different parts of this great music, you have to keep a cool head while at the same time being totally involved.

Have you talked with other conductors about Mahler?

Blomstedt: No. What I know about Mahler comes only from my studying his scores. I didn't study Mahler with a teacher.

Would you agree that Mahler's roots are in song?

Blomstedt: I think so, yes. He is almost at his greatest in his early songs; they are fantastic, the *Kindertotenlieder* [*Songs on the Death of Children*], the *Lieder eines fahrenden Gesellen* [*Songs of a Wayfarer*] – they appeal very much to me because they reveal another side of Mahler that is perhaps less familiar: the more restrained Mahler, the more internal Mahler.

He and the voice were one. He wrote very little chamber music, as we know; he was an orchestra man, but he was also a man of the opera. He constantly worked with singers, and I am sure he worked with some wonderful singers who gave him an idea of what the human voice can express.

When you started to study Mahler you were already a great Bruckner conductor. Do you think Bruckner influenced Mahler, bearing in mind that Mahler wanted to study with Bruckner?

Blomstedt: We know of course that Mahler studied with Bruckner, but it must have been for a very short time. I think that Mahler's symphonies would have been impossible without Bruckner's music. The scope, the greatness of thought surely influenced Mahler, and Mahler of course performed some of Bruckner's music, in his own way, with many changes and cuts, which was standard at that time. Today, it would be a crime to do that, but we should not judge Mahler by today's standards, but by the standards of his own day. After all, he was one of the first conductors to perform [Bruckner's] *6th Symphony*, although he didn't perform all the movements and made large cuts.

When I compare the two, what surprises me is how modern Bruckner was compared to Mahler. What Bruckner wrote in 1868 is much more daring than what Mahler wrote in 1890, harmonically speaking. And he did it with the same orchestra as Beethoven used. The harmonically daring language of Bruckner's *1st Symphony* is just unbelievable. When you hear Mahler's *1st Symphony*, it sounds very commonplace, harmonically speaking. It has, of course, many new kinds of expressions and a whole new world is already opening up in it that Bruckner never would have written, but harmonically speaking, Bruckner is much more advanced than Mahler. Perhaps in 1908, 1909, 1910, 1911, by the time he began the *10th Symphony*, Mahler would have approached something like this; there are also some harmonically daring progressions in the

9th. But the Mahler of the 1890s was not going in that direction. He developed other parts of his musical language which really made him Mahler. He didn't have to be more modern; he had to be more Mahler. So it's not that Mahler was not as advanced as Bruckner, but harmonically speaking, Bruckner was very innovative and daring. The clashes in his 9th are unbelievable!

But I am so glad that we have both. As different as they are, we love them both and we cannot do without them.

From a practical point of view, are there differences when you rehearse Mahler and Bruckner?

Blomstedt: There are enormous differences. When I conduct Bruckner, I always feel that this is the truth, some objective truth. It's very personal music and it's full of emotions, but not Bruckner's emotions. It's like Beethoven's music – he speaks for us all. Beethoven was not telling us about his being afraid, about becoming deaf or of his anguish. He speaks for man as a species. I feel the same with Bruckner, whereas Mahler speaks absolutely for himself and he shows us that this is also part of us. We can have sympathy for him and he appeals to us – "Oh yes, I have something similar in me." And that's why we like him so much; "He suffered just as I do."

But Bruckner's music is on a different level. It's very personal, but not as subjective. This is why I feel that with Bruckner's music you get a sense of the truth; it is like it is. It's real. One of the most wonderful passages in Mahler's music is the one where he gives an idea of an ideal world, of ideal happiness, in heaven – in his *Wunderhorn-Lieder*, "I long to be in heaven." And you have a wonderful feeling that this is where you want to be. But with Bruckner's music, you are there. And it's *real*, you know. It's not just a vision that you forget three bars later. Mahler's says that it's something to be hopeful for, but it's not real, it doesn't exist, but you must not forget to dream about it and hope for it and work towards it, even though it actually doesn't exist. Whereas Bruckner creates a situation where it *does* exist, and it's *here*!

These two composers are very different; they appeal to different aspects of our personalities.

When you rehearse, are you looking for the long line with Bruckner and for the mosaic with Mahler? Or is the technical aspect almost the same with both composers?

Blomstedt: Well, with both composers you have to have a complete overview before you start painting details. This is as true for Mahler as it is for Bruckner. Mahler's music may seem to be more kaleidoscopic; a series of snapshots. Perhaps this is also why it appeals so much to today's audiences. They don't have much patience; they want to be stimulated all the time. It's like when you're watching TV – you have three seconds of this and two seconds of that, and when you have ten seconds of something, you think it's boring [*laughs*]. Mahler's music is *always* changing and this is part of why it fascinates us so much. Because we know that our existence is so fragmental. But Bruckner's music tells us there is also a line, a vision, and hope for eternity. For Mahler, eternity is only a dream, but for Bruckner it's real.

How do you imagine Mahler's personality?

Blomstedt: He must have been a great man. He was a difficult man when it came to art; he demanded absolute fidelity to what he was aiming at, and he was not prepared to make any compromises. Of course, life taught him that things don't always develop the way you want them to. He suffered great tragedies in his personal life – his children died, his wife deserted him – terrible things. That a person could create such great music in such circumstances is a miracle. Just as it's a miracle that Bruckner created such great music being the man that he was – in many ways a very simple man.

Do you see Wagner's influence on Mahler as well?

Blomstedt: Yes, of course; without Wagner there would be no Mahler. And I am sure he was a great Wagner conductor and he knew his works very well. But it's interesting that Mahler and Bruckner, since we are compairing them all the time, were not opera composers. Wagner played a great role for them, but Mahler only had some curious attempts at arranging opera; his world was the symphony. And so was Bruckner's. Bruckner was in a monastery, he was an organist, but his world was the symphony. He wrote some wonderful church music, but compared with his symphonies, it was a minor part of his output. It's great music, wonderful, he was a wonderful organist, but he wrote no organ music; he improvised.

His organ was the orchestra …

Blomstedt: His world was the orchestra! And he had that vision without having an orchestra at his disposal. Mahler had an orchestra at his disposal, it was his everyday work. He heard what was possible; he was a fantastic conductor.

But with Bruckner you would never predict that he would develop into a man of the symphony. I think this is also important to bear in mind when you judge Bruckner. You put him into a corner – he was a church man, he was very religious, he was very pious; we admire that and we would like to be like that ourselves, but unfortunately we can't, that time is past …

Mahler was, of course, an extreme romantic and as a conductor, he also wanted to test the limits. He caused the orchestra to do what no one else had done; he enlarged the orchestra as he saw fit; he felt no compunction in using unconventional instruments – he was simply experimenting. In this respect, he was also a child of his time. He said to his students, "If something in my music does not work in terms of balance, change it", or "If you feel that the oboe is too weak here, use the clarinet instead, and if it's still too weak, double it, triple it, or put the piccolo on top", and he not only gave his students free rein to do so, but he said that they *must* do it. This is completely alien to us today, when everything Mahler wrote is sacrosanct – you don't change a note, you don't change one instrument. The job of the conductor is to adjust the sound balances so that everything can be clearly heard, and so on, but you don't change the *colours*; that's a crime!

What would you have asked Mahler?

Blomstedt: I wouldn't have nearly as many questions for Mahler as I'd have for Bruckner because Mahler was much more specific, to the last detail, when he wrote his scores. For me, Bruckner is more enigmatic than Mahler. I feel that Mahler's message is pretty clear to me. That doesn't mean that I know it for all time. Tomorrow, I might have other ideas. It's like that with any great music; you can never come close enough to it.

Of course I would have loved to meet both of them. But I am afraid if I had the privilege of meeting them, I would just go numb and admire them … "Is this really you?"

What did Mahler want?

Blomstedt: Well, he certainly wanted to stir our emotions and to make us take part in his world, which was very intense – and to share his loneliness. He wasn't really an outcast because he had many admirers, but I think he never completely felt at home. Only when making music could he really express himself and only then was his world complete. As soon as a rehearsal or concert was over, he felt lonely – "only me and a few people who perhaps sympathise with me" – it might have been a thousand or 3,000 or 5,000 people, but not many who really understood him. I think that he wanted to try to communicate with people.

That feeling of loneliness, I think, is not foreign to any musician – we are so specialised, we can share our world with only a very few people. We are happy when a thousand, 2,000, 3,000 people listen to us, or when 100,000 buy our recordings, but that does not really make us less lonely. After the concert, there is this emptiness – after we've had a great emotional experience, a great intellectual experience coupled with an emotional experience, there is this great feeling of excitement and fulfilment, but when it's over, after 10 or 15 minutes, you're alone. I think every musician basically feels that.

I think it was Goethe who said in a wonderful commentary that he felt that the whole world was like a desert. But then suddenly you find somebody with whom you can share your thoughts and feelings on special subjects, and suddenly the desert starts to bloom and is like an oasis. And when that person is not there anymore, then it's a desert again.

The basic temperament of a musician is melancholic.

Where would Mahler have gone?

Blomstedt: That's an interesting question. Judging by what we know from the *10th Symphony*, he was certainly going into a period of extended harmonic language. I don't think he would have reached the same dead end as Sibelius, who simply felt he could no longer go on and just stopped. His own self-criticism became too great and it destroyed the *8th Symphony*. Mahler had an even bigger ego than Sibelius and he was too convinced of his own talent. It is not possible to predict, but I think he would have continued on his own way. But it's an interesting question because that was when Schönberg was finding his own way – and Stravinsky, too.

(Vienna, 17/02/2011)

Pierre Boulez

"One cannot refer to the biography to explain the music"

Do you remember the first time you heard Mahler's music?

Boulez: I think so. In France he was not performed at all when I was young. But it was the *4th Symphony*, and I remember being surprised by the *Schellen* [*sleigh bells*] because it was very unusual to hear such a sound, especially at the beginning of a symphony. Paul Kletzki was conducting.

And then the other time I heard Mahler, that was *Das Lied von der Erde* [*The Song of the Earth*], performed in 1952. I don't know if that was for the first time in France, but it was the first time I saw it programmed there. Although I don't remember the performers, it was very impressive. But I was disappointed, I remember, by the long oboe solo in the last movement because it was much too repetitive for my taste at that time. I mean, it was a very extreme time in my studies, so I heavily rejected all that was influenced by or was part of tradition.

After that, I think I began to know Mahler better, and when I was in Germany, in Baden-Baden, I remember we discussed it with Hans Rosbaud. He told me, "Listen to this symphony", and it was the *9th Symphony* recorded by himself, and I was really very impressed, so I began to form an opinion of Mahler that I couldn't have had before because of my lack of knowledge.

You succeeded Leonard Bernstein as chief conductor of the New York Philharmonic. Did you talk with him about Mahler?

Boulez: No, I wasn't in close contact with Bernstein. I met him, of course, from time to time, but we didn't discuss music because our tastes were so different that a discussion would have led nowhere. And I think we had a kind of agreement not to touch on the subject.

Bernstein made Mahler popular in the States. It was in a way his responsibility. I was told, for instance, by musicians I knew in the orchestra, that when Mahler's *7th* or *5th* or *6th* was performed in the 50s, the auditoriums emptied because it was considered too long and boring.

Bernstein conducted Mahler very emotionally. Did you feel that weighed on you when you took over?

Boulez: No, I didn't try to fight or change anything. I simply did it my way. And of course I noticed that some features of his performances were still there, which I can very well understand. Dimitri Mitropoulos was also very emotional, not only Bernstein. And probably the least emotional was Bruno Walter – I mean, emotional in the sense of exaggeration. Personally, I think the emotional side should be there because it is in the music. I was discussing with Barenboim how one cannot constantly refer to the biography to explain the music – it doesn't explain the pieces at all.

When he composed, he had a kind of mesh of motives, of themes, and he organised them very carefully; so it's not a kind of emotion which is forever improvising. It's very important to me that the organisation is part of the emotion.

But was it your goal to make Mahler more down to earth for the American public?

Boulez: No. I didn't have a goal, as a matter of fact. I was simply busy trying to figure out the music for myself. Because you know, in the French tradition, pieces – orchestral pieces at least – are always rather short. And even in the Viennese School pieces are really rather short. But in Mahler you have a movement which is 30 minutes long, or even more, which you have to organise. You certainly can't just go along and say, "Well, I have this emotion at this moment. I am waiting for the second one", and just play from time to time with holes in the middle.

I think one of the crucial points is the tempo. Mahler wrote censoriously of a conductor whom he heard, criticising the lack of flexibility of the tempo. How do you feel about that?

Boulez: Well, the number of times he writes "*nicht eilen; nicht schleppen*" ["*don't rush; don't drag*"], it's always negative. And he was afraid that the weight of the emotion would make you exaggerate what he wanted, and that's exactly the point. So if you're excited, you risk pushing the tempo to the maximum, although there is absolutely no reason for the tempo to be that quick.

You really have to go from one pulse to another without anyone noticing the exact moment you do it. And that is very important, especially in the 6th, where it happens in the last movement. It happens a couple of times, but especially at the end. Sometimes he wants to precipitate the tempo, and so instead of four beats you have two beats, instead of two beats you have one beat; and it's very important to accomplish that as smoothly as possible – not chopped up, but continuous.

And the relationship between the various tempi is very important to me, especially when you have to find some sort of coherence between the tempi, like in the second movement of the *8th*.

Do we now have more perspectives on Mahler?

Boulez: Yes, we certainly have more perspectives. But Bernstein was not the only one at this time. You also had Sir Georg Solti, for instance – and I say Solti because he was one of the main performing forces at the time – or Zubin Mehta. So I don't think Bernstein was overpowering. But there were already people rebelling against this kind of over-romanticised performance. You know, there was certainly no total agreement.

What did the composer Boulez learn from Mahler's scores?

Boulez: Well, quite a lot. I mean, first the distance, the long distance let's say: how to organise a long work, like I did recently with *Sur Incises*, 45 minutes of music without stopping; you have to organise your concept of time differently because you have to make the ideas renew themselves and at the same time still be recognisable. And that's not easy at all, but I have learnt that from Mahler, and Wagner, too, from conducting his music. It was the same problem for the French. I mean, the French were very often left short of breath because their pieces were shorter; they were very refined, but mainly they were short. And so there was this long distance; it was very important to me to know it and to benefit from it. That's the first thing.

The second thing was the use of the orchestra. Not that it can be used the same way now, but I mean certainly the weight of the instruments is very well calculated in Mahler, as well as the dynamic proportions. They are very important because when he has a fortissimo for some instruments and a pianissimo for others, he absolutely knows the weight of the instruments, of the register, of the colour. And you know, generally, when you see some scores – even in the 20th century – you find a kind of general dynamic for the entire orchestra, and that's a very primitive use of dynamics.

Mahler was very advanced in that way. And you can see the difference in the experience. For instance, when Berg wrote *Op. 6*, the third piece especially, you have problems of balance and you have to adjust the dynamics because with the dynamics he has written, it will simply not sound good. And you will not hear what is important, on the contrary, you will mainly hear things you do not want to hear.

Would Mahler have revised his 9th Symphony?

Boulez: No, I don't think so, the *9th* is very well put together. Maybe the sketches of the *10th*, especially the Adagio. Here he would maybe have changed a couple of things. But I think he was so aware of the possibilities of the orchestra, and that's also a kind of gift.

But he had to fight for it. Writing the 5th Symphony he said he felt he was an absolute beginner.

Boulez: Yes, well, he said it, but I don't believe it. [*laughs*] No, I mean, he had to think again because the music is very developed from the *4th*, and even from the *3rd*, which uses much more counterpoint, and certainly he had some difficulties, but he knew what he was doing. The difficulty came from the fact that the substance of the music was different, was much more complex. But he didn't have to re-learn how to use the instruments. That, certainly, I don't believe. That was frivolity.

What were the first Mahler works you conducted?

Boulez: The first one I conducted was the *5th* because it was very rarely performed at the time – '65 or '66, I don't remember – and then the BBC was my way of finding out how I could do it. And I don't remember the performance; I don't think it was the peak of performance I have ever done, simply because it was the first time.

When I was conducting it, especially the Funeral March, it reminded me of Chopin more than anything else. Of course because I played [Chopin's] Funeral March on the piano when I was a child – it was kind of cliché for me. And I had quite a lot of difficulties entering into this cliché.

But you continued to conduct Mahler. So there was something …

Boulez: Yes. I certainly didn't want to give up. I wasn't entirely set on Mahler, and then, what you said is exactly what I thought myself. I had heard, especially from Theodor W. Adorno, that Mahler was the source of the Viennese School, so I began to think back, to think Schönberg, Webern and Berg, and to go back to Mahler.

I was able to understand *Wozzeck* better when I knew Mahler, especially the military march and all the vulgarity: well-conceived, the kind of vulgarity you find in *Wozzeck* with the Captain and the Drum Major. I discovered this with Mahler retrospectively, and I said yes, I can see where it comes from.

Speaking of Schönberg and the influence of Mahler, even Schönberg had a lot of problems with it at the beginning.

Boulez: At the beginning, yes.

Can you understand that?

Boulez: Schönberg was an idealist, and didn't want vulgarity to intrude. You know, the kind of stylistic collage that Mahler sometimes created; and by instinct Schönberg was rejecting that because he wanted a pure style. And Schönberg was always looking for purity of style. Always. Yet his system of 12 tones is not even purity; it's asceticism. And therefore I can understand his initial reaction. But comparing, for instance, the music of Mahler and even the 'vulgar' music of *Moses and Aaron*, I can understand that there is the influence of Mahler in that very small, isolated segment of Schönberg.

In which direction would Mahler have proceeded?

Boulez: Well, especially if you look at the *10th Symphony*, the Adagio, or even the *9th*, he certainly would have pushed towards expanding tonality. I don't think he would have given up, as it were, the grammar of the tonality, the classified chords, but he would have pushed the relationship between the chords very far. I am quite sure of that.

Barenboim told me yesterday that when he starts to conduct a new piece, he starts it slower, and when he feels more comfortable, the tempi become faster. You are the contrary, he said.

Boulez: Yes.

You become slower?

Boulez: I suppose there is some truth in that, yes, because personally, I want to push because I am afraid that I will be boring. I calm down when I master the thing.

Is there a relationship between life and music?

Boulez: There is certainly a relationship, but not literally. I mean, you have many people who have suffered anti-Semitism even more than Mahler, but who have never written the *9th Symphony*. You cannot really confuse moral and aesthetic points of view. You have very moral people who write very poor music; and you have people who are not moral at all, who have sides to them that are absolutely inacceptable, but who write good music. You know, Debussy was anti-Dreyfus and Ravel was pro-Dreyfus: fine. But you cannot find an equivalent in their music.

Do we understand Mahler better after the catastrophes of the 20th century? Did he anticipate them?

Boulez: No, because otherwise you would just regard all Jewish composers as being representative of the catastrophe, and as I say, morality has nothing to do with talent – unfortunately or fortunately, I don't know – but they are two different things. Take Hanns Eisler, for example: He suffered – although he was in exile – but if he had stayed in Germany, he would certainly have been killed. That's a fact – and we sympathise with that fact – and without being crass at all, would I say that Eisler is a better composer than Berg? Certainly not.

But when the soloist sings: "O Mensch! Gib acht!" ["O man! Take heed!"] …

Boulez: Well, Nietzsche wrote that long before the holocaust.

So it is a general topic?

Boulez: That's a general topic, yes, only it was actualised, so to speak, by the Hitler situation. As I say; with anti-Semitism, if one makes Wagner responsible for Auschwitz, no, that's also an exaggeration in the opposite direction. He was anti-Semitic like many people: if you read the letters of Modest Mussorgsky, anti-Semitism is there constantly; Stravinsky wasn't very cautious either. You know, in Russia you have a lot of anti-Semitism, and in France, too, just like during the Dreyfus affair – and, like I say, Debussy was against Dreyfus.

So we should separate this? No influence?

Boulez: No influence, certainly. You can really suffer from a situation, that's for sure, and Mahler suffered. But don't forget that he also became a Christian at the beginning of his career, just because Christianity was necessary at the time to be head of an opera house. They were all converting, Schönberg too; it was like a passport in that society.

If Mahler would have lived another 30 years, would the influence of Schönberg have been different?

Boulez: I don't think Mahler would have accepted the 12-tone theory and system.

But how about Schönberg? If he had felt the great Mahler on his side, would he have composed differently?

Boulez: Schönberg was independent enough, I am quite sure. Maybe Berg would have been less influenced by Schönberg, that's possible.

This would have been two worlds coexisting.

Boulez: Yes, yes.

Debussy attended the French premiere of Mahler's 2nd Symphony – and he walked out.

Boulez: Yes. Well, that's a kind of legend, no one will ever know if it is true or not. Apparently, he left because he wanted to smoke a cigarette, and he went out and never came back because he found it was better outside. But you know, it's a legend, that's all.

But maybe the reason was that Mahler never was part of French musical education.

Boulez: Perhaps. But not only Debussy had that attitude; it was the attitude of the whole musical class. There was no interest in Wagner. Strauss was invited regularly to conduct in France, even before the First World War. And as a matter of fact, Debussy wrote a long article on the way Strauss conducted because they were practically the same age: 1862 for Debussy, 1864 for Strauss.

But would you say that Mahler is completely accepted now in France?

Boulez: Oh yes, well internationally. But not Bruckner.

Would Mahler have been possible without Bruckner?

Boulez: I think maybe, yes, but I'm not sure. Certainly the last Bruckner symphonies were influential, 8 and 9.

In terms of the energy of massed forces?

Boulez: Yes. But you know, for instance, Mahler's scherzos are much more complex than those of Bruckner, which are A-B-A-B-A, or A-B-A simply.

And even Shostakovich …

Boulez: Don't speak to me about that man. I really cannot understand the success of his music, it's so trite. It's like a collection of clichés, which is really embarrassing sometimes.

Why did Mahler, the opera conductor, never compose an opera?

Boulez: Because he knew too much about the opera houses. This was a joke. Maybe because he lacked the time: that I can imagine. Because as much as he was able to concentrate on a limited amount of work in the summer, I don't see him composing something like *Meistersinger* [*Mastersingers*] in three months.

So we can say that his symphonies with chorus and soloists are a kind of musical drama?

Boulez: Yes, that's a kind of substitute, especially the *8th Symphony*. But what is very strange is that the Faust scene is not the most dramatic music he wrote. The finale of the *6th* is much more dramatic than the second movement of the *8th*.

He deleted the third hammer blow in the 6th.

Boulez: Yes, that I can understand because it does not fit at all. That's not the same context. With the first two hammer blows you have a main melody playing with the trumpet. The third time it's the introduction which comes back, and the hammer has nothing to do with this reprise, this repetition, from the very beginning. And so there is no hammer there.

It has nothing to do with reasons outside the music?

Boulez: No, I don't believe anything else. Well, maybe he wanted a third one, but ultimately he found that it was absolutely illogical to have a third one in the context. And what Alma later wrote about the drama; I don't believe a word of it. She invented quite a lot of things.

So we should protect Mahler from these legends?

Boulez: From Alma, yes, but it's too late now. [*laughs*] It's true what Barenboim was telling you, that one speaks much too much about his psyche, about his difficulties, psychoanalysis and so on and so forth.

When I hear the 1st or the 2nd, I can understand that the outbursts, "Durchbrüche", as Adorno said, shocked the audience. This was unknown territory.

Boulez: No, I don't think so. Strauss also had quite a lot of energy. It was part of the times.

What was it in Mahler that startled people?

Boulez: The length, that's all; the length and the complexity. They didn't understand the continuity of things. And it was not surprising that the first thing to be generally understood was the Adagietto of the 5th.

And the use of the material: funeral marches, soldier songs.

Boulez: Yes, well, Mahler's material is very limited. You have funeral marches, you have military marches, you have Ländler, and that's it.

Birdsongs.

Boulez: Yes, birdsongs, but that's very sporadic. It's certainly not Olivier Messiaen. It's especially in the 1st and in *Lieder eines fahrenden Gesellen* [*Songs of a Wayfarer*], but apart from that you don't have many birds. No, he really only used three things – the other material is himself – the material you can see permanently in his work, from the very beginning.

And was it new how he put it together?

Boulez: Yes.

For me this technique of montage and collage is very similar to Varèse.

Boulez: Better, better made: Varèse is much more primitive in that sense.

But he did the same thing, in terms of technique.

Boulez: Yes, exactly, but that's primitive compared to the way Mahler used it. Apropos material, you have Charles Ives in America, which uses not funeral marches, but marches, military marches, fanfares, and also tunes, let's put it that way. But how he uses it all is infantile compared to Mahler, or not even comparable to Mahler! So it's not only the material that counts, it's also what you do with it.

What was Mahler's greatest achievement?

Boulez: Well, using such basic, rather trivial material and transforming it completely.

(Vienna, 28/04/2009)

Riccardo Chailly

"Mahler's *First* was the great emotion of my youth"

Do you remember the first time you heard Mahler's music?

Chailly: Yes, very clearly; it was in the early 60s in Rome, at the Auditorium del Foro Italico with the RAI Rome Orchestra. I attended a rehearsal of the *1st Symphony*, conducted by Zubin Mehta, who was very young at that time. I was there because my father was working at the RAI Rome, programming classical music. He had to leave for a meeting and said, "Stay here for one hour and don't move, don't talk, don't do anything!" When I heard the power of the music it left me feeling at a complete standstill. I didn't know what to do, how to react … it was the great emotion of my youth.

When did you start to study the scores?

Chailly: Well, much later. I would say around 10 years later, when I decided to become a conductor. I found it very difficult to study and understand Mahler at that time, so I sort of deliberately postponed it until the late 70s.

Would you say that you had instant access?

Chailly: When I decided to try to learn about the universe of the ten symphonies, and strangely enough, I did start very, very early with the *9th* and the *10th*, it disclosed to me a barrier-free universe and opened up his language. Starting with his latest style of music almost helped me. Much later though, I became close to *Das Lied von der Erde* [*The Song of the Earth*] – but that's another story. I think the key for me was really the *10th*, the *9th* and the *8th* symphonies, and then everything that came before. And it's very strange because when I was studying in Milan, I happened to be at a rehearsal of maestro Ozawa at La Scala, of the *8th Symphony*, which, until that time, I had never heard performed live. This was kind of a repeat of the same emotion that I had with a live orchestra rehearsal when I was younger and with the *1st Symphony*.

In Amsterdam you were chief conductor of an orchestra with a tremendous Mahler tradition. When you started to conduct Mahler there, did you feel something of that tradition?

Chailly: Very strongly. The orchestra is incredible with regard to the pauses, the culture and the tradition in the silences between the notes Mahler wrote, the as it were lengthening of the tempo, where he wants a fermata not to be a real fermata, but just a broadening of one note. They are very clear and unique.

When you start a Mahler concert, you see the orchestra placing themselves on their chairs in a position that will not change for the remaining hour, or hour-and-a-half, to follow. There is a unique kind of collectivity; members participate even when they are not playing the music, sometimes having to wait minutes and minutes because only one section is moving along. This is an example of complete commitment to music, both mental and physical. And last but not least, we have to consider the tradition of the chief conductors; for half a century, Willem Mengelberg put Mahler regularly, almost daily, on the orchestra's programmes. Maestro Van Beinum and maestro Haitink followed this great tradition of superior quality.

Have you listened to Mengelberg's recordings?

Chailly: Yes, the very few: unfortunately, just the Adagietto of the 5th, the complete 4th and the *Lieder eines fahrenden Gesellen* [*Songs of a Wayfarer*]. It certainly is fascinating to hear, even in these few pieces, how extreme his way of conducting Mahler was – but also how flexible it was. The word rubato had a different meaning in those days from today's *rigore filologico*. Consider the freedom and the attitude of taking this music in its own way by talking and living with the composer himself – and also the quality and flexibility of the Concertgebouw Orchestra of those years. The confidence is very clear. When you hear Mengelberg's recording of the Adagietto of the 5th, the quality that he achieved in those years is quite astonishing.

Comparing those few recordings with Bruno Walter's, we see that even in the beginning of a Mahler tradition, the approaches were very different.

Chailly: I think Bruno Walter can be seen as the opposite of Mengelberg – the man of rigore, the man with the neoclassical thoughts, the man who came strictly from the Viennese School – from the Classic to the Romantic. I think this also added a very clean vision of the shape of Mahler's music, which was necessary because of the expansion of his form. That meant a lot of rigore, if not some kind of rigidity, not getting lost sometimes with the approach of freedom and *libertà interpretativa.*

Even today, Walter is a keynote [Mahler] conductor – I would say, along with Otto Klemperer. The only recording by Oskar Fried of the *2nd Symphony* is very important too, of course, because we know that when he conducted the piece in Berlin, he had many discussions with Mahler, who described his own way of interpretation and his choice of tempi. So, in a way, that recording of the *2nd Symphony* is the result of those intense, involved discussions between Fried and Mahler.

But what is the right approach today, when there have been such extremes from the very beginning?

Chailly: I doubt there are limits when talking about a genius like Mahler. We know that Leonard Bernstein, who was one of the paradigmatic Mahler conductors, went to extremes – yet those extremes always matched the spirit of his own way of interpreting Mahler. When considering the half century separating Mengelberg from Bernstein, those extremes somehow make sense.

When I conduct Mahler, I am not too loud; maybe in the future I will tend to such an extreme. It is an impulsive nature that makes you want to take such liberties to such an extreme. Still, in the case of Bernstein, we have an example of one of the greatest interpreters who ever lived. I still remember a performance with the Vienna Philharmonic of the *9th* at La Scala in Milan, where the finale reached indescribable degrees of emotion – and Bernstein's courage, even though the acoustics for concerts is rather dry at La Scala, to stretch the last two or three pages of the piece to the extreme, making it slower and slower. The power and the tension he achieved are still very strong in my memory.

Is there a danger of overpowering Mahler?

Chailly: Mahler, as only a genius can, has overcome that. Because the inner power of his music speaks so strongly, it is not necessary to overpower Mahler. At least it would not be my approach. Composers like Rossini sometimes seem completely wrong and unidiomatic. And you suffer, listening to that – but in the end, you say "Oh, what a bad interpretation", not "What bad music" – the music has survived. He made it. In the end he wins *la guerra de la composizione e l'interprete* [*the war between the composition and the interpreter*]. With a genius like Mahler, the composer always wins against the performer.

Would you say that there is a specific Mahler sound you want to create when you conduct Mahler in Leipzig, or in Amsterdam, or in Berlin?

Chailly: That depends on the nature of the orchestra's sound. However, I think that, with regard to Mahler, it is always important to have a romantic sound. 'Romantic' in the sense of the depth of the sound, the nature of vibrato, the cultivation of portamenti, which is becoming increasingly rare in symphony orchestras all over the world. This is an extremely delicate matter in Mahler's music, where you can easily become tasteless or purist. It would be easy to abolish portamento, but it would also be wrong. Of course, Mahler has a very strong impact when you work with an orchestra like the Gewandhaus in Leipzig, which is one of the greatest German Romantic orchestras in terms of sound.

How do you see the relationship between his difficult life and his music?

Chailly: I doubt that his relationship with Alma, although she was an interesting and very musical woman, made his life easier at the end, for too many reasons. But I also think that his inner conflicts stemmed from the world around him, from the way European culture perceived music. He kept studying and even conducting important scores, important operas by his fellow composers. He kept informing himself very much about what the world around him was doing. His relationship with Arnold Schönberg is also interesting. I think he consciously decided to go his own way, to follow his own path – fortunately! The famous dinner in Vienna comes to mind, where Schönberg described the concept of *Klangfarbenmelodie* to Mahler, which, according to Alma's diary, apparently left Mahler totally indifferent.

However, when you look at the final pages of *Das Lied von der Erde*, you see that the *Klangfarbenmelodie* is already there. I think he was constantly trying to increase his musical vocabulary, to explore a new way of music-making. But at the same time, he kept very faithful to his own style until the end. You see a unique unity of language when you look at Opus 1, *Das klagende Lied* [*The Song of Lamentation*], and then you make a jump to *Das Lied von der Erde*. In this context, I can't help comparing him to Puccini. The 'linguistic' development from *Le Villi* to *Turandot* is completely unpredictable.

With Mahler, the genius and modernity of *Das Lied von der Erde* is, of course, unforeseeable when one starts with *Das klagende Lied* – but a unity exists, nevertheless, which is unbelievable. I am a particular fan of looking at the *teatralità della musica pucciniana* in comparison to the theatrical moments in Mahler's music. There are many common elements, for instance the introduction of Act III of *Tosca*, where the Roman bells are playing. This is one of the things that can surely be connected to the cowbells in Mahler's 6*th* – but in a completely different environment of sound and music. But there are many moments where I can somehow see one composer having an influence on another.

They met in Graz at the premiere of Salome, *1906, when Strauss and Mahler met, too. There is that famous photo of them coming out of the opera house.*

Chailly: I remember …

Strauss the tall, slim man …

Chailly: … and that was the last time Puccini and Mahler met, in Graz; but I think that there certainly was always a discrepancy of character between the two. It is a great shame that Mahler never composed an opera. Would it have been similar to Weber's interesting approach to the opera house and the theatre with *Die drei Pintos* [*The Three Pintos*]? A man who lived there his whole life yet didn't want to compose an opera – it's absolutely astonishing, I have to say.

Where would Mahler have gone if he had lived longer?

Chailly: Look at the Adagio of the *10th*; I think that's the answer: the vertical chord of nine pitches – three short of 12-tone music. I would say that he would have certainly gone beyond harmony, beyond the burden of the harmonic system, and that he would have reached the 12-tone system by himself. Puccini did the same with *Turandot*, by the way. In the sketches that Luciano Berio showed me of the finale, there were pages which show a 12-tone series, which unfortunately Berio finally did not include in this orchestration. With Puccini and Mahler, I see two composers who were so interested in the new, always moving forward in their own different ways, always expanding their musical vocabulary.

Why did you come so late to Das Lied von der Erde?

Chailly: Probably because it's definitely his most difficult score. I doubt there is any other piece in Mahler's oeuvre that is as complicated. And there is always, to any conductor, a guarantee that there are many unresolvable moments. Somehow, the complexity of his music, which sometimes moves vertically into different tempi, creates more freedom than might be expected. However, some things are sure to remain unresolved. And the non-solution of those questions is probably due to the fact that he never heard the piece. If he had heard it and learned how difficult it was to conduct and to interpret, he might have made it somehow easier.

Look, jumping back to Opus 1, *Das klagende Lied*; in the original version there is an offstage orchestra, which plays in a completely different metre – it is written in three beats against the orchestra in four beats. This kind of overlapping of two different independent tempi, which is extremely complicated to perform, happens in the orchestration of *Das Lied von der Erde* many times, especially in the *Abschied* [Farewell], especially in the last, the *fifth* movement. Although Mahler's instinctive idea to do that is fantastic, it is, in a practical sense – for a conductor – extremely complicated.

He didn't hear his 9th either. Do you think he would have revised some pages there?

Chailly: I most definitely hope not. Even if I have my doubts with regard to *Das Lied von der Erde*, I don't have any, not even in one bar, with the 9th. I think the 9th is beauty to perfection. I think that, in a way, his language was almost moving towards Schönberg's Chamber Symphonies.

Schönberg built the fundamental things, but from his emotions and from their understanding of the world, I think Berg and Mahler were much closer.

Chailly: I agree. You can clearly hear how Mahler influenced Berg in *Wozzeck*. We know how much Berg studied Mahler's symphonies and that he made transcriptions for piano.

Which parts of Wozzeck *do you mean?*

Chailly: The famous interlude in the third act, before the *Hop, hop!* scene. This is really not Berg composing, this is Gustav Mahler, it's so clear. Many other places, but that's the most obvious one.

Or the marches ...

Chailly: For sure, the marches are fundamental to both composers; in a way, they were obsessed with marches. If you look at Mahler's *2nd*, for instance, after the introductory bars, you can already hear a march. The *3rd* even starts with a march, with the horn and then what follows. Then the *5th* starts with a march, the *6th* starts with a march, and the *7th* with the *Trauermarsch* [Funeral March] – it's unbelievable. Mahler's musical obsessions have often been described, as has his kind of rhythmical form.

But how does one deal with his irony?

Chailly: I think that he was a man of smiles, not of laughs, as you can see in his pictures. That's a major difference; his irony is always provoking a smile. His witty side is expressed in the Lieder, like in *Lieder eines fahrenden Gesellen*, where you can occasionally see moments of it. However, it is even more clear in *Des Knaben Wunderhorn* [*The Boy's Magic Horn*] – this is the cycle where you don't even have to search for pleasure, for there are countless moments of serenity and wit. We call it in Italian the *sorriso*, the smile. *Non la risata, ma il sorriso* [*not laughter, but a smile*].

How do you see his personality?

Chailly: There is a new book by Gastón Fournier-Facio which shows a different kind of Mahler; it presents us with many anecdotes from his friends and acquaintances. We get to know a side of him that was full of humour; he was always ready for jokes. This is an aspect of Mahler that we hardly ever see. The book also provides us with a different physical description of when he was younger, how physically fit and muscular he was, etc. It is very interesting that we can look back at Mahler today, and see a Mahler who is so very different from the one that has been described for so many years.

That's very interesting; he was not an athlete, yet he had a trained physique.

Chailly: Absolutely.

He was not always weak and suffering from heart trouble.

Chailly: No, no. That was a very important new chapter for me to read and to learn.

What did Mahler want?

Chailly: I think he was more than aware that he would leave masterpieces of composition – not just "very good music" – behind. Music that was unique, of a kind that, at that time, no other composer was writing. Mahler did something unbelievably big; he really opened up a universe of new language. And I think that is what would answer your question; that was what he wanted, what he achieved.

(Salzburg, 05/08/2010)

Christoph von Dohnányi

"Mahler composed inwardly"

Do you remember the first time you heard Mahler's music?

Dohnányi: Yes, I remember very clearly. It was during the Nazi era, when my father said to us children, "Come in here, I have something you might like to hear." He played us *Das Lied von der Erde* [*The Song of the Earth*]; he had likely got the shellac recording from somewhere abroad.

How old were you then?

Dohnányi: I was 10, maybe 11.

Can you remember how you reacted to the music?

Dohnányi: Well, it was a child's reaction – but the music did make a great impression on me. Perhaps that has less to do with the music or my musicality than the fact that my father was playing us something that was very special to him.

Your father was acting like the underground movement at the time; Mahler was of course forbidden.

Dohnányi: Yes, Mahler was forbidden. My father closed the windows before he played the music.

When did you begin to conduct Mahler?

Dohnányi: I think it was back when I was in Lübeck – certainly in Kassel, where Mahler worked as a conductor for a while.

It is a phenomenon that Mahler emerged from the marginal repertoire into its centre with a vehemence which is quite singular in the history of music. Simon Rattle told me that Mahler was a "kind of joke" in England, and Pierre Boulez said that Mahler didn't figure at all in musical education in France … how did you experience the Mahler renaissance?

Dohnányi: First of all, it was at Tanglewood, when I was studying in America. I was attending a course which Bernstein sometimes taught – including, of course, a lot of Mahler.

The fact that Mahler was misapprehended in Europe for so long was a relic of Fascism – and that was not only in Germany, as we know. Anti-Semitism was everywhere until its crime led to such inexplicable horrors in Germany and Austria. Mahler converted to Catholicism so he could become the director of an opera house. Those were confused times.

Do you think that the rejection [of Mahler's music] had more to do with Anti-Semitism than his music itself?

Dohnányi: Mahler's work was not so different from others' per se – young Richard Strauss was already working, for instance. His relationship with Mahler was something between friendship and competition. Bernstein always said, "Mahler is an end, not a beginning", and that is certainly true for the most part. The influence of Brahms on Schönberg and much music to come is perhaps greater than Mahler's – as a composer, he was too subjective to be primarily oriented towards the future – he wrote his music without having any other expectations of life.

The Schönberg circle had sensed that the musical materials were being exhausted; they all looked for new forms. Schönberg's famous words, "Somebody had to do it", basically means that we all tried to advance, to find new paths, each of us in our own way. Almost all of the major composers of the time were looking for new forms – from Busoni to Hindemith.

Do you see Mahler as the last offshoot of Late Romanticism?

Dohnányi: Absolutely. I'm always interested in the ambience in which those people lived – a time so incredibly in flux – politically, intellectually, philosophically. Mahler's interest in politics is underestimated; he even went to Freud when he was having problems with Alma. He was very strongly integrated into his time, a time which determined the shape of the 20th century – but Mahler composed [in] his time, not the 20th century.

Maazel said he was 40 before he really understood what Mahler wanted, in purely musical terms, because Mahler's use of street music, folkloric sources, was a world which did not open up to him at once. How was it for you?

Dohnányi: When does one 'understand' music of genius? It can only be a question of continuously working to come closer to it.

I don't want to do things I understand. I want to work on things I'm trying to understand. For me, it's much more interesting to be involved in something I don't yet have the answer to. If I know that I understand Beethoven ... heaven forbid, one mustn't even say that! Conducting Mahler 'for fun' is fatal, in my opinion.

Mahler has now become fit for the masses ...

Dohnányi: ... And I don't think this is a positive thing. He is likely the first great composer after Wagner who appealed to broad, democratic popular structures. He appeals to people who understand nothing about music – he even appeals to unmusical people, to 'highly sophisticated' intellectuals, and to musically educated people. This is an effect which has almost become inexplicable as well as hazardous.

Where do you see the hazard here?

Dohnányi: The hazard of misunderstanding – that the inner voices aren't perceived at all, that the result is a yapping away, breathlessly greedy for the upper voice and the effects. Mahler is similar to Wagner in that he can very easily be misunderstood.

Mahler composed inwardly. He was a very extrovert conductor and an often introvert composer, whose tenderness in my opinion is too seldomly heard.

And the explosions and outbursts which occur in almost every symphony?

Dohnányi: They are part of the music of his time. Subito effects – you find them much earlier, like in Beethoven, where his subito dynamics – subito pp, subito ff – were especially admired. Think of the beginning of the fourth movement of the 9th. Today, we can scarcely imagine how people must have reacted back then to such a clash after the 3rd movement trails away. God knows, that was an explosion written using other means for other ears.

That's to say that Mahler was firmly rooted in the Classical tradition, like Bruckner and Wagner. Bruckner's symphonicism lives off subito dynamics.

Bernstein said that Mahler anticipated the catastrophes of the 20th century. Would you agree?

Dohnányi: I don't think much of such analyses. You can't 'compose' Auschwitz – before or after. Surely Bernstein meant that Mahler felt the world could be about to sink into chaos.

Bernstein popularised Mahler. Many people say that, basically, he overemotionalised Mahler. What would be the right approach?

Dohnányi: For me, such a question is very hard to answer since, in that sense, there is no right and wrong in art. Rather, there is a wrong. If there were a right, a composition would eventually become exhausted. We're all looking for the right and if we're lucky, we sometimes get close to it.

But if you were to tell me that there's someone who thinks their interpretation of Mahler is right, then I would be very sceptical. Bernstein took a lot for himself from all the music he made and this was the fascinating thing about his performances – especially for a performer who also composed.

But it was important then that other interpretations arose, with a different orientation: those of Pierre Boulez, for instance. In my opinion, one can reproduce these things differently without being wrong – but one cannot claim to be right.

What would you define as wrong in this context?

Dohnányi: If the interpretation becomes personal – for example, when conductors 'have a good cry' when they do Mahler. I always have to think about Beethoven writing the *Heiligenstadt Testament* during a fundamentally personal crisis, like the *2nd Symphony* – one of the most affirmative and sunny works he ever composed – both created around the same time.

Rudolf Kolisch once said in an interview that he felt so sorry for conductors when he saw them conducting slow movements because they always looked so sad …

When you say that Mahler composed 'inwardly', does that mean that broad swaths of his work are conceived in terms of chamber music?

Dohnányi: No, I didn't mean to imply that. For me, 'inwardly composed' means to have emotionally sounded oneself out and to have given the music form and expression corresponding to one's view of the world, one's aesthetic and the emotional world developing deep within.

Mahler was seriously involved with the philosophy of his time; he was an aficionado of Schopenhauer. I believe our time evinces how little the future can be calculated or grasped. For me, art is misunderstood if one says that Mahler formulated the future. He communicated precisely the time in which he lived, just as Bach did during his.

Is there a work of Mahler's which is especially important to you?

Dohnányi: The 1st, over and over – and the 4th. I don't conduct the 8th. On the other hand, I like the 9th very much …

Why the 1st so much?

Dohnányi: Its language is so overwhelmingly honest.

You have performed the 2nd and the 3rd relatively seldom.

Dohnányi: I haven't done the 3rd yet, but the 2nd, yes – although it only seemed successful to me when I approached it very 'formally'. I often hear it so weepily – I don't like that.

Why not the 3rd? Where do the difficulties lie?

Dohnányi: I can't really explain it. Perhaps – like the 8th – it's too closely bound to its time. I don't see any music of the future – to me, the proportion of expenditure to statement isn't right.

Is it too bombastic?

Dohnányi: No, bombastic would be the wrong expression. I listen to them and read them sometimes, but I'm not yet close enough to them.

Perhaps I'm wrong, but I detect a certain reserve in you regarding some of Mahler's expressive forms. Can that be?

Dohnányi: No, not at all, actually. You have to be capable of self-appraisal. At my age, I have to know where to find the contact which also contributes to my understanding of a work, not just for me, myself. I haven't achieved that yet with the 3rd – but that's not a judgement, it's just an acknowledgement.

So it's not an aesthetic criterion?

Dohnányi: No. You know, I like it when I think I'm helping a bit with the interpretation, too – so that some things become clearer to the listeners and to me.

You are a celebrated interpreter of Brahms. Mahler is certainly not in the Brahmsian tradition of motivic-thematic work – and I believe that, fundamentally, Brahms didn't understand Mahler – Mahler was formally too free for him.

Dohnányi: They had little to do with each other, although the theory of total antipodes is exaggerated. Wagner's attitude towards Brahms, for instance, was not as bad as they say – and Brahms, for his part, analysed the *Tannhäuser* overture with his pupils. They were not such personal enemies as the story would have us believe.

I think that Wagner thought much more of Brahms than we assume.

The case of Brahms vs Bruckner is similar. Both were of course incredibly different personae, but I imagine back then it was more of a fight amongst 'Twitter fans'.

How do you see Bruckner's influence on Mahler?

Dohnányi: Rumour has it that Mahler allegedly helped Bruckner pick up the pieces after the premiere of Bruckner's *3rd*, which was disastrous. The audience laughed and the musicians laughed. That is the worst that can happen to a musician – to be laughed at. But Mahler was standing backstage and he helped Bruckner – he took Bruckner very, very seriously, I think. Wagner was certainly another great influence – but Mahler was also very interested in Berlioz; he conducted the *Symphonie fantastique* various times.

His energy on the podium was legendary.

Dohnányi: Here again, we must recall Mahler's origins: a three-room flat, seven children, his mother pregnant with an eighth child. They were living very much in their father's Jewish tradition. He had to prove himself, even at home.

His power of self-assertion was certainly enormous – that's why he made so many enemies, as we know – not only in Vienna, but also in New York, where he was Toscanini's rival. Klemperer allegedly said, "Mahler is a thousand times more than Toscanini"; of course, Klemperer sensed what an extraordinarily dynamic artist Mahler was. But I don't think much of comparisons on that level.

Klaus Schultz once told me that when Mahler was in New York and whenever he had conducted *Tristan* or other major opera, he closed the score and said one single word. At that time, there were many immigrants in the orchestra, and at some time or other they asked one another, "What does he always say then? – It's always the same word … " and an immigrant answered, "Yes, he always says the same word: *Schmarr'n*." [roughly translated as "rubbish"]

Maybe he was just being ironic.

Dohnányi: Yes, but I can imagine him wanting to brush away his deep involvement with the piece by saying that. When you conduct *Tristan*, you are utterly exhausted, both inwardly and outwardly – drained, and then you can well say "*Schmarr'n*". Mahler was no stranger to parody, was he?

What would you have asked Mahler?

Dohnányi: I would have asked him how he managed to withstand living in a world which didn't understand him at all. It must have been unbearably difficult – and then there were also his personal matters, the conflicts with Alma – his life would have been so desolate without his music.

Certified Bruckner specialists such as Günter Wand, Herbert von Karajan and Christian Thielemann – none of them are Mahler conductors. Is that mere coincidence or is it significant?

Dohnányi: Well, Günter Wand is the product of a time when Mahler was unknown in Germany. He was certainly not against Mahler; basically, he simply had no opportunity to approach [Mahler]. His music was banned and many were the musicians whom it baffled. Let's just say that Mahler somehow became categorised as "like Bruckner, only kitschy".

Bernstein also suffered from it, until he was able to work on Mahler with a younger generation and new musicians. You should ask Thielemann personally about that – I would find his Mahler intriguing.

Karajan was a man whose greatness included his ability to adapt. He was able to adopt a mentality which was foreign to him relatively quickly. That is a gift and even a prerequisite for a professional musical performer. He came very late to Mahler; I knew him quite well and I experienced how Mahler truly fascinated him when he began to look at him seriously.

Did you talk about Mahler with Karajan?

Dohnányi: Yes. He became very involved with Mahler because Mahler had now 'arrived' – a situation completely different from Karajan's youth. But by the time he got older, the Berlin Philharmonic had played Mahler and they were waiting for Karajan's Mahler.

So the world of Bruckner and the world of Mahler are not a priori mutually exclusive?

Dohnányi: Well, we can read Proust and Thomas Mann, can't we? The worlds of both survive, they persist. There is one cosmos, where great art will always break through, undisturbed and irrespective of opinions.

(Hamburg, 16/082012)

Gustavo Dudamel

"Wow, Mahler!"

Do you remember the first time you heard Mahler's music?

Dudamel: It was years ago, and rather funny; my father played the trombone in a salsa group and was also playing with an orchestra. I remember finding the third trombone part of Mahler's *1st Symphony*. I recall taking my father's trombone and trying to play [*imitates a trombone*] ... I was maybe 11 or 12 years old at the time, and I was playing the violin. But I remember a recording of the *1st*; I received it as a gift from an uncle. That was the first Mahler I ever listened to. It was a very special experience because, even though I found it difficult to understand at the beginning, later when I started conducting, it was the first big piece that I performed. It was amazing because that was maybe three or four years later. I was 16 when I had that first experience with a Mahler symphony. So that was how I got into Mahler, listening to the orchestra playing his music in my home town, and especially through that recording I received from an uncle.

Did Mahler's world appeal to you immediately?

Dudamel: I think that Mahler's music creates a very special atmosphere. The kind of colours of nature, animals or that feeling of space that you have with Mahler are very unusual. It's almost a kind of 3D music. Not only do you hear things, but you feel them, feel how these elements surround you. The first experience of this can be really strange because first you listen to Beethoven and Mozart, to the classics, then you arrive at Mahler's music, and to experience all these elements is very special, almost crazy.

You worked with Claudio Abbado on Mahler's 5th Symphony in Caracas. Can you tell me about that?

Dudamel: I conducted the first and last movement of the *5th* for the first time in 2001, or maybe in 2000. I was rehearsing at the time with the National Children's Youth Orchestra, which would later become the Simón Bolívar Symphony Orchestra. Then, in October or November 2003, I conducted the symphony. I then went on to win the Mahler competition in Bamberg for which Mahler's 5th was the principal piece to conduct. The most beautiful thing about that was the experience with the orchestra, especially a German orchestra with a Mahler tradition and a tradition of that sound.

I felt like I'd received a gift from heaven when Claudio came to Caracas in January 2005 to conduct Mahler's 5th with the Simón Bolívar Symphony Orchestra. I thought I knew the score – but I was mistaken. A lot of things opened up for me then. I discovered that a certain element was related to another symphony, which could be from the *1st* Symphony all the way to the *9th*. Mahler's music follows one line. All of his music is one complete symphony. When I watched Claudio studying the score and when he told me all the details that one has to work on, I thought "Oh my God! This is the real Mahler world!" It was an amazing experience.

Conducting Mahler is difficult and not difficult. It is difficult to find every detail, but finding the essence of the piece is not difficult, because it is so clear. It's like when you see somebody and you can immediately understand their personality.

Then I remember I went to Israel to conduct Mahler's *5th Symphony*. It is a symphony that has become a part of my life. I was conducting it with the Bolívar Orchestra as part of a huge tour, during which I performed it 20 to 25 times. Later, I conducted it in New York with the New York Philharmonic and in London with the Philharmonia Orchestra.

Did Abbado talk to you about technical aspects of conducting, how to organise difficult parts of the symphony?

Dudamel: He told me, for example, about Willem Mengelberg. I think he had copies of Mengelberg's score, and when you see those scores, every bar and every note has a marking – it is really crazy. Sometimes you cannot even read the score because there are so many markings. For instance, I remember the beginning of the second movement [*sings*], where you have a ritenuto [*sings the same phrase again*]. And he told me the best way to do it, which, to my knowledge, he had seen in Mengelberg's score. He said that it was too difficult to do the ritenuto [*repeats the phrase*] … "Let's do a misurato" [*repeats the phrase slightly differently*] in three instead of two [*sings the phrase again*]. These kind of technical elements were wonderful. He told me things like that. I think you can learn a lot from seeing Claudio conducting, his easy gestures for example. Having this close relationship with Abbado was a very important thing in my life.

You conduct Mahler very emotionally. Is there a danger of overpowering his music?

Dudamel: It's funny, actually. I am thinking of what Sir John Barbirolli once said, not about Mahler, but about Jacqueline du Pré. He said that if you don't exaggerate when you're young, then what are you going to do when you're old?

Mahler was very passionate. He was not a conductor who was detached from the music and its passion and life. There are sketches of him making faces, jumping and moving and waving his hands even when he was conducting opera and other composers' music. This is an example of how his music has to be. And as remote and as serious as his music might be, there is a lot of passion there.

I think that there was always a child inside of Mahler that people sometimes don't see. They only see Mahler thinking of death, they see him thinking in a tragic way. But even in Mahler's tragic approach to life, there is this childlike part of him, made up of his memories, the memories of his country and the atmosphere of where he grew up.

You are conducting Mahler's 9th Symphony now. Can you talk about your relationship to it?

Dudamel: It's a very special kind of music, oh my God! It's breathtaking, it's like someone stealing your heart. I feel this symphony is like time. It's as if somebody said, "I will give you five minutes more of life", and you can do with it whatever you want. When you arrive at the adagissimo on the last page of the score, it is in the last two minutes that you can do something with your life. But it is a continuation of what has gone before because all of the last movement is about trying to find something. He is trying to embrace an eternally elusive hope. And you must go on, cherishing this hope, even though you don't know if there is an eternity after death.

The music is perfect. You don't have to do anything. The notes are there and the indications, 'faster', 'slower', 'pianissimo', 'sostenuto', 'marcato', everything. The only thing you can add is the energy and the vision. I love how Leonard Bernstein used to give titles to each movement. And I love the name he gave to the last movement, which he called 'Let It Go'. You know, "let it go, it's okay. This is what I have now; let's try to suffer a little bit more." It's not only his physical death, it's his spiritual death, too.

He did not have an easy time with Alma. And the most tragic thing is that he knew it was his fault. It is often like this with relationships. You do this or that wrong, and then, when the relationship finishes, you know that it was your fault. And that happened to Mahler; you can feel it in the symphony. He is pleading "Please, please, I am giving you my soul!" But nobody is listening because he didn't say it to her in words. He was in his little room, writing that music and trying to say it in private, screaming. When you visit those places, those little houses where he was writing, you can feel that he was screaming "Please, please, I am here! I love you!" But he was saying it to his music, to himself. That is the duality of his music: life, death. Love, no love. Hope, no hope.

I waited a long time to conduct this symphony. I have done almost all of them, and only this year I began to feel "Okay, I'm 'ready'." Not like [*puts on a mocking voice*] "Oh my God, I am the Mahler conductor; I know everything now!" Rather, I feel that I may be ready now to say something with this music or to try to say something about Mahler.

What would you have asked Mahler?

Dudamel: I don't know. Sometimes you don't need words with that kind of personality. To see him conducting or talking or walking ... You just have to enjoy: "Wow, Mahler!" It would be so terrible to ask him "Maestro, do you think this is in four or in three?" What could I ask Mahler? Many things or nothing. But I would have liked the chance to be close to him.

What did Mahler want?

Dudamel: Let me give you an example – let's say it's like with Pablo Neruda, the famous poet. We now know his letters, not just his books. Mahler's compositions were his private letters, his love letters. Writing music was his only way of communicating with the world. In the beginning, he expressed memories from his childhood. Then he composed the *Resurrection Symphony*, which came too early, but there it is. And then came the other symphonies. I think he was trying to show his soul – and his vision of the world. Many people say his vision of the world was political, but it was not – it was love. He was saying, "I am here! Maybe I am ashamed, maybe I am distant, but I am here! This is what my life is about, this is my soul!"

On the one hand, the most powerful conductor – on the other hand, that sensitivity. Someone with such a personality could explode ...

Dudamel: I think he had a very strong personality. He brought about big changes in the art of conducting, and not just in Vienna. Back then, the profession of conductor did not yet exist in the modern sense; composers conducted their own pieces. Maybe there were a few conductors at the time, but Mahler was like an emperor among them. Our profession emerged from that – he created the maestro conductor.

If you have that kind of power, you have to deal with it. And he did, but he suffered – so many problems and tensions were heaped upon him, sweeping over him like a wave. But he was very strong.

You conducted Mahler's 1st Symphony in your first concert with the Vienna Philharmonic at the Lucerne Festival in 2007. Was it your choice?

Dudamel: Yes! We were thinking a lot about what to do. And of course it was a challenge: Mahler with the Vienna Philharmonic! It was amazing when one of the players came up to me and said, "You know, my grandfather played under Mahler." I learnt a lot, just from the Viennese sound. It is a tradition that has been developing for more than 150 years. And this tradition is preserved, not because the players are the same – that would be impossible – but because the tradition has been passed on from one player to another. Many of today's players are pupils of the generation of musicians before them, and so on. What an experience!

Also: Barenboim was around. He was my soloist in Bartók's *1st Piano Concerto*. He is also close to Mahler and he helped me too, in a way. I had already conducted the symphony many times. It was my very first Mahler piece and I had been building on my interpretation for seven years before I conducted the Vienna Philharmonic. You cannot imagine how much I enjoyed it! It was like a dream come true.

Your self-confidence was impressive. During a rehearsal you asked the first violins how to use the bow on the G string at a certain place. That must have taken courage.

Dudamel: Yes! Of course you have the orchestra and they have their standards and expectations. But sometimes you have to create the sound that you have in mind – naturally with respect to the tradition and to the sound of the orchestra you're conducting. It's like when you have a Stradivari; you cannot force the instrument because it has its own sound. But you do have to coax it in your own way to create the sound that you want it to make. That's a conductor's life. [*laughs*]

(Vienna, 08/09/2010)

Christoph Eschenbach

"Mahler is certainly the greatest symphonist ever"

Do you remember the first time you heard Mahler's music?

Eschenbach: Mahler wasn't very popular in Germany during my childhood, for obvious reasons; he was banned during the Hitler years. Only slowly did Mahler symphonies return to concert programmes. I was living in the country, in Schleswig-Holstein, so I didn't have many opportunities to go to concerts anyway, but I remember listening to Mahler records. There was a very famous actor at the time, Gustaf Gründgens, whom I knew, and he introduced me in 1961 to the *2nd Symphony*. It's very interesting that it was him.

What did Gründgens tell you about Mahler?

Eschenbach: Well, first of all, he said that it was great music. And he talked of the journey, the voyage, from the first movement into all of the other movements, into the transcendent ending – which was already there in Beethoven's 9th, but here it is extended in enormous measure and formal scope. He talked very much about form. He particularly loved and talked about the Ländler, too. I wasn't very familiar with Austrian music, except for playing Schubert on the piano and loving it. So I naturally felt a connection between Schubert and Mahler.

Did you feel from the beginning that, in some way, you had an understanding of his music?

Eschenbach: Yes. The door opened very quickly. And there are other composers, for example, with whom I have struggled, not understanding them for years and years, and then the door suddenly opened: Shostakovich, for example. But with Mahler it was very, very fast.

What is the biggest challenge when conducting Mahler?

Eschenbach: You have to try to understand everything. I mean, it's not easy to understand everything intellectually, and you shouldn't be totally intellectual in your approach to understanding Mahler. Don't forget that his music is written at the time of Sigmund Freud, when psychoanalysis was emerging. Therefore, his music deals with big emotions – like Brahms and Beethoven – but also with pinpointed insights into the soul. You can discover that intellectually, but it's better if you go from the heart and from the soul itself, and try to figure out for yourself: "Why does this phrase go like that? Why does it break off so abruptly? Why does it switch all of a sudden to a totally different mood?" – because so much is happening inside; Mahler takes a big step further, breaking rules of form, going further than Brahms, for example.

You conducted Mahler's 3rd in Prague recently, and you told me that you had to work on the sound very much. Is there a special sound required for Mahler?

Eschenbach: No, but his sound scope has enormous amplitude; it can change from a *fortissimo* outbreak to an intimate scene *in pianissimo*. The amplitude is enormous and you have to work on that. You can't tolerate a *mezzo piano* where a *pianissimo* is necessary. You can't tolerate that in any music, but in Mahler it would be senseless.

Is there a danger of overpowering Mahler?

Eschenbach: Not of overpowering him, but of being on the verge of tastelessness. If you don't understand why certain things are called *'trivial'*, which are not actually trivial, and you let them be trivial, but take away the inverted commas, then there is a danger. There's very much irony in Mahler: irony in the Aristotelian sense of things which are seen from two sides at the same time.

How does that irony translate, in terms of performance?

Eschenbach: You have to grasp it, you have to see it that way, you have to investigate, and you also have to constantly ask the question: "Why? Why? Why?"

Are there conductors who influenced your understanding of Mahler?

Eschenbach: Well, I'm a strange person. I rarely listen to recordings. Especially when I'm performing pieces, I never listen to other people's recordings because I don't want to be influenced.

Certainly Bernstein influenced me and brought me further into Mahler, but that's a long time ago, and now I need myself – my insight – to listen to Mahler. I don't need others to give me insights. It sounds a little pretentious but it's not, it's just how it is.

Did you talk with Bernstein about Mahler?

Eschenbach: Yes, very much. And he was very, very serious. He also talked about that triviality which is not trivial, but which people see as trivial. Those marches, for example, or those really blatant Ländlers, or the Bohemian dance in the *1st Symphony*, *2nd* movement. And of the danger of exaggerating those things: he did not. People often say that he 'milked' Mahler's music – exploited it. It's not true. He was a wonderfully classic, 'classical' Mahler conductor.

But the first Mahler prophet for the people, after Mengelberg and Walter, was Stokowski. He brought Mahler to America. Bernstein wasn't the first after Bruno Walter. It was Stokowski. He gave the first American performance of the *8th* – in Philadelphia, of all places – in 1916. And eight years later, I believe, once again the *8th*, and then all of them. He was one of the great conductors anyway, in my view.

What was Bernstein's main advice for conducting Mahler?

Eschenbach: He was very careful with advice, actually, and especially with Mahler, because he himself was always so overwhelmed after conducting a Mahler symphony. I remember after the *9th Symphony* at Tanglewood when I went to ask him something, but he didn't answer. He was just totally overwhelmed, which I can understand.

Or after the *2nd*. It wasn't that he didn't want to give advice, he just lived the music: how to be so intensely in the music, and identify so intensely with the music. That was his best lesson actually, that he was so totally worn out afterwards, sweating. But he was not sweating with his body, it was his soul that was sweating, and that was his advice.

Did he talk with you about his understanding of Mahler's personality?

Eschenbach: No, not per se, but he always said he *is* Mahler. Yes, he identified with Mahler. He always said that when he was in Maiernigg, in the house where Mahler composed, he had a vision that he himself was Mahler. It was, of course, slightly exaggerated. But Bernstein was not pretentious, he was always *echt*. He was such an honest man that even things which poured out of him like that were as true as they were spontaneous. He had a vision that he was Mahler, therefore he didn't talk about Mahler – "He is *me*." [*laughs*]

Would you say the struggles in Mahler's life influenced his music?

Eschenbach: Well, yes and no. I'm always amazed by the contrast of composers like Beethoven, for example, who wrote his *8th* – which is the happiest one –

when his health was worst; Schumann's *2nd*: the same thing. It's about thinking positively to overcome suffering, almost like a formula, a medicine. But of course the suffering is there, and composed, and so an interpreter must work very, very hard to identify with all of that.

But would you go so far as to say, as Bernstein did, that the first movement of the 9th deals with his heart condition?

Eschenbach: Yes; it's obvious, actually. I think his irregular heartbeat, at the beginning and then in the climaxes, in the *fortissimo* where it's really desperate, is quite obvious and a bit like Shostakovich's *2nd Cello Concerto*, at the end, where the heart-and-lung machine was ticking.

Mahler wrote about how to organise his symphonies, especially about the flexibility of the tempi. Does that influence you?

Eschenbach: Well, I'm all for flexible tempi anyway, and I'm always being attacked for my flexible tempi and for seeing flexible tempi in compositions. That's like speaking or breathing; you don't speak like a metronome, you don't breathe like a machine, you don't think like a machine, and you don't sing like something or someone who doesn't breathe. So tempi are flexible because phrases have to have space around them, and with Mahler especially, since he expressed so many thoughts and so many emotions, and so many enigmatic aspects of the psyche. He needs space and time, and I think it's very important that you realise that as an interpreter, and that you never forget it.

How do you see the relationship between Bruckner and Mahler?

Eschenbach: First of all, Mahler loved Bruckner. He did the first complete performance of Bruckner's *6th Symphony*. And I think it comes from Schubert, who influenced Bruckner enormously, and then Schubert, who influenced Mahler enormously. He brought Austrian folk music into classical music for the first time, in his earlier works, which was very important; all those marches with trios – the trios were really from nature. And in his Ländler, in his dances, and then further on in his symphonies: look at the Scherzo of the *C-major-Symphony*, for example. Bruckner adopted very much of that rustic music into his style, and so did Mahler then from Bruckner. That is how I see the connection.

And regarding the masses, with the huge orchestra – was Mahler influenced by that?

Eschenbach: Yes. Bruckner was more erratic in constructing blocks. Mahler didn't use that technique so much, except of course the lengths of the symphonic arc, which Mahler carried over – and even prolonged. His symphonies are the biggest, longest symphonies, using everything possible – singers and choruses – and lacking only a narrator. Mahler is certainly the greatest symphonist ever.

How do you see Mahler's influence on the Viennese School?

Eschenbach: Certainly there are hints, especially in the 9th, which suggest his music's influence. For example, at the end of the first movement of the 9th there is a big flute solo, which is an 11-tone row, an exact 11-tone row, and the 'missing' component, the 12th tone, comes with the F sharp of the violin solo.

Schönberg claimed in his famous speech in Prague two years after Mahler's death that Mahler was a saint; so he really confirmed him as a visionary, and a visionary who influenced him and certainly Berg.

This is highly speculative, but if Mahler had lived another 30 years, in which direction do you think he would have proceeded?

Eschenbach: In the direction of Berg, I guess. And in which direction would Berg have proceeded after 1936, who knows? But Berg's *Drei Orchesterstücke* [*Three Pieces for Orchestra*] and Mahler's 6th – you might think they are by the same composer.

You conducted the 8th in Paris, and you tried to have as many singers as Mahler had in Munich in 1910.

Eschenbach: Yes; it had to do with the venue. It was Le Grand Palais des Sports, which seats 12,000 people. So we looked at the oval shape and took one side of the oval as the stage, and had one-and-a-half orchestras – that means the Orchestre de Paris plus all the members of our academy, the young people. Then we had three choirs: the Vienna Singverein, the London Symphony Chorus and the Orchestre de Paris chorus.

And we had 300 children from the *banlieue*, the suburbs of Paris. That was a wonderful initiative, a wonderful effort made by people to get underprivileged children to sing Mahler. They rehearsed for three months. I had a rehearsal with those children one month previously, and I still shiver when I tell you about it now; it was so wonderful, so overwhelming to see how those children were living the music, and wanted to do their best – and at the end, they were so fantastic.

That added up to 800 people – it wasn't a thousand, but it was close enough. And there was the spatial aspect; we had 9,000 listeners, and in the other part of the hall were the performers, and there was a bit of space between them.

Is it possible to bring Mahler's monumentality and his structural modernity together when you conduct his music?

Eschenbach: Yes, of course. The symphonies are masterpieces of composition. Sheer monuments of skilful craftsmanship. Everything is clear with Mahler, nothing is questionable or leaves you saying, "Oh, this is not so well composed" – it's perfect, perfect.

Why was it so hard for audiences to accept Mahler's music during his lifetime?

Eschenbach: Well, Mahler himself said, "My time will come." The symphonies were monsters for the audiences; they had never heard anything like them. The 8th was actually his greatest success. The others were kind of semi-successes. He conducted them in Essen, in Krefeld, and those are not really musical capitals – but he didn't dare to conduct them in Vienna because he already had so many enemies.

Would you agree that Mahler anticipated the catastrophes of the 20th century?

Eschenbach: Yes. Oh yes! In a non-outspoken way, but, for example, if you take the last movement of the 6th *Symphony*, this is a catastrophic movement. Therefore, there is a connection to Berg's *Drei Orchesterstücke*, which were written just before the outbreak of World War One. And they are certainly visionary of the catastrophe, and not the catastrophe of *a* war – there were many wars – but of that very First World War, which was so different from other wars before it, because it was the first modern one in a horrible sense. And I think Mahler, especially with the movements of the 6th, captures that same thing. Because from the beginning of the 20th century, there was something in the air that was in many, many ways opening minds, opening the whole way of thinking of mankind, and with it the possibility of the destructive catastrophe. The opening of abstract art, of psychoanalysis, of modern theatre, and at the same time, the evil force, which – not always, but often – goes with a creative destructive force. And one would hopefully learn from this, but mankind and learning is problematic to say the least.

When Mahler met Strauss, he asked himself: "Am I made of different material?" How do you see his character?

Eschenbach: He was a very courageous man actually, very courageous in every way: courageously fighting against anti-Semitism in Vienna, for example; courageous in going to a new continent, to America, to create something new there; and courageous in seeing himself as a loner in creation. But Strauss was actually conservative, or turned to conservatism when he saw that things were difficult in the reception of his music. So he went from *Elektra* and *Salome* to *Rosenkavalier* [*Knight of the Rose*]. In my view, it's a pity. Mahler, in the short time he lived, went so much further. He died in 1911 and touched the whole century, the 21st century as well. Mahler is so modern today. No wonder people like Boulez conduct Mahler all the time.

A contemporary of the future.

Eschenbach: Exactly.

What did Mahler want?

Eschenbach: I think Mahler wanted to tell us to be aware, to be receptive, and even to enjoy every moment in life. Because his life was so short, he certainly did, and he expressed it in music. He wanted us to discover that alertness to every moment in life: whether it's people, nature, transcendent things, metaphysics, or simply the physical and metaphysical in oneself.

(Schwarzenberg, 26/06/2009)

Daniele Gatti

"Mahler should be performed simply and humbly"

Do you remember the first time you heard Mahler's music?

Gatti: I was nine or ten when I began to study music. And of course the names familiar to me were Beethoven, Mozart, Chopin, Rossini, Verdi – but not Mahler, not at all. Once I heard my father say: "Mahler, Mahler – there is a symphony of Mahler on the radio", but I was unimpressed. Later on, when I was growing up – I was 12 or 13 – almost every evening he would bring home a new record. They covered the entire repertoire – from Mozart to Stravinsky – and that was how he tried to introduce me to the orchestral sound. I remember he brought Mahler's *1st*, conducted by Bruno Walter, so the first time I listened to his music was with my father in our sitting room – at least 20 minutes of the *1st Symphony*. And there I was, listening, without any particular emotion – but subconsciously I was absorbing his style.

My next encounter was much stronger; it was when I was studying at the Milan Conservatory – the *6th Symphony*, the European Community Youth Orchestra, conducted by Claudio Abbado – it was in the late 70s, I believe; I was 14 or 15. The concert was fantastic – the experience of my lifetime! I remember I went to the Conservatory library to borrow the score of the *6th* the very next day. I bought the record and spent weeks and weeks listening to it with headphones on, reading the score at the same time. That was my first, really deep impression of Mahler.

When did you first conduct Mahler?

Gatti: The first Mahler symphony I conducted was the *4th*, in Venice in 1989, at La Fenice. I was 27. I remember that during the first half hour of the rehearsal I didn't understand a thing – it all seemed to be a lot of noise coming from here and there. I didn't have the feeling of being in control of the situation. I remember during the break I went to my dressing room. I was alone and I thought: "I'll have to change the programme." I was supposed to be in control of Mahler; I had studied that symphony day and night, it was in my blood, but I couldn't control it! During that 15-minute break I said, "No, no – I have to control the situation." So I returned and began to rehearse almost bar by bar. Until then I had conducted Tchaikovsky, Mozart, some Beethoven symphonies, but not the complex polyphony of Mahler. It was a shock, but also very useful that it had that kind of impact on me – and then to gain control of it.

How did you proceed?

Gatti: Since then I have conducted the *1st*, *4th*, *5th*, *6th*, *9th* and the Adagio of the *10th*, all the *Lieder* except *Das Lied von der Erde* [*The Song of the Earth*] and *Lieder eines fahrenden Gesellen* [*Songs of a Wayfarer*]. And time after time I have tried to understand what Mahler is saying with the notes he put on paper. Recently, I attended a concert of his *5th*. It was a good performance, but no one, to my mind, was paying due respect to the music on the page. The initial triplets are marked "*flüchtig*", just to leave a sort of looser flexibility – but the tempo made them terribly rushed. Then, where Mahler marks "*vorwärts*" or "*schwungvoll*", I heard a ritardando. That annoyed me because I couldn't understand why the conductor was imposing his personality on the music to make it different from what Mahler wrote. We have to rein ourselves in, I think, and especially with Mahler, return to the essence of the tension that the music can create.

How should a conductor approach Mahler properly?

Gatti: For conductors today, Mahler seems to be the most personal composer. I don't want to be too critical, but sometimes there is too much freedom. Why are we so careful of playing Beethoven or a symphony of Mozart, attending so much to the text, yet with Mahler we take so many liberties? Instead, I think Mahler wrote all those indications, the *Anmerkungen*, in the scores in order to instruct the conductor carefully. Probably because of this kind of romantic idea of being a performer, i.e. of 'consuming the music' and creating a new piece, this can become a bit extreme, as it did in his time. We know that Wagner brought a lot of freedom to the conducting style; a lot of new ideas. On the other hand, during Mahler's time, Toscanini began to bring back more purity to the music. Not so histrionic, not so much personal feeling, but just trying to find what is behind the notes.

Which Mahler conductors have influenced you?

Gatti: I am more attracted today by Kubelík, Klemperer … straightforward, temperate yet profound interpretations totally respecting the score. Or take the

Boulez recording of the *3rd*, which I absolutely adore. Pierre discovered something new in the music – it sounds almost modern.

We can talk about the nostalgic aspect of Mahler's music, but sometimes that nostalgia makes for viscosity, like molasses. It's clear that he wanted the Adagietto to be conducted in seven minutes, or in seven-and-a-half minutes. I am unable to do so. I manage it in nine minutes, or no more than ten. But then I also think: "Why is the Adagietto so slow in performances?" It becomes an adagio grave – whereas, if you consider the score, it seems that it is actually a sort of 'Lied to Alma', a kind of love letter.

Also, the position of the Adagietto in the second half of the symphony, if we split it in two – the first two movements are a very dramatically desperate world. And then, when the Scherzo begins, it's like opening a window in the morning and listening to the postilion's horn. It seems like a totally new symphony, composed by another hand.

Would you agree that Mahler anticipated the catastrophes of this century?

Gatti: It is very difficult for me to say. What I feel in his music is a sort of depression. And there is a sort of depression also when he wins – and he is an overwhelming winner. If I compare him with Beethoven when he is winning, in the finales of his symphonies, everyone knows he is truly victorious. Mahler needs to say, "You see, I'm winning. You see, I am here, I am still alive." And in some overwhelming finales like the 5th, the 7th, the 1st, it seems he probably wants to show even more that he is a happy person.

But behind that, even in the fortissimi, in the brightness, there is a sort of melancholy, of 'tristesse'. We are living in a time in which the Internet is the metronome of our lives. And we are unable to stop time and to think for a moment about our lives. Today, we cannot enjoy progress because progress is consuming us. And in humans I think there is also a sort of melancholy, because even if you are able to obtain and achieve something, if you take a step, there will still be something else you have to achieve – it's a race against time.

I am a man of this century. I don't know what happened in Mahler's time. I think his music makes me uncomfortable in a way, and I sometimes feel like I'm eating a cake that's too rich. Then I need to drink water to wash out my mouth. But take the last page of the *9th Symphony*; that could have been written by Anton Webern.

Which of Mahler's symphonies is dearest to you?

Gatti: Probably the 9th. I waited before conducting it. I was 37, and probably still too young. Now I'm 47 and gradually getting older … I'm happy to have done it at that age because it is one of the scores that you live your life for. And it's nice to see how it can develop. But it was probably a bit too risky for me to conduct it at the age of 37.

Is there a risk of overpowering Mahler?

Gatti: I think Mahler is sometimes used by performers to show how good they are. We have to be very cautious about that, because he was a man who suffered so much. We cannot use his music just to show that we are fantastic. So I have been waiting to do the 7th and the 3rd. Now it's time to do them, but only after more than 20 years of conducting.

Sometimes I think it's a shame he didn't compose an opera. He was certainly one of the greatest opera conductors of all time; I like to find the theatrical aspects in his symphonies. There is always a tension between characters – and you see the two, three, four themes.

When I work with an orchestra and there are a lot of string portamenti that Mahler asked for, and if the players are unable to understand that kind of portamenti, I say: "Don't play the portamenti as a technical thing but just as a result of vocal thinking." If you render the passage like a singer making a portamento, it's probably what Mahler desired. He knew the voice very well, he knew the repertoire. There is that connection between the human voice and the music he wrote.

Pierre Boulez told us that he found his way to Mahler through Alban Berg. If you look at it from the other direction, in which way did Mahler open the doors to the Viennese School?

Gatti: The first answer, technically, is the 12-tone chord in the *10th Symphony*: the Adagio, when he uses it for the first time. We can also go back to the last Beethoven quartet if we are looking for a kind of technical solution. From the three composers of the Viennese School, Alban Berg is probably closest to Mahler – due to the sense of nostalgia. And whereas Berg was Viennese, Mahler was a guest, a visitor. I think they are very close because there is a sort of lyricism in the music of both composers where the harmony may be unclear, yet there is always some kind of hiatus, like a cadenza.

The background of the Viennese School is surely contrapuntal – the lessons from Bach, fugues and canons. I see Berg and Brahms more related in the sense of control of form and the way they are able to work with the old forms: variation, passacaglia and also the sonata – how they were able to keep invigorating them, find fresh material. Mahler, on the other hand, didn't use the variation form in his symphonies.

In *Wozzeck* and with the monorhythm of *Lulu* in Act 1, I think Berg is closer to the composers of the Classical school, the First Viennese School, than the late Romantic composers. Apart from the technical point of view, listening to Brahms and Berg, you hear the music going fluently, although it is built up note by note, mathematically. From my standpoint, this is the connection between the two composers. Listening to that music, it seems as if it comes so fluidly from the pencil – yet it is the result of utmost work à la Beethoven, in a sense.

Mahler probably had a different impact on the technical aspect of composition. The sonata form dominates, but then he goes to a dance, Lieder, and rondo form. And the only contrapuntal movement he ever wrote was the Rondo-Burleske.

How do you see Mahler's influence on Berg?

Gatti: Berg fills his scores with indications like "Ausbruch", espressivi, crescendi, diminuendi. Every bar is indicated with a sort of 'rise and fall' dynamic. This is quite close to Mahler.

If we are talking about orchestral sound, Berg and Mahler are characteristically quite close. But Berg didn't have a chance to review his last works before he died: the *Violin Concerto*, the *Lulu Suite* and the opera itself. They are miracles of orchestration. We then have *Das Lied von der Erde* [*The Song of the Earth*] and the *9th Symphony*, which Mahler never heard. That is very sad.

Would Mahler have revised his 9th? It was the only one of his symphonies he did not hear.

Gatti: Probably, yes. Just to get the transparency of the voices you really must have a top-notch orchestra to play it properly. I do not retouch the orchestration – some conductors put the bass drum on the second note in the last bar of the finale in the *1st*, for example. I totally disagree with this because it is only the finale which is orchestrated with percussion. It's not an echo but a very empty sound, just strings and the winds playing the second D, without percussion.

(Vienna, 13/05/2009)

Valery Gergiev

"Mahler's *Seventh* made me sleepless"

Do you remember the first time you heard Mahler's music?

Gergiev: I remember it very vaguely. It was the *1st Symphony*. Obviously, I was a very, very young man, but I remember that final movement when the horn section suddenly stands up and continues to play while standing. It's a very powerful statement of desire in this symphony. That was very memorable.

That was a long time ago and, of course, it was also a long time before I started to look at Mahler's symphonies – although when I was preparing to participate in the Herbert von Karajan Competition for young conductors, I saw that Mahler's *1st* was on the list of pieces to prepare. That meant that if you prepared it, you could be asked to conduct the second movement, part of the finale, part of the first movement or just a couple of tempo transitions at the end – they don't give you the entire symphony to conduct.

Was Mahler played regularly in St Petersburg when you were growing up?

Gergiev: No. Just occasionally a great conductor performed him; Kondrashin conducted the symphonies, but Mravinsky did not conduct Mahler. But there were, of course, guest conductors – I remember very well Erich Leinsdorf and Zubin Mehta, both with the New York Philharmonic. Zubin conducted the *9th*. It was long ago and we considered that repertoire as being relatively unknown, although the *2nd Symphony* was performed – it was somehow thought to be very grand and successful, maybe because of the huge choir and voice.

Did you have recordings?

Gergiev: Very few. What people thought about the cycle of Mahler symphonies was unknown. Of course, there were great people like Leonard Bernstein, Klaus Tennstedt, Georg Solti and Rafael Kubelík, but it took many decades before the cycle of Mahler symphonies became part of what you could call the property of many great orchestras and audiences everywhere. Even in Vienna it took time and it was not that easy for Mahler himself in Vienna, as we all know.

Mahler visited St Petersburg. Can you compare the Mahler tradition there with Amsterdam, where he also was performed when he was still alive?

Gergiev: Well, he went to St Petersburg twice. He conducted music by other composers, especially Beethoven, but he also conducted his own *5th Symphony*. It seems that he was extremely impressed by the orchestra. He got a good response and was given a very welcoming reception. When he went to St Petersburg, it was not an unhappy period in his life.

On the other hand, in Amsterdam, he had Willem Mengelberg. He was not only one of the most loyal and most gifted conductors, but also one of the most powerful because he already had a huge following. He was in a position to do what he found most interesting and most important. Also, St Petersburg was already heading towards disaster. Things were already looking somewhat dangerous in 1905. There had already been a famous bloody event which was followed by smaller but equally dangerous incidents. The system was already shaken. The Mariinsky Theatre, of which I have been artistic director for 22 years, was one of the leading houses in the world, if not the *pre-eminent* one. All of the composers were there – Schönberg, Debussy, Strauss, Mahler, Bartók, Hindemith and of course all the big Russian composers. Stravinsky was there all the time because his father played first-desk contrabass in the orchestra; so he came to the rehearsals as a boy and heard many great performances. So did Prokofiev, including *Kitzeh* and some Wagner operas. So they were all practically children of that tradition. At the same time, tsarist Russia was reaching perhaps its most dangerous period for centuries. The last years were the most difficult for the Romanovs.

The Imperial Theatre was becoming increasingly popular and after Tchaikovsky died, when Rimsky-Korsakov was still alive, St Petersburg was practically flooded with the great musical names. Everyone was coming – Nikisch, Bülow, Hans Richter, and not just for single concerts – they were performing entire festivals. Hans Richter twice conducted the Festival of Wagner Operas, as it was then called. And of course there were also others, including Karl Muck, Felix Mottl, Weingartner – to name them all would make for a long list. But it was a fantastic time in St Petersburg – or Petrograd, as it was called before the Revolution. It still continued, even when the Bolsheviks were there, until the late 20s, early 30s. Klemperer, Bruno Walter, Alexander von Zemlinsky, they all came. Unfortunately, Mahler had already been dead for a long time, but Zemlinsky continued to come; Erich Kleiber was there several times and did a lot of work there. And some of those conductors would perform Mahler symphonies. They were big scholars, especially Sollertinsky, who was one of the first influences on Shostakovich, making him open his eyes and ears to the cycle of Mahler symphonies. That was very important.

Is Mahler now completely understood and accepted in Russia?

Gergiev: I think Mahler is respected in Russia and I think my orchestra and I contribute to that more than any other conductor or orchestra in Russia. We have performed in about 10 cities. We played the 8th in Kazan, for instance. We used a local chorus along with our own. It was a huge event and it was great to see how many young musicians were there, practically hanging from the chandeliers. The hall was overflowing and there were a lot of young people sitting and standing.

In Yekaterinburg it was the same story; it repeated itself in my native city of Vladikavkaz, where we played Mahler's 5th. That was also very special. We gave a huge performance in Nizhny Novgorod, in Moscow and in St Petersburg ... So it started to look like a tradition or even a movement was developing.

Would you say that the audiences in Russia understand Mahler because of their familiarity with Shostakovich?

Gergiev: I think that helps me – maybe other people, too. I certainly feel much more secure when I approach a Mahler score with all my experience of Shostakovich. I hear certain things which other people may not find immediately. And it's not about a certain interval or tonality; it has to do with the musical intensity – the way the music tries to express what is in your heart and your mind – of speaking out musically. And this is where Shostakovich and Mahler are in some ways similar. Of course, Shostakovich was someone who followed, someone who heard his, if not mentors, then certainly his great predecessors.

Maybe Shostakovich's *4th Symphony* is closest to Mahler. He didn't really borrow the musical material; it is quite different, much more dissonant. It's a fantastic symphony, but I strongly believe that Shostakovich, although he was a very Russian composer, couldn't avoid, or maybe didn't want to avoid, the most fundamental emotional power he was given by Mahler and his symphonic cycle.

And he said that if he could take only one record to a desert island that he would choose Das Lied von der Erde *[The Song of the Earth] ...*

Gergiev: Yes, certainly. It was absolutely clear that a lot of time was spent in the late 20s analysing Mahler. Those people probably also had a chance to look at some of his scores when visitors were there. I am sure they talked about

Mahler, not only with Klemperer, but also with many others coming from Germany or Czechoslovakia or Austria. This was clearly the case.

You once told me that you had difficulties in finding an approach to Mahler's 7th Symphony.

Gergiev: I had problems conducting it; always at some point in the final movement. I went with the Rotterdam Philharmonic to perform in several cities and I remember very well a concert in Prague, in the Rudolfinum. After the concert – although the acoustics were good and I couldn't possibly complain about anything – I felt that I still didn't have the key to fully understanding that problematic symphony.

So, to be honest, I spent a sleepless night in London before the recording and I made some very radical decisions, because I felt I had to stop trying to present the symphony gigantically. I wanted the finale to sound, in a very simple way, like something you could call a Rondo-finale – although it is orchestrated much more powerfully than famous Haydn finales, it is still after all a Rondo-finale. And I felt that I had to find a combination of power and intensity along with an ethereal feeling of lightness, one that was not deeply pensive or portentous. Because sometimes a final movement can draw back from an important statement, like going back to normal from a dramatic moment in your life – looking forward to something else. That's how I saw it.

One could compare it with the finale of the 5th Symphony.

Gergiev: In many ways that is true – except that the *5th* is shaped in such a way that you don't want to add anything and you don't want to take anything away from it because it's just perfect. With the *7th* you have to spend some time on it and perhaps be your own severest critic. That's what happened to me. Finally, when the recording in London took place, I felt for the first time that I was close to making [the *7th*] start to work. That was maybe one-and-a-half or nearly two years ago – and quite an involved story with me and that symphony.

How important are Mahler's instructions for you as a conductor?

Gergiev: Mahler was a great conductor, so he made it nearly impossible for a conductor to impose his own personality on the performances, to take one of his scores as if it were a quick sketch and improvise his way through it. His music is so calculated and clear that it is next to impossible to distance yourself from it. But still there is a bit of leeway – the performance venue is always important because the acoustic aspect is crucial. Listening to Mahler's Adagios must be a miraculous feeling, for example – playing them must be ultra-special, particularly as regards the sonorities you can achieve.

Which Mahler symphony do you feel closest to?

Gergiev: That is very difficult to say right now. I recently conducted the *10th*; I spent a lot of time trying to make it sound like a piece of music written by a composer who was mysteriously approaching his last months; his death was imminent. But when I am performing this music, I still make a big effort to incorporate the composer's smile, if not his laughter – because even if the music is not completely hopeful, it is still somewhat optimistic. You see the difference between complete hopelessness and some sense of hope. I also always do this with Shostakovich's music – I refuse to think that Shostakovich had anything to do with propaganda or dictators, Stalin or Hitler. That's not why he composed his symphonies.

Shostakovich composed his symphonies because he wanted to compose music. If Mahler had written his autobiography, if he had lived another 10 or 15 years, maybe he would have given us explanations and would have made it easier for us to understand why he composed the Adagio, which is strange in so many ways. Strange to us, that is; but then the music of Berg or Webern or Schönberg and many others can make Mahler's sound like a first statement of the New Viennese School, as opposed to waiting for Schönberg to theoretically explain the Viennese School with its techniques of composing atonal music.

So we are still not entirely clear on this and I think the Adagio should sound like yet another statement about human life, about nature and this huge musical world in which we constantly want to progress, small though we may be.

What questions would you have asked Mahler?

Gergiev: Well, I would certainly have asked him to conduct at least one of his symphonies for us. And I certainly wouldn't have missed it.

Are there any questions that you would have liked to ask him about his scores?

Gergiev: When I look at a score of a Mahler symphony, I can't help asking myself why he indicated some of the things he did. He will write "*kräftig*", for instance – OK, that's clear; he wants it to be powerful. But then he will warn you not to rush or not to drag, "*nicht schleppen*", so that you don't make the audience feel like they've just taken a sleeping pill. Mahler's scores are famously full of such indications.

Why didn't Mahler compose an opera?

Gergiev: Maybe because of the greatness of the operas that he conducted. His *8th Symphony* might be his opera, in a way.

Mahler conducted Mozart, Beethoven, Wagner and Tchaikovsky. I conducted *Iolanta* in Vienna in 1992; it was one of my very first performances here. And Marcel Prawy, who was in the audience, told me: "You are the second conductor to conduct *Iolanta* in Vienna. You know who the first was?" And he didn't even give me time to think before he said: "It was Gustav Mahler."

What did Mahler want?

Gergiev: Well, maybe it's my turn now to ask you what you would have asked Gustav Mahler if you were given the chance to talk to him. Maybe you would ask him that question. It's very difficult for me to talk about music and especially to talk about Mahler and his deepest thoughts. I am quite sure that he wanted to be a happy man and a happy musician. He was a man who sometimes went so far beyond the usual that, famously, some of the musicians, especially in New York, simply didn't understand him.

He was a gigantic musician, making music of the highest calibre. And if anyone could, then it was he who could explain things and demand from any orchestra in the world certain things in order to constantly raise the quality. There is no doubt that he knew everything about every instrument, about orchestration and so on. But the truth is that even very experienced musicians found it difficult to understand him – even in New York, back then. I just conducted the New York Philharmonic – they are completely different now: a wonderful orchestra that can play anything.

But at the time, Mahler had trouble just making himself understood. Sometimes, [the American musicians] made this known in an unpleasant, even rude way. But they just didn't know what the conductor was talking about. A lot of them didn't care whether he was a composer or not because his symphonies had not been performed. But sometimes a conductor is what I call so far ahead of the average level of some of his fellow musicians. Perhaps that was part of Mahler's tragedy. Maybe it was not that often that he had a hundred musicians who would share everything with him, who would put some love and warmth and their whole heart into the symphonies.

Do you think that was one of his most painful experiences?

Gergiev: Yes. Because it is bad enough if you conduct a Beethoven symphony and you see that your colleagues onstage do not understand your intentions, but for this to happen with your *own* music, for it not to be understood, not to be supported … It could in the best case be ironic, but in the worst case it could be interpreted as aggression towards Mahler and his compositions. That might have been a major factor in his early death.

(Vienna, 29/05/2010)

Michael Gielen

"Bernstein turned Mahler into kitsch"

Do you remember the first time you heard Mahler's music?

Gielen: I remember very well. It was around 1956 in Vienna; Mitropoulos performed the 6th with the Vienna Philharmonic. I admired Mitropoulos very much; I was also his assistant at the opera.

I had read through the 6th, but I wouldn't say that I knew it. As a conductor, I was still a beginner, but it was clear to me that the symphony was so under-rehearsed that it was barely recognisable. Of course it is a very complex work – the third movement was wonderful, but the second turned out to be very problematic, due to the changes in metre and the syncopations – and I would describe the finale as noise.

How has your understanding of Mahler developed over the years? You worked with Julius Patzak, for instance, and he had worked with Bruno Walter.

Gielen: Patzak was a phenomenon, a wonderful musician. His voice literally cut through the music – he was still able to carry the day, even when he basically had hardly any voice left. Around 1958, I stepped in for Paul Kletzki at the Musikverein for *Das Lied von der Erde* [*The Song of the Earth*], and Julius Patzak sang, if I'm not mistaken. I had only a few days to learn the piece; it was a dire situation. There is even a recording of it; it's not too bad, but Erwin Ratz, the president of the Mahler Society at the time, an old friend of the family and of Eduard Steuermann, said to me afterward: "Michael, that will not do" – and he was certainly right.

Patzak told me important things about the piece – for instance, that only two horns, not four, must be allowed to play so that, in the first song, the tenor can come through at the place with the apes. He also told me where I should replace a piano with a forte – not for the entire orchestration, but for certain instruments which the tenor would cover over. He was very experienced and I was very grateful to him for his help. Of course I would have tried to tone things down so that he came through – but when you know what you should tone down, then it's much better.

Josef Polnauer told me that the students would always go to the standing-room section at the Vienna Court Opera to see if Mahler was conducting, because the conductor's name was not given on the programme leaflets yet. If Mahler came out into the pit, the students stayed. Apparently, they could tell the tempo from his walk – the orchestra musicians said that, too. He had such an incredibly suggestive aura; he must have radiated much energy.

Polnauer said that Mahler conducted very wildly because he wanted make what he wanted clear to every musician; apparently, he had too little rehearsal time. But his style became calmer later on. On Steuermann's recommendation, I studied music analysis with Polnauer. Erwin Ratz had provided bread for Polnauer during the war.

Did you immediately realise back then that such a world would be captivating you your whole life long?

Gielen: I've been asked about that many times. I started off with music of the modern era, the music of my own time, especially the Schönberg school. Thus, for instance, in 1949, when I was still playing the piano, I performed all of Schönberg's works in Buenos Aires for his 75th birthday, and after that, I gradually mastered all the symphonic works. By contrast, normal development would have been starting with Mozart, Haydn and Beethoven, and then working through the Romantics up to the moderns – depending on whether Mahler counts amongst the moderns. But mine was precisely the other way around; I began with the Schönberg school, first as a pianist and then as a conductor.

Promoters soon realised that I wanted to perform modern music and that I could, too. And I was penalised for that because they only engaged me for modern music. That's no way for a conductor to develop; one needs to work through the great repertoire. So I would ask again and again for tonal pieces – for pieces that audiences could grasp and from which I could learn my trade.

Eventually, Hessian Radio had me conduct Mahler's 5th – that was when I still lacked the necessary conducting experience to do the piece. I heard a recording of the performance a couple of years ago; it's terrible; I simply had no idea what to rehearse. It wasn't just the tempi and the rhythms which gave me problems – I had trouble getting through the piece at all. But let's not forget that the music of the 5th *Symphony* is sometimes very complex.

Is Mahler's music autobiographical?

Gielen: That's difficult to answer. What Alma reports about the metre changes in the Scherzo of the 6th – that they represent the children romping about – is certainly wrong, like almost everything she handed down to us. I believe she made that up – this music is not about children. Mahler's fatal mistake was prohibiting Alma from composing – that wrecked their relationship; she never forgave him for that. He did not recognise what she actually wanted from him – I don't understand that. His poor health in his last years certainly had something to do with her. There are people who defend Alma – but I am most certainly not one of them.

I do not believe that his music is meant *expressis verbis*, autobiographically – I think that every artistic statement is autobiographical, intentionally or not.

In terms of Mahler's aesthetic: Bernstein went so far as to say that the beginning of Mahler's 9th reflects his coronary problems.

Gielen: Yes, but Bernstein was a simpleton in that regard. We are dealing here with a musical phenomenon, not a biological one. We know that Mahler had an irregular heartbeat – well, so do I. But I do not think that my beating would be different if I were in perfect shape – I think that is nonsense.

Speaking of conducting style: Bernstein popularised Mahler. On the other hand, he was accused of overemotionalising Mahler.

Gielen: He turned Mahler into kitsch.

You would agree with that, then?

Gielen: But of course. Bernstein makes a huge thing out of everything; he is devoid of objectivity – he transfers his personal emotions onto the interpretation of the music. My feeling is that his emotionality was more important to him than the score. I believe it is a huge misunderstanding to say the great Mahler renaissance began with Bernstein, because he sentimentalised and exaggerated everything. Perhaps it's nice to hear 'Bernstein's Mahler' – but to a large extent, that is not what is in the score. Bernstein brought the aspect that one could call popular music to the forefront.

The sound of the 7th points much more towards the later modern era – i.e. the contemporaneous compositions of Schönberg and Berg – than one would assume when listening to Bernstein, who underlined Mahler's regressive elements. That's also why I would say Bernstein was such a great success: because he, and not only he, conducted Mahler completely ignoring the 20th-century elements of his music – people's inner turmoil, societal conflicts, which are material components. But I do admire him in other things.

Should we be protecting Mahler from his admirers?

Gielen: I believe we must have the courage to waive a certain part of our success by playing Mahler less fulsomely, by not drowning everything in lavish sound. We must gear our work to the polyphony, the multiplicity of the sounds. We should not shove the vertical onto a standard, romantic orchestra sound – on the contrary, we should be trying to bring out the individual lines.

Bruno Walter and Otto Klemperer both knew Mahler personally; have you been influenced by their recordings?

Gielen: I don't know all of them. I heard a great performance of the 2nd by Klemperer in Vienna. But I don't know of a recording of the 7th; I think he deliberately avoided making one. It is a very tricky piece, and one generally has less success with it than one would wish. Of course I know Walter's recordings, the various recordings of *Lied von der Erde* and one of the 9th. But I'm not sure when that recording of the 9th was made; I assume that there are two versions – there is certainly a live taping from the 1930s and most likely a studio production from America.

One of Walter's major concerns was to smooth Mahler over, to help him to his breakthrough. I think he didn't conduct as resistively, as roughly, as inelegantly as he should have, according to the score. Walter avoided the actual problem of the sound – a predecessor of Bernstein, so to speak.

Would you say that the Bernstein School founded a Mahler tradition in opposition to the music?

Gielen: With every conductor who attempts Mahler, it's always a question of the education he has had, his schooling. There are issues to be addressed, such as the problems with Beethoven, whether the clarity of the entire texture and the polyphony were already crucial for conductors a century before Mahler, whether to unify or to soften. If you take Beethoven too seriously, he can be an unpleasant composer – play him too slowly and he can seem very tranquil – which he was absolutely not, in my view.

People compensate in time for what they wreck in playing Beethoven too slowly by playing Mahler too fast. Mahler himself said he could already see that generations of conductors would take the entire Scherzo of the 5th too fast. Listen to the entire phalanx; I don't think anyone adheres to it – they just plunge right in.

You mean that exaggerating the effects in Mahler actually masks his modernity?

Gielen: That's it exactly, yes.

Where would you begin if you were to attempt to define Mahler's modernity?

Gielen: With the content, definitely. As I said before, Mahler's subject matter is the turmoil of the individual and of society in the 20th century. That must be perceptible even if the music is momentarily peaceful. Otherwise, [the subject matter] is jeopardised, the rug continually pulled from under its feet, so to speak. All hell breaks loose in the development of the first movement in Mahler's 4th – which is always called 'Haydnesque'. If it is presented properly, and not smoothed over and stroked, then the rug really is pulled from under your feet. With many famous conductors, the Adagietto of the 5th takes between 16 and 17 minutes – but even if it only takes 14 minutes, it's still too slow. It was timed during Mahler performances – at the world premiere, perhaps he was very nervous, but it lasted eight minutes – later on, the Adagietto never took more than nine minutes – it mustn't ooze sentimentality.

I think Visconti's film [*Death in Venice*] reinforced all of that; he did a terrible disservice to Mahler – the audiences identified the actor with Mahler, too. Perhaps the film was excellent, but it was outrageous to make Mahler's music so unrecognisably slow merely for the sake of the film. You have to know Mahler very well to deal with that film – it's a shame there's no law preventing something like that – I mean, seriously.

Have there been fundamental changes in your approaches to Mahler in coming to terms with his music?

Gielen: No, not really. But I learned this profession and those pieces slowly. When you are facing a symphony lasting 80 minutes, you have to have rehearsed and conducted it often to be able to do it properly – instead of being preoccupied with yourself. This is a problem that confronts every conductor sooner or later: being involved with the music, not with oneself. If a conductor is struggling with himself, he cannot get to grips with the subject matter. But if he has enough stylistic sense to find the right tempo and get the right notes from the players, and if his dynamics are clean, then he has a better chance than a conductor who projects himself through the music.

Two different schools of conducting continue to emerge; the first pair of opposites being Mendelssohn and Wagner. Wagner was certainly Furtwängler's model; he conveyed the poetical material, but I think it wasn't always related to the subject of the piece at hand because the tempi weren't right. To refer again to Beethoven; Furtwängler often conducts him far too slowly, although there are metronome markings for the symphonies.

This aspect does not apply to Mahler, since unfortunately, he did not write metronome markings. Playing his fast movements too quickly would not be so rampant if he had. Even if conductors do try to ignore metronome markings, they can't block them out completely. The average image of Beethoven has changed greatly since Furtwängler's time, especially due to Toscanini. But even he didn't concern himself too much with metronome markings – he constantly conducts marches, for example, at a pace which is by nature very fast.

Looking at the relationship between Mahler and the Viennese School; to what extent did Mahler make it possible?

Gielen: First of all, he did it personally. Although Alma helped out with money, I don't know how it was with him. But he was very convivial, he often invited Schönberg and Berg to dinner – Webern, too, as far as I know.

Yes, there is the anecdote where Mahler said they must read Dostoyevsky and Webern replied, "But we have our Strindberg."

Gielen: [*laughs*] Dostoyevsky was probably too old-fashioned for him. Schönberg and his pupils worshipped Mahler – foremost, I think, because he so energetically challenged tradition at the opera, and because his conducting style was so remarkable. Apparently, no one in Vienna had heard such Beethoven and such Schumann before Mahler came along – which was certainly one of the reasons why he was hated so much. The fact that Mahler and Schönberg both invented things at the same time which shaped a style is fundamental, even if Mahler's dissonances aren't as radical – but he was born in 1860, 14 years before Schönberg.

Although both of them were Jews, I don't think their origins were determinative for their style. I believe transmitting subject matter was more important than emancipation for Mahler. And personally, I am very, very grateful to him for expressing 20th-century subject matter in a language that audiences accept. Schönberg's language is still not accepted by the general public – Berg's is somewhat more, but I think that's because he wrote operas.

The catastrophes of the two World Wars are also 20th-century subject matter ...

Gielen: Look at the *6th*; in the Finale, there is certainly a vision of a catastrophe – the catastrophe has already happened in the *9th*. The first movement attempts to cope with people, with why they are the way they are.

Mahler was interested in Charles Ives' music – the story goes that he took the score of Ives' *3rd Symphony* with him, intending to perform it. As we know today, that didn't happen and that score has not been found in his estate. Who knows whether Mahler lost it or threw it away? Ives was very interested in popular music – and there are many vulgar passages in Mahler's compositions.

What do you admire most about Mahler?

Gielen: The scores. He conducted almost every evening, yet he was still able to write meaningful music up to 70 minutes long during the 2 1/2 months of his summer holidays in Maiernigg, Toblach, etc. And he orchestrated and refined that music, too, although he was at the opera almost every day during the season. I don't know how much work was left to do during the summer – you can see from the facsimile of the *10th* that he always sketched in a great hurry. He was not in Vienna at the time, yet he knew he had only that one summer, because he was obliged to travel to New York.

Where would Mahler have gone?

Gielen: I have no idea – I don't think it's important, either. Mahler achieved so incredibly much in his short time. He was an exemplar of operatic work and a paradigmatic composer. It amazes me that he managed to reconcile them – he had to earn his living, too, and he couldn't do that with his symphonies. I think, if given the choice, he would have done less opera.

What I do not understand is why Mahler did not reconvert to Judaism, as Schönberg did in 1933 – simply as an affirmation of the Jewish people.

(Vienna, 24/09/2009)

Alan Gilbert

"In New York he was kind of giving up"

Do you remember the first time you heard Mahler's music?

Gilbert: I couldn't swear that it was the first time I heard his music, but my first memory of Mahler is very clear. I was nine years old and my parents decided that it was time for me to hear all of his symphonies. The New York Philharmonic was playing a Mahler festival in Carnegie Hall, I think it was in September or October of 1976. They bought me a ticket and I heard all of his symphonies. I think the first one was the *5th* and – maybe because it was the first or maybe because there was this incredible trumpet solo that really struck my nine-year-old fancy – that's the one that stayed with me. But I did hear all the symphonies.

It was back when the seats in Carnegie Hall were not reserved for the boxes, so whoever came first had the front seat in the box – now they are numbered – so I would make my father get me to the concert early and I would run up the stairs, and there was one other young guy who wanted to be in the front as well and we would race up the stairs and it was always the two of us in the front of the box. That was probably a life-changing experience for me, to hear Mahler's symphonies.

As a nine-year-old hearing this complex music, wasn't it just overwhelmingly loud?

Gilbert: You know, I liked music and I liked going to concerts. For my 10th birthday, which was a few months after that, my piano teacher gave me a pocket score of the *5th Symphony*. I didn't think about it then, but it must have been because I had spoken about the experience – obviously, it had made a great impression on me. I still have the score, it's a treasure … it was the first score that was my own, and it was the *5th Symphony* of Mahler, the piece we just performed the other night in the Musikverein.

Do you remember who conducted in 1976?

Gilbert: Absolutely. Erich Leinsdorf, James Levine and Pierre Boulez shared the nine symphonies and they also did most of the orchestral songs – it was a major Mahler event in New York. Actually, they did the Adagio from the *10th* as well.

Very different approaches then ...

Gilbert: Yes, completely!

Your parents are or were members of the orchestra. Did they know anyone who played under the baton of Mahler?

Gilbert: I don't think so; I think that was too far back. You know, it was really Leonard Bernstein who was responsible for the Mahler renaissance in the United States. The symphonies, back in the 1960s when he was conducting them, were not so well known and not so commonly played. I think that's the history of Mahler performances; he was obviously an incredibly important musician in Vienna, Prague and Hamburg, and all the places where he was chief conductor, and then finally in New York, but for various reasons he suffered an unjust neglect for a while. Then came Leonard Bernstein and I think he thought he was Mahler. He not only conducted the music brilliantly, but he really identified with the soul of the music and made an incredibly convincing case for it. I think for a long time there were a lot of musicians who felt that the only way to do Mahler was the way Lenny did it. Now, of course there's a myriad of ways to play the music. But I really am grateful, and I think we are all grateful to him for championing the music the way he did.

At the same time, Bernstein was blamed for overpowering Mahler. Is there a danger of overpowering his music?

Gilbert: I think so, although you can't really argue against his interpretations of Mahler because they were his interpretations and he was such a great musician and such a great man that you were convinced when you heard him conduct the music.

There is such a huge Mahler tradition in New York. Could you define it?

Gilbert: Well, I have always felt that the New York Philharmonic has an innate understanding of Mahler's music. What I like about that orchestra is that they really bring great feeling to everything they do. The thing that I find amazing about Mahler's music is that it can really withstand many different approaches.

You can hear very different performances of Mahler that still sound convincing.

Some conductors say that with Mahler all you need to do is follow the directions, because the scores are so carefully notated and because he was such a wonderful conductor himself that he knew precisely what he wanted. So, if he says "slow down", then you slow down and if he says "don't slow down", then you don't slow down – it's very clear what he wanted.

But having said that, there is an incredible range of possibilities in the way you approach Mahler. Let me just talk about some performances I have heard; I have enjoyed Mahler played by the Vienna Philharmonic – you somehow feel that the folk aspect and the traditional Austrian dances are just so natural with them. Then you might hear a British orchestra play and you don't have that same sense, but there's a clarity that might be very telling for the music. When the New York Philharmonic plays Mahler I think there's a wonderful mixture; there's an intuitive understanding of the folk side, but it's not as pronounced as when you hear, say, the Vienna Philharmonic. But in New York I do appreciate a deep feeling of pathos and of the life experience that the orchestra imbues with every note.

Arturo Toscanini felt that Mahler could be dangerous for him in New York because he was such a tremendous conductor. Have you looked into that?

Gilbert: Well, I have read a great deal about Mahler and it appears that every place he went he was in competition with other great musicians in the area. He must have been a difficult man in a way and he had some kind of need to be the one and only. Toscanini also had some of that, I'm sure – he famously said to one soprano who proclaimed herself a star that, when the sun is out, you don't see the stars. And I'm sure that Mahler felt that way, too, somewhat. When you have two such giants in the same city … just imagine what a time it must have been, to hear Toscanini conducting the *Ring* and then to hear Mahler conduct Wagner operas – what a terrific opportunity for New Yorkers.

Yet it seems to me that Mahler stopped struggling to be number one when he was in New York.

Gilbert: Well, I think he was kind of giving up, he was letting go of life. He seemed to have lost his spirit by then. He was a hypochondriac and I think that while he wanted to remain optimistic, somehow there was a pessimism that crept in, which is a sad way to live. It's a shame he only lived for some 50 years –

that wasn't really long enough; he seemed to be just reaching his stride as a composer when he died.

The Mahler renaissance started very late in Europe, during the 1960s, 50 years after his death, but it probably would have started earlier had it not been for the Second World War. Why do you think it took so long for Mahler to become popular in the United States?

Gilbert: Who can say. There are other composers who have been neglected and who finally came back. Bach was neglected for a long time in Germany. Maybe Mahler was ahead of his time, maybe he really did foreshadow something not yet comprehensible. He was so brilliant and he had such an imagination of what an orchestra could be. I even think there has been no composer who has really exploited the possibilities of an orchestra quite the way he did. If you listen to the power and the richness of experience that he could create with a large orchestra, yes, but with an essentially traditional orchestra – there was nothing unusual about the instruments he used. Yes, he added an organ and he used eight horns rather than four, but essentially it's a traditional orchestra and the colours and the power and the richness of texture that he could create – unequalled before or since, I believe. And the message he was trying to convey – he was so consciously trying to say something – and that's perhaps why he started to use voice and songs in his music, because he must have felt that there was a limit, eventually, to what he could express with instruments only. He was trying to say so much that maybe it was more of a leap than people were able to take. He was there himself, at first, to champion his own works and to be his own advocate, but after that, maybe there was no one else who was able to carry it on at that time.

But in New York he didn't conduct his own music very often …

Gilbert: That's true, he didn't do a lot of his own music; I get excited when I read about the range of his repertoire and the music that he liked – Italian opera and, of course, a lot of German music, and composers we have never heard of. And he really knew those scores; he would revise them and rewrite them. He was obviously intimately and deeply involved in an incredible amount of repertoire, so I'm sure a lot of people didn't even think of him as a composer.

Have you studied the Mahler scores which are now in the New York Philharmonic archive?

Gilbert: Studied, no, but I have seen many of them; it's fascinating to see his own markings. Even in his own scores there are changes which haven't appeared in even the newest editions, and it's not clear whether he wanted them to be definitive changes or if they were based on the moment. He was above all a practical musician, so if there was one musician in the orchestra who may not have been up to playing a particular line, he would put it in another instrument or if he felt some instrument wasn't playing loud enough, he would double it somewhere else or add percussion to emphasise something. It's not clear and I don't think we'll ever know for sure whether he wanted these markings to remain or whether they were just based on one particular week when he wanted to get the best performance he could. But it's amazing to see his brain, and his writing is so neat and meticulous. He was obviously an incredibly thoughtful composer.

Almost all the chief conductors of the New York Philharmonic have been great Mahler conductors – Bernstein, Boulez, Mehta, Maazel. Do you feel the tradition, that heritage in the orchestra, in the sound, in the articulation?

Gilbert: Absolutely! And that's not only true for Mahler and the New York Philharmonic. Great orchestras bring something to the music they play which really affects conductors. I think the challenge and the secret to working with orchestras like these is knowing how to accept what is offered, but not to let it completely drown you. I have enjoyed conducting many composers, but with Mahler there is definitely a special will that the orchestra has and there is a current that compels you to go with it. It's really a pleasure to conduct music that the orchestra feels so strongly about. I think they love to play Mahler and they know that they sound good when they do, so there is always a special energy. No matter who conducts Mahler with the New York Philharmonic, and I have heard different conductors do it, you can still feel the personality of the orchestra coming through very, very strongly. This is true for a number of composers, but maybe for Mahler most of all.

What did Mahler want?

Gilbert: [*laughs*] What did Mahler want? That's a very hard question and I certainly don't think I can answer it. But I guess that he wanted music to be very important to people; he was a complete musician in that he was a performer who performed his own music. His compositions were genius, but I also really admire that he recognised the value and the quality of so many other composers throughout history. I think that, to him, music and life were basically the same thing. He wanted happiness and he obviously experienced tragedy in his life and, while he wanted to express that through music, he also wanted to transcend it through music. He must have deeply believed in the power of music to not only represent life, but also to enhance it. And I'm guessing and hoping that this was what he wanted, that he wanted music to be truly meaningful to people in their lives.

Was his music referring to his time, to the fact that everything was headed for collapse soon after he died?

Gilbert: Undoubtedly. The *fin de siècle*, especially in Vienna, was obviously an incredibly fraught, difficult time where the old was going out and the new was coming in. And I think Mahler is a very emblematic composer in that way, because he took the symphony and kind of destroyed it and turned it into something absolutely brand new. This makes him a very pivotal figure in the history of music.

Which of his symphonies is closest to you?

Gilbert: You know, I have a very soft spot in my heart for the 7th; I love it very much. You seem surprised by that answer. I find the 7th just so mysterious, and sometimes I think it's my favourite. I know this is a provocative answer, but I mean it. There is something about the 7th that just draws me in, in a very bizarre way. But the 1st is also an amazing work. It was written earlier, of course, and it's a terrific explosion of energy. It reminds me of Don Juan in that it's an early work by a younger composer who has a well of experience and life force that somehow just had to come out in a completely fresh and new way. The 1st is amazing to me in that way, what Mahler was able to do in it. I think the 9th maybe goes the furthest emotionally and philosophically. It's not quite as bizarre and twisted as, say, the 6th, 7th and 8th. I think he goes back to a more direct and more sincere musical language. So, I would say maybe the 1st and the 9th in that way, with a special allowance for the 7th.

Where would Mahler have gone in other circumstances?

Gilbert: It's hard to say. He didn't write that many pieces and his oeuvre is relatively limited in terms of genre, compared to other composers, and he did seem to create a kind of 'closed arch' in his work. I really couldn't say where he would have gone. He didn't seem interested in writing an opera, which is strange, because people say that he might well have been the greatest opera conductor ever. He also wrote very little instrumental or chamber music, except for maybe one piece. But symphonically, he made a very convincing statement through his works and it's a real canon ... I wish I knew.

How do you see Mahler's influence on the Viennese School?

Gilbert: I think it's enormous. And that's why I have often programmed Mahler and Berg together. I think it's very instructive if you hear, for example, the unfinished *10th Symphony* and then go straight into Berg's *Drei Orchesterstücke*, because it really could be a completion of that symphony. Berg started with his sensibility of Mahler and took it one step further. I don't know if Mahler himself would have gone there had he continued to compose, but Berg and then even Schönberg with his highly serial music – I think that disintegration of the traditional approach to composition started with Mahler. You can hear it in the *9th Symphony*, which becomes virtually atonal and is completely off the map as far as traditional harmony goes. Maybe the next step was what was picked up by Berg, Webern and Schönberg.

What would you have asked Mahler?

Gilbert: I'm always interested in what might be a very mundane, musician's, insider-type question, but I'm always curious about the tempos – what tempos he would have taken, for example, the Adagietto in the *5th Symphony*. If it's a love song, should it sound drippingly sentimental and pathetic or should it have a freshness, an eager, young, springtime character? The tempo can affect that a lot and it's hard to glean from the score. He says *molto adagio*, extremely slow, and I wonder what that means because 'slow' is obviously a relative concept. I'd be very interested to ask him first of all what he thought the right tempo was, but also how much latitude he would allow other performers. He didn't hear other people perform his music and so I don't know if he thought his music could be that freely interpreted, and I'm curious what he would make of the variety of approaches people take today when they perform his music. So, I would ask him what he thought about that.

(Vienna, 17/05/2011)

Bernard Haitink

"I always found Mahler alarming"

Do you remember the first time you heard Mahler's music?

Haitink: Of course. The first Mahler I ever heard was on old 78 rpm records; it was *Das Lied von der Erde* [*The Song of the Earth*]. With Charles Kullmann, Kerstin Thorborg and Bruno Walter – probably names that don't mean anything to you anymore, except for Bruno Walter. It was 1946.

Was Mahler immediately accessible to you?

Haitink: Not in the least. He was forbidden in my country until 1945, and before that I was simply too young. Bruckner always appealed to me. I remember a radio broadcast of the 8th in 1938; I was nine years old. But that was all – after that, it took quite a long time; in September or October 1945 the Concertgebouw Orchestra performed Mahler's 2nd in Amsterdam. That was of course a symbolic deed, with the idea of resurrection.

There was also a Mahler Festival in 1920. One could say that Amsterdam was the very first city to appreciate and recognise Mahler.

Haitink: The Mahler Festival in 1920 must have been a great affair – Willem Mengelberg was at the height of his career. It's interesting that he performed Mahler less and less after that festival.

Does anyone know why?

Haitink: I believe it was because he thought that the Mahler Festival had been enough. He did do the 1st and the 4th after that. There is that recording of the 4th where you have to be very attentive – it's somewhat distorted. He was a bit too free – and probably a bit too vain, as I've been told. But times were different then.

Traditionally, Amsterdam is a tolerant city. Could that be why Mahler was accepted there at such an early date?

Haitink: Amsterdam has always had a very significant Jewish populace – incredibly musical – and Mahler was a true favourite. They always hoped for performances, they wanted to hear Mahler – and they were fans of Willem Mengelberg.

Unfortunately, Mengelberg was surrounded by controversy during the Occupation. He was a great conductor, but he was not very sensitive. He never had an instinct for sensing what he could or should say. He would simply say stupid things – even if he believed what he said, he should never have spoken them. But that's how it was; and after the Occupation he was *persona non grata* – which is a terrible shame.

The Jewish populace who came back after the war – decimated, but nevertheless – were always trying to get Mengelberg back. They loved music and Mahler passionately. But I'm treading on thin ice when I talk of political matters – I'd rather not talk more about that now.

Amsterdam can be very proud of that tradition.

Haitink: It was a great thing for Mengelberg to bring Mahler to Amsterdam. He was still young at the time, the structures were much stricter then and he once wanted to take a weekend off so he could go to Düsseldorf to hear a very gifted composer conduct his *3rd Symphony*; the composer was Mahler.

Then he performed Mahler's *4th* on a Sunday afternoon with the Concertgebouw. After the interval he turned to the audience and said, "We are going to hear the *4th* again – but this time, Gustav Mahler will conduct." Fantastic! Amsterdam had a treasure in Mengelberg. Amsterdam is a tolerant city, and I hope it remains so.

Have you performed with musicians who played under Mengelberg?

Haitink: Certainly. My violin teacher had played second violin in the orchestra – not at the Mahler Festival, he was too young, but he was a member of the orchestra in 1930 or 1935. He admired Mengelberg passionately – but as I said, Mengelberg wasn't conducting Mahler anymore by then.

What happened after the war?

Haitink: I've done a bit of research on that. It all began again, very slowly. The return to Mahler was difficult; in Amsterdam – for the orchestra, too – there was no longer a Mahler tradition and so the music was de facto new. I remember that Erich Kleiber performed the 3rd – but that was much later.

Bruno Walter had already conducted Mahler in Amsterdam before the war; afterwards, he came back and performed the 4th again. That was his piece. The difficult works, such as the 7th, the 9th and the 6th, had to wait a long time. Rafael Kubelík and Hans Rosbaud came; both of them performed the 9th.

Bruno Walter had worked with Mahler – his style was completely different from Mengelberg's.

Haitink: Yes, he was much stricter. I've always admired him greatly; he was like a role model for me. I attended some of his rehearsals – he conducted the music warmly, classically and very masterfully.

Did you have contact with him?

Haitink: No, I was far too shy. I got a short thank-you letter from him; I had it framed. I was with the orchestra in Los Angeles and I had sent him flowers – "From an admirer" – and he answered, "My dear colleague …" – wonderful!

I find it surprising that you didn't sense any Mahler tradition when you took over the Concertgebouw.

Haitink: There wasn't one anymore, especially since so many of the Jewish musicians didn't return to the orchestra. It all had to be built anew. The sound was different, too – leaner, less lush. My predecessor Eduard van Beinum was a wonderful, very aristocratic conductor, but he was so terribly in Mengelberg's shadow, and he had distanced himself from Mengelberg's style. Van Beinum also performed Mahler's 7th – that was heroic because no one had performed the 7th then. The style had changed. I don't think he performed the 8th – that piece is somehow 'too peculiar'.

Did you study Mahler with a teacher?

Haitink: No. I only learned about Mahler in the concert hall. Back then, I was a very young, fascinated music lover who lived around the corner from the Concertgebouw building. I heard every one of the concerts.

Is that how your grasp of Mahler grew?

Haitink: I always found Mahler alarming. Bruno Walter and Hans Rosbaud opened up Mahler to me, but when I was younger, his music alarmed me.

Bruckner always gave me inner peace, even though I'm not a religious man – Mahler always agitated me because there is never a personal affirmation.

What agitated you so?

Haitink: Those moods are more superficial – but I don't want to analyse that too much now. The thing that irritates me about the Mahler cult these days is that there are people who only want to hear Mahler. I think that's a terrible shame.

I once got a letter from a music lover who had heard Mahler's 3rd. He wrote that he had wept through the entire piece. I tried to answer him very carefully; these things can be very tricky: "If so, then perhaps you need a psychiatrist. Your behaviour is not really healthy – there is still a lot more music."

I conducted the London Symphony when I was young; they wanted me to do Mahler, but he was not at all popular at the time and the concert halls were half empty. But I experienced that attendance was increasing more and more. Today, when orchestras go on tour and want to be sure that the halls will be full, they play a Mahler symphony. Many of my colleagues also conduct Mahler because he's in demand. Am I happy with that? No.

I know Mahler said, "My time will come." But I'm not sure that he would have been happy with this avalanche of performances – some of them are excellent, of course, but some are too loud and gimmicky. I don't think that serves Mahler's life's work.

I'm also cautious because I know what a chain of performances is like. It's not good for Mahler's work. Somehow, performances of Mahler must remain exceptional – like Bruckner symphonies – they should not be churned out on a conveyor belt.

Are we already overfed?

Haitink: Yes. It's overkill.

Can the emotions also be exaggerated?

Haitink: Yes, because Mahler already has so many emotional instances. Do we need to emphasise them as well? That is a big question. Personally, I've never tried to do more than what is already there. Then I've been criticised for being cold. But that's how this business is – and I don't think I am cold; certainly, compared to Bernstein, but that's another matter.

In my view, Mahler wrote symphonies, not rhapsodies with enormous eruptions. Of course there are enormous, incredible eruptions, but the symphonic form has its limits.

How important are Mahler's conducting instructions for you?

Haitink: I am aware of them. Sometimes they seem superfluous today, yet they must not be ignored. Why? He wrote in those instructions because there was no tradition at all back then. It was a different time: "nicht eilen", no?

Which of Mahler's works do you feel closest to?

Haitink: I love the 4*th*; it has such wonderful chamber-music tenderness. I am very cautious with the 9*th* – it's still something very special and it should not be performed too often. I'm also cautious about the 2*nd*, even though I love the instrumental parts very much. The first movement is wonderful, and so is the semi-sentimental second movement, and the third movement as well. It's all wonderful; the 'little red rose' is miraculous – but I could live without the fifth movement.

Because you are not religious?

Haitink: I wouldn't put it like that. The idea of resurrection is not for me. I'm also against after-the-fact completions. Which is what is now happening with Bruckner's 9*th*; discovering sketches and commissioning composers to write a finale. I've done Mahler's *10th*, the Adagio, quite often; I was always uncertain, the differences in my tempi were always incredible – unintentionally, which is unusual for me. I also think that the Adagio is simply unfinished; I'm sure that Mahler would have added or omitted something – you must be very self-confident to complete the *10th* as, for example, Deryck Cooke did.

Would Mahler have changed the orchestration of the 9*th?*

Haitink: No, and no one should. It's Mahler's last thought and that should be respected. Of course, he might have changed things – but that's his business, not ours.

How do you see his personality?

Haitink: We must be careful here. The impression left is a unilateral one. He must have been a complex man, like many of us, but he was also a wonderfully gifted man. Of course, he made many enemies – a director of the Vienna Opera has many enemies before he has even moved into his office. Mahler himself said it: "If I want to know if I'm still director, I knock on my door – and if someone says, 'Come in', then I'm still director." But you're familiar with that …

Every year you hold a kind of 'conducting workshop' in Lucerne, where you pass on your experience to young conductors. What would you say to them with regard to Mahler?

Haitink: I would say that it's not as easy as it seems: the tempi, the transitions. Those are very tricky things with Mahler. They have to work seamlessly – and it doesn't happen by itself.

Do you rehearse Mahler differently from Bruckner?

Haitink: It's different music. [*laughs*] With Mahler, it's important that the dynamic gradations come through clearly – that everything isn't a mezzo forte soup. That is very important because there are so many details. And of course there are Mahler's own indications; he was always trying to make the music more transparent.

Karajan once said that there is only one climax in a piece, pointing out how important it is not to try for that climax too soon. You must take it gradually – even in the *2nd Symphony*.

Where is the climax in the 2nd?

Haitink: At the end, of course.

Did Bruckner influence Mahler?

Haitink: I don't hear it; Bruckner's orchestra isn't so large. Bruckner always had the Vienna Philharmonic in mind when he was composing. It wasn't his way to use exotic instruments as Mahler did – the Schellen [sleigh bells], the cowbells. It's very important to deploy such instruments appropriately with Mahler. Of course, he also gives very precise instructions – "as if from afar", for example.

Another interesting thing with Mahler is that there is always a 'but'. He is never too direct.

Haitink: Exactly.

It seems to me that you have difficulty hearing Mahler played too harshly over and over again.

Haitink: When it is supposed to be harsh, then I'm the first one to want it that way. Think of the 6*th*; there are terrifying moments which need to be worked out. But we mustn't load everything with effects – that must be kept in mind.

What would you have asked Mahler?

Haitink: I don't know. Probably too much. I don't think I would have dared approach him.

What did Mahler want?

Haitink: That question cannot be answered like that – better to listen to his music; that is where the answers lie.

(Salzburg, 24/08/2012)

Manfred Honeck

"The rubato is essential when conducting Mahler"

Do you remember the first time you heard Mahler's music?

Honeck: I remember it very well. I was a member of the Austrian Youth Orchestra; we went to Berlin to participate in the Karajan Competition. Several youth orchestras from all over Europe were taking part; I heard the Junge Deutsche Philharmonie performing Mahler's *1st Symphony*. I was extremely impressed right away, not only by the big sound – other symphonies have a big sound too – but also by the way Mahler treated the darkness and the special significance of his music, particularly in the third movement.

It might have something to do with my own experience of losing my mother. She had nine children. I took part in the funeral, of course, and the way it was conducted reminded me a little bit of this music. I must have been 13 or 14 years old at the time and it was remarkable. It was probably one of the most important moments for me. I was almost shocked that this could happen with music, that it could come into my life and into my heart, where it has stayed ever since.

We are here in Vienna, where Mahler enjoyed great success as a conductor at the Opera. At the same time, he was attacked in a way composers rarely are, and faced such struggles. Where did those conflicts come from?

Honeck: Well, I'm sure it was partly his personality. He was an extremely proficient conductor and he wanted everything to be perfect – he demanded it from himself and from the musicians and singers with whom he worked. So in a way, he was very radical.

And the other thing that always amazes me when you go back to the time in which Mahler lived is what happened to the symphony per se. The symphony was still the holy grail – Beethoven, the hero, of course Mozart and Haydn, Schubert and Schumann, Brahms and Bruckner – they treated the symphony as a whole and as a 'holy art form', so to speak. And then along came a composer who started to write music that one hears in a salon orchestra. We have to bear in mind that at this time, and also later on, many of the musicians of the

Vienna Philharmonic, of the 'Hoforchester' [Court Orchestra], spent their free time at wonderful summer retreats, playing in salon orchestras. There they played transcriptions of *Tannhäuser*, for example, as well as music by Johann Strauß, marches, galops, polkas, waltzes, everything.

When they came back from their holidays and played again in the Vienna Philharmonic, they suddenly experienced a composer who was putting all those elements into his compositions. So you can imagine how the musicians at the time thought this was something cheap and trivial. Nowadays, we understand it, but at that time they didn't. And even lately, when I was playing in the Vienna Philharmonic, some members told me that they didn't like Mahler because they found his music trivial.

Do you remember any specific Mahler experiences which were important to you during your time as an orchestra musician?

Honeck: I played Mahler's 6th under Leonard Bernstein – that was very impressive. I also played the 7th under Lorin Maazel's baton – he has an exceptional love for Mahler's music. Then there was also Claudio Abbado's love for Mahler's music that impressed me tremendously. I had the opportunity to organise the first concerts of the Gustav Mahler Youth Orchestra in my capacity as Abbado's assistant.

Can you compare their different approaches to Mahler and to your own?

Honeck: I think it's like a puzzle you have to put together. But I would say, after having heard all those different interpretations and played and conducted Mahler myself, I developed an increasingly strong interest in old Austrian Bohemian folk music.

I was forced by my father, who was a very simple music lover and did not have a great knowledge of music, to play the zither – an Austrian folk instrument. I didn't like it very much, but because my father wanted me to, I played it.

I spent two years with a teacher who could hardly read music. I had already had violin lessons at the Hochschule [University of Music and Performing Arts] in Vienna – but that teacher always wanted me to play in a certain way, and I protested, "But it doesn't say that in the music", yet he persisted, "You have to play it in this rhythm", and so on. So we had this little battle; I played all the minuets, all the marches, all the waltzes on the left hand, learned how to produce the sound on the zither, and to accompany, play the bass ahead of the melody or behind it. He was very stubborn. He said, "That is our tradition!" I stopped after two years.

Later on, when I was working and studying Mahler's scores, I was back in this world and I realised that those two years had been crucial to understanding Mahler's music – because the Viennese way of playing is sometimes very different to what we hear and experience even here in Vienna. You don't play what is written in the score, but you mustn't improvise too much either.

So how does one do it? What I had learnt was the art of rubato playing. And this is also in the music of Mahler. The way that musicians a hundred years ago played in the salon orchestras – it was natural for them because they were trained to play the waltzes of Johann Strauß in a certain way; they didn't have to write it down. And neither did Gustav Mahler. He wrote a lot of things down in his scores that are very important, but he didn't specify those bits because the musicians played them that way anyhow.

So for my interpretation and my understanding of Mahler, that is very important. Recently, someone told me: "Your recording of Mahler's 1st sounds extremely modern and new", and I said, "No, it's not really new. I was simply trying to go back a hundred years and think about how the rubato was to be played." To our ears, a hundred years later, this actually sounds new and modern, but it isn't, really.

Talking about different interpretations – Leonard Bernstein is often criticised for overpowering the music. On the other hand, there is an approach to Mahler which renders his music somewhat meek and dry. Where does your way fit in?

Honeck: I always try to work out the meaning of the music. The music tells you what you have to do. I am a big fan of chamber music, I have always loved it. I grew up with chamber music: Haydn quartets, Schubert, and even the Bruckner Adagios – this is great music for learning to listen to one other and exploring the depths of the music.

When Mahler asks for a certain dynamic and a certain way of reading the music, you always have to think of chamber music, in my opinion. How can you make an explosion, how far can you go? If everything is loud, then what is left? If everything is soft, what is left? So you have to point out the climaxes – and to avoid any misunderstanding, climaxes don't equal loudness for me. Climaxes can also mean softness. And there are hundreds of moments in Mahler's music when you have the climaxes in the silences, which is great. And I want to work this out.

In the first movement of the 3rd, for example, it's not only the beginning; it's not only the third movement which describes a countryside idyll; it's also in the last movement when the first moments of the first movement suddenly come back. But they come back as an idea, like childhood memories, so it must sound far away. This is one of those incredible moments – the softer you get it, the better and stronger it is.

On the other hand, some of the explosions that describe his desperation also need working out. Or the beginning of the second movement of the *1st* – it cannot sound rustic enough because he wanted to establish a heavily rural Ländler in this music, so I would not feel that it is light and joyful circus music; rather there must be a deep understanding of the 'Lederhosen' sound that we experienced in the old salon music.

So this is the way I see it and this is the way I think Mahler's music should be treated. But Bernstein is one of my heroes and he was so honest in his music-making – he felt it like that. And it was always convincing, I think. It was great.

Would you say that Mahler's complicated personal life influenced his music?

Honeck: Definitely, because Mahler was honest himself. He brought all of his different emotions to his music – his desperation as well as his feelings of exaltation. You will feel his childhood experiences everywhere in his music – in the fourth movement of the *4th*, for example, with the angels and *Des Knaben Wunderhorn* [*The Boy's Magic Horn*], the boyish element in it …

So all these childhood experiences are there in his music – his disappointment in love, his first loves as well as a sense of desperation. Also, he was thinking about the meaning of life, at a time of transition, at the turn of the century, when Vienna played a very important role, politically as well as musically. There was this feeling that the world would be destroyed, an apocalyptic view of the future. But he also incorporated a feeling of being in heaven; he put everything into his music that was in his heart, in the heart of someone I would call a great human being. But then again, he demanded so much that he could also be a little bit arrogant and nasty to other people. But what a thinker! Personally, I think he loved people very much and demanded a lot from them.

Together with Anton Bruckner, he anticipated the entire 20th century. What we experience now, in the Mahler years of 2010 and 2011, our problems with nature and the environment – isn't there already something of this in his music, all these apocalyptic elements? I think so, and I find this is what makes his music so modern and so fascinating, even though it was composed a hundred years ago.

So you agree with Bernstein, who said that Mahler anticipated the catastrophes of the 20th century …

Honeck: … and the beauty of the 20th century – we must not forget that. The catastrophes are very important because they create that sort of effect, but the beauty is also there. I was born after the war; there has not been a war; isn't that great? But many people have experienced wars. There was probably no time in history as terrible as the 20th century. But in the second part of the 20th century we experienced the beauty of life – a great life with its technological advancements and developments.

What would you have asked Mahler?

Honeck: That's a very difficult question, but I would probably have asked him to compose more music, especially for soloists. I would like there to be a Mahler violin concerto, or cello concerto or a piano concerto. Or better still, an opera – we know that he loved opera very much and that he conducted a lot of it. He was the director of the Vienna Court Opera, so why not compose an opera?

On a more personal note, I would have asked him what he thought about the meaning of life, about death, about what happens after we die – that would have been a very interesting conversation, I think. He already provides a lot of answers in his music, but answers that we first have to search for.

What did Mahler want?

Honeck: Well, first of all, he describes his own life in his music, which has led some people to believe that there was too much of his own ego in his music and that he didn't write for the people. I don't think that is really true. He was so honest in describing his own feelings. He wanted, and probably needed, to write down what was in his head, like all great composers, just like Beethoven described it. All great composers wanted to impart a message to the people – Mahler wanted to have people share his own experiences. He also wanted to answer problems people might be experiencing. For instance, how many people tell me that they start to cry when they listen to the *2nd Symphony*, the Resurrection? Why do they cry? – because Mahler was able to create an atmosphere of heaven, an expectation of a glorious life after death. The same thing that Mozart described once in a letter to his father: "Don't be afraid of death. Death is my best friend. I never go to bed without thinking that I might not wake up again the next day."

Mahler was extremely interested in these questions and he probably knew that every human being was born to ask them. Someone somewhere always asks them at some point in their life. But a lot of people don't want to provide answers or look for them. And I think Mahler realised that he could provide answers through his music and that's what he wanted to present to the audience. He knew that at the time in which he lived people probably wouldn't understand his music, so he wrote it not only for himself and the people who did understand him, but also for future generations.

He knew that we would understand him. And don't we understand him now? We understand a lot. To me, he is so wonderfully close when I am studying the score that it feels as if he were sitting next to me.

What is the biggest technical challenge for a conductor performing Mahler?

Honeck: Conducting the rubato. We know that conducting for instance *Parsifal* or other music by Wagner – although it has many challenges, don't get me wrong – can be much easier than conducting Johann Strauß. He is extremely difficult because you have to move a hundred people at any moment in a different direction, and if you make a mistake, it results in an unnatural and artificial interpretation. I think the same is true for Mahler's music. The challenge of conducting rubato is immense with Mahler, but it also lets me give the musicians a certain freedom, and find something new for myself in the very moment that I am conducting a concert, provided that I find the right way to play and conduct the rubato. This makes Mahler's music an extremely great adventure, if you can achieve it.

Of course, you can rehearse everything and you don't need a conductor, so to speak. But then it is rehearsed and the audience will probably hear that it is rehearsed. In my concerts, I would like people to feel that everything is natural and very Viennese or Czech or Hungarian – in true Austrian tradition. It's true in the moment and it's right to do so, but it takes a lot of effort.

Do you think the sound of the Vienna Philharmonic influenced Mahler?

Honeck: I'm sure it did because they were a great orchestra. We know that Mahler was in Kassel and had another orchestra in Germany, in Hamburg; that he also heard the Czech Philharmonic and that he came to Vienna and worked with the great musicians of the time. I am sure there were many moments when he was thinking about certain Viennese instruments which we still have today. But we also have to bear in mind that he worked in Amsterdam and in New York, where some different instruments were used. So I am sure that Mahler's main interest was to project the message in his compositions.

By the way, he probably needed to rehearse a lot more than we do today because nowadays, musicians are technically much more advanced than they could have been at that time. I think Mahler would have been overjoyed with the standard of today. That might also be why he sometimes got angry during rehearsals and personally insulted individual players in the orchestra. It was because he was not getting the result that he wanted. If a string player wasn't using the whole bow, he would bully him.

There is one other thing that is very important to me personally, which has nothing to do with the interpretation – the set-up of the orchestra. For Mahler, I use the original set-up, how he would have heard his symphonies, with the second violins on the right and the celli and bassi, together with the first violins, on the left. It's fascinating how Mahler's music becomes more transparent because of this. He once wrote in a letter: "Why don't the second violins play more? I have composed it in this way." This means that if you sit in the audience, you will have a stereo effect, with the first violins on the left and the second violins on the right, so if they enter into a conversation with each other, the music will come from two different positions. This is very interesting, especially for Mahler's music. This set-up changed after the 1920s or 1930s into what we know today. So I think it might also be very nice to hear Mahler in that way.

Why did it take so long for Mahler's music to become popular?

Honeck: I think it definitely has to do with his Jewish background. As we know, anti-Semitic sentiments were growing in Vienna at the time. And during the terrible 20s and 30s, there was no way Mahler's music could have grown in popularity. We have to be really thankful to Leonard Bernstein and especially to Rafael Kubelík – we mustn't forget that wonderful conductor, who started the Mahler renaissance long before Bernstein joined in.

The second reason is that his symphonies were misunderstood. They still have the reputation of being trivial, of not really constituting high art or of containing too much folk music, as I described earlier. This probably prevented some people from loving his music, especially in German and Austrian culture where Beethoven was revered as a hero, and Schubert, Brahms and Bruckner were those who created symphonies. Gustav Mahler went too far in their opinion. That was a gross misunderstanding, but good music, particularly the best music, will have its time, and that time began to arrive in the 1960s.

(Vienna, 25/05/2010)

Mariss Jansons

"With Mahler you have to give everything"

Do you remember the first time you heard Mahler's music?

Jansons: I remember that the first time I heard Mahler I was so impressed, it was like I was in heaven. I understood that he was a genius, a great composer, and I suppose that when you are young in some ways you always think, "That's my composer." So I would say that Mahler immediately, from the beginning, conveyed the feeling that he was my composer. So I had this big love for it immediately, and it never disappeared.

I'm not one hundred percent sure, but I think the first Mahler symphony I heard was the *3rd Symphony*, which I'm conducting now in Amsterdam. I was probably around 16–18 years old.

What was Mahler's reception in Russia like at that time?

Jansons: Well of course people didn't know much about him, didn't hear much. One of the first conductors who introduced his music was my teacher in St Petersburg – or at that time Leningrad – who taught at the conservatory, Professor Rabinovich. He did Mahler's symphonies with the student orchestras and even with the Radio Orchestra. And of course Kirill Kondrashin was another one; he was one of the leading conductors, he liked Mahler very much and he conducted his music and made it more popular in Russia – you might say 'invented' it there – and he did it very well.

We know that Shostakovich loved Mahler …

Jansons: Yes, you know, he said that *Das Lied von der Erde* [*The Song of the Earth*] was the piece he would like to take with him to heaven. Those were Shostakovich's words. 'Slawa' [Mstislav] Rostropovich told me that.

How did Shostakovich know Mahler's work so well? Were there performances of Mahler's music, even in the Stalin era?

Jansons: Oh yes, of course. Mahler was not a forbidden composer; I think he was probably just not so well known. He was played in the Soviet Union, but

I remember very well the audience's reaction, and how his popularity and the strength of public feeling for him grew. I don't like to use the expression 'understanding' because to me the idea of understanding music is curious. You can understand language, but I'm not sure about music – perhaps it has a different meaning in this context. I think that talking about people's feelings and relationships to music would be a better way to describe it – but that is a theoretical question.

Is there a connection between his life and his music?

Jansons: [*laughs*] Of course I know that there is the view that his life, what the composer says, or writes, or thinks, has nothing to do with the music. Music is music. And we know that Mahler wrote programmes and then changed his mind and said he didn't want them, and so on. But for me, as a conductor, it is very important to know his life, to know what Mahler said, what he wrote, what his moods were. And it's not only Mahler; I would say it's my way, or my method, that I generally use for preparing my pieces. Whether I conduct Beethoven or Shostakovich or Bartók, it doesn't matter; I need time to immerse myself in the world of the composer.

Because, as a professional conductor, I can prepare very quickly technically, you could even say that I have already conducted almost everything and just repeat it, but this is nothing if you really want to have what I would call a 'cosmic' performance. By that I mean that you would not be on the Earth anymore; you would be in another dimension where crescendos, diminuendos, accents, and tempo relationships don't exist anymore.

Mahler was looking for titles for the 3rd *Symphony* and he used an image of Pan; there is an interesting story about that. He got a letter from [Anna von] Mildenburg around the time he was writing it and on the envelope was written PAN – it stands for Post Amt Nummer [Post Office Number] – and he took that to be a sign. And maybe that's nothing, but it really inspires me. I can't explain it, but it gives me something very special.

When you came to Vienna to study, did you hear Mahler often?

Jansons: Oh yes, but not only Mahler. Being in Vienna was like a holy time to me. Of course I had a wonderful education in St Petersburg, because I have to say that it was perhaps the best conducting school in the world. We were given a fantastic opportunity, which was not so prevalent in Western countries; we had a professional orchestra to practise and rehearse with and a professional opera house where we conducted ballets and operas. And so I started to conduct operas and ballets at a very early stage. That was very important because, as a conductor, this is your instrument. And then I was in Leningrad, which is a more Western area, and I had wonderful teachers who were great examples to me. The first of them was Mravinsky – he adored Bruckner and Brahms, so in that sense he was not only a Russian conductor – and also my father, of course, who grew up in Latvia; and my teacher Rabinovich, who was very interested in Bruckner, Mahler, Mozart, etc.

But of course to come to Vienna, to this centre of the world, was a godsend, it was something unbelievable; to be in the Music Academy with Swarowsky and Karl Österreicher and all the other professors was just unbelievable. I learned so much about old music. Professor Josef Mertin, the great music specialist, was very funny because he would always forget people's names, so he would say, "Äh, Herr Leningrad, kommen Sie bitte." ["Er, Mr Leningrad, please come here."] [*laughs*] I was so lucky to hear all those great conductors and opera performances – I tell you, I went to the opera house or the Musikverein or a concert hall every day. And on Sundays, I almost always attended three performances: morning, afternoon and evening. I think the people who checked the tickets all knew me, so sometimes when I didn't have one they just let me in. I earned a lot and since that time, Vienna has been probably the city I love most.

Are there Mahler conductors who have influenced you?

Jansons: Yes, of course, there are many conductors who do Mahler and there are many, many recordings. I think they all influence a young conductor in some way.

Of course in the beginning I think we were all incredibly influenced by Leonard Bernstein. He was great, one of the greatest, and he had such a wonderful personality. And of course he conducted Mahler with such passion and emotion, and we were very influenced by him. But later, now that I am older, I wouldn't say that I don't like his Mahler or that I'd criticise him, but I can see that I would perhaps take things in a slightly different direction, compared to how I was in the beginning.

Would you agree that in your approach you try not to exaggerate or overemotionalise Mahler's music?

Jansons: You know, I think this is a question which can be applied to all music, and to exaggerate anything in music is not good. Mahler's music is so complex and so emotional it tempts you to exaggerate, so of course it's very dangerous.

You could say it's completely different, of course, but you could say that exaggeration is very dangerous with Tchaikovsky, too. My father always used to say something good, which I'll never forget. "Never put sugar with honey, please. It's too sweet."

How much are you influenced by Mahler's remarks, for example in the first movement of the 3rd Symphony: "Von hier ab Halbe zu schlagen" ["beat half notes from here on"]? Do you take them very seriously?

Jansons: Honestly, I must say I analyse this, but I don't take it word for word. I try, of course, to follow it, but sometimes I don't. For example, he writes *"noch in vier taktieren"* [*"continue to beat in four"*], and I go in two. And you know, I think if it doesn't destroy the tempo relationship, or let's say the accelerando or ritenuto or the tempo markings, sometimes there actually isn't a big difference between conducting in two or four. Mostly it depends on the orchestra, whether it suits them best to have it that way. And sometimes you need, let's say, to conduct in six, when you have (*sings rhythm*) to help a little, or you might conduct it in three. It depends on the orchestra. But in general, you have your tempo, so these are not big things which need a lot of attention.

What would you have asked Mahler?

Jansons: I would need to look at the scores to answer that. I would not discuss his views on interpretation and his concepts; I would perhaps rather ask him specific things. For example, I would say: "Why have you written a glissando here and not here? Do they have the same function in the music, and do you have something very special in mind or not? Or sometimes I know that it should be like this because you understand the logic, but …" There are many things; you know how it is with interviews, I really need to bring a score to show examples.

Is the secret to forget that you have studied everything so carefully when you are on stage, in order to perform freely?

Jansons: No, I wouldn't say so. When I conduct rehearsals, I prepare the orchestra and everything so that it's how I think it should be. And then, of course, when you come to the concert, then you try to go further and if you succeed, it's really wonderful, and sometimes perhaps it's not. But I think in the concert you really have to let this kind of spiritual yearning, you might say, come through. But that doesn't mean you forget to use your brain, which is always a terrible danger.

The question is what the balance should be between expression and emotions, and the analytical, controlling side. If you choose only the controlling side, it's terrible.

Secondly, I think we, people on stage, are performing for listeners – of course for ourselves, too, but generally speaking, we are artists and we know that to bring joy and to pass across this energy gives 'fire' to the public. If you want the music just for yourself then you sit at home and play it quietly, but on the stage you are performing art for the listeners. This is one of your tasks.

I'd like to come back to Shostakovich and Mahler. Shostakovich's 4th Symphony is a homage to Mahler; he cancelled the premiere because he was afraid that Stalin would put him in prison. When you compare Shostakovich and Mahler, what connects them and what distinguishes them from each other?

Jansons: I always feel that in Mahler's symphonies and in Shostakovich's symphonies, "here is Mahler himself", or "here is Shostakovich himself". I think there were forms that both composers used which were quite often similar, and their ways of expressing emotion, too. Also, they both knew the orchestra extremely well: instruments, and what you can get out of them. I think in this respect Shostakovich was unbelievable because in his music you very seldom need to change dynamics and make adjustments.

They both – perhaps I exaggerate a little – are tragic people, if you speak of their inner worlds. Of course for Mahler, there was not such a real danger, but for Shostakovich it was always imminent. If he had been a writer, Stalin would have killed him. Since he was a composer, and music is a very abstract art, it is very difficult to judge, but he was really in great danger. He knew that the KGB might come for him, and he had prepared things that would help. So they were different, but I feel that they both survived very much. And they both kept things to themselves, and did not express them, perhaps more so with Mahler because he was in fact a very expansive person. Shostakovich was too, but he actually didn't talk much at all. If you asked him something, it was very difficult to get anything out of him.

Did Mahler anticipate the catastrophes to come? Would you agree that the march in the 6th Symphony does this? Or do you think that this music is absolute and had nothing to do with subsequent events?

Jansons: Not consciously, of course, because that's not possible – he was not Nostradamus, saying "This is how it will be." But I think he embraced and expressed the whole world in his music, and I think in his nature there was somehow an anticipation of the future. He spoke about global things and these things exist forever, and they come around again in circles. So in this way, yes, his music expressed what would happen, but I think that's only because it was so complex.

What did Mahler want?

Jansons: I think he wanted to express all of this, you know, these questions that in one way or another almost every human being asks sometime. He was a highly intelligent man, very rich inside, and of course he raised enormous questions, even the question of whether there is life after all of this: you can simply believe there is or not. It's a tremendous, unanswerable question. I ask myself such questions sometimes, thousands of them. And I think Mahler was trying to raise these questions, but I don't think he wanted to solve them, even the question of *Auferstehung* [*resurrection*].

I'm not sure that he truly believed one hundred per cent in a resurrection. In some way, Mahler is like Leo Tolstoy, analysing everything, including one's inner world. I think for Mahler, this complex, inner world was the best world, a universe without borders.

Does Mahler demand everything of you, as a conductor, for a good performance? Do you have to give everything?

Jansons: Absolutely everything, yes.

You said that your approach to Mahler had changed over the years. Can you describe this?

Jansons: Of course it is hard to judge myself, but I think I became more profound, and more understanding of his world.

I hope that today I can successfully sustain much slower tempos in Mahler, which of course is very difficult in any music, but especially in Mahler. Take the finale of the 3rd – the slower you can make the tempo, the richer, in terms of inner feelings, you can make the music. If you don't feel the emotions, you take a faster tempo because you have nothing to say.

Metronome marks are a tricky one, whether to follow them or not. I can think of times when I myself tried to follow the metronome marks of Shostakovich, who sometimes wrote crazy things, and Mravinsky said, "Just ignore them." And many times I have done a first performance of a piece by a modern composer – where you would think you must really follow the metronome marks because these days they are very important. And then I come to the first rehearsal and I think, this metronome mark doesn't work, so I say to the composer, "Can I do it like this?" And he says, "Yes, of course, forget about it."

What Mahler writes at the end of the 3rd is remarkable.

Jansons: If you look at the end of the 3rd, you could say that it is a triumph, but a very curious sort of triumph. You are not speaking as God, you are already on that level. Looking closely at it, Mahler only writes one forte in the brass, and I hink this is like a hymn to God and to the heavens, but it's not a triumph, not a victory. So this is another example where it isn't an ending, but a glimpse of eternity. I must look up what it is that he writes there because it is very important; people can misunderstand it: "*Nicht mit roher Kraft. Gesättigten, edlen Ton.*" ["*Not with brute force. With rich, full sound.*"]

This tells me, "Ah, I don't think that they're in heaven, you must be *edel*." He would have used different words if it were about something which was not on the Earth. I think he wanted to say, "I am happy that I'm here." This is my clumsy interpretation or feeling.

I saw in the rehearsal today that the finale was not a flood of sound.

Jansons: That was deliberate, which is what I just said. And I think it is right, otherwise he would have written something different. I think he was afraid that he would have exaggerated it, and he didn't want that. Will you come to the concert tomorrow?

Yes, I will be there.

Jansons: Please come and see me after the concert, then you can tell me if it was okay or not, if it was good or bad.

In the rehearsal today, at the beginning of the 4th movement, you mentioned the colours and you pointed out the incredible darkness.

Jansons: Yes, grey, grey.

Do you search for colours in Mahler?

Jansons: Yes, I generally like to do that. For me, it's like it is underground at the beginning of this movement. He is speaking about the human being. I like colour generally, I think sound is very important.

(Amsterdam, 02/02/2010)

Lorin Maazel

"I would never have asked him anything"

Do you remember the first time you heard Mahler's music?

Maazel: The first time I conducted a movement of a Mahler symphony was in Tanglewood. I was a young conductor – I was 20, I think – and I conducted the first movement of Mahler's *2nd*, and that was my first contact with his music.

When did I first hear it? Well, sometime in my teens, rather late I would think. I was a member of the Pittsburgh Symphony for three years; I played in the violin section, first as a *2nd* and then as a *1st*, and I do not remember ever having played a Mahler symphony during those three years.

Mahler was extremely unpopular at that time; no one was really interested in him after the Second World War, despite a great deal of effort by Bruno Walter and several other conductors to try to popularise his music. Barbirolli was a great Mahler fan. I remember going to concerts conducted by him as a youngster, and – this was at one of the first concerts I ever heard – I remember people walking out of Carnegie Hall. I think I was 17 or 18, so this was after the Second World War. By the end of the performance there was nobody there. So when he said *"Meine Zeit wird kommen"* [*My time will come*] – he was right, but it took a long time.

Did Mahler's world immediately open for you?

Maazel: No. I enjoyed the challenge of each new experience of a Mahler movement, but it was a challenge. It was very difficult for me to come to grips with the music and to meet the challenge of it; it was a world and a mentality completely foreign to me. Like everybody else, I had grown up with Bach, Beethoven, Mozart, and so on, and I was also interested in a certain amount of contemporary music: Berg, Webern. So it wasn't that Mahler was beyond me, because I was very happy with the music written up until his birth and after his death; but that whole period was foreign to me. It took me a long time to understand his music, movement by movement, symphony by symphony, and I was already in my mid 40s by the time I finally came to grips with the entire Mahler repertoire – very, very slowly. I am glad that it took so long, because it gave me the opportunity to get into his music movement by movement, slowly and thoroughly.

What is the biggest challenge in conducting Mahler?

Maazel: Well, I think the first thing one needs to do is not to have any preconceptions about Mahler, his person and what he was trying to express. There are many conductors who bring literary conceptions to another language; music has nothing to do with literature. There are literary overtones, there are philosophical dimensions explored by the music in the language of music, but coming to Mahler and saying, "Here is a person who was born to weep and every phrase must be a tragic spirit" – nonsense! Mahler was, like all composers, primarily interested in composing music. What that music might mean was important to him, but first and foremost he was a composer, a technician who wrote music.

He was interested in sound, in balance and sound combinations, and all this has little to do with philosophical connotations.

Leonard Bernstein is quoted as saying that Mahler anticipated the catastrophes of the 20th century. Would you agree?

Maazel: Well, there was that period before the First World War when every sensitive person felt that there was a tsunami in the making; things were too quiet, things were too peaceful. If you look at painting at that time, there was a kind of unease, that calm before the storm, and Mahler, being an extremely sensitive person, undoubtedly felt that, as well as many other things. He wasn't thinking about the catastrophes of the 20th century when he wrote his 4th. Yes, there are nostalgic, rather reflective, perhaps even sad moments in that symphony, but basically it's a very happy work.

What about the last movement of the *5th*? So many people hold it against him that he had the nerve to write a Rondo, a happy piece of music. Well, he had every right to be happy too, and the reason he wanted to write something like that was that, purely from a compositional point of view, he needed a counterweight. He had said all that he wanted to say about tragedy and irony and conflict, nostalgia, *Sehnsucht* [longing] and so forth, and then, after the smoke cleared, there is a happy and glowing statement. It's a compositional matter, marvellously put together, and it is supposed to be just that. He wanted to write a Rondo, and why not? You see, that's what the problem is with people – preconceptions: "Ah well, that's one of his weaker movements." Not at all; it's one of his best movements, both philosophically and compositionally.

Mahler wrote instructions for conductors in his scores, such as "Von hier ab Halbe zu schlagen" [beat in two from here]. Do you follow these strictly?

Maazel: Oh, he was a marvellous conductor and he knew exactly what he was doing. I don't always agree with what he writes, but then he probably wouldn't always agree himself. I write music myself, and I think that I have prepared it perfectly with a foolproof orchestral score, and then when I start to conduct it, I begin to make changes. Today I was rehearsing a piece with the Vienna Philharmonic that they commissioned many years ago, called *Farewells*, and I saw a 5/8 bar followed by either a 2/8 or a 3/8 bar, and decided it was just badly written and right on the spot I came up with a better idea, and it was put into the parts and I had to relearn how to conduct those three bars – but why not? It's just a small edit to a rather well-written piece, and one does make changes. Sometimes I'll write little agogics like *più mosso*, let's move this tempo here, and then I'll discover that it's not a good idea. I wrote it because somehow I became impatient – composers are always impatient when they conduct their own music, and this is born out of embarrassment; they want to get on with it. I'm always rushing through my own music, and I'm trying to stop that practice because I'm doing my music a disservice. It has its own speed and I should accept it and not fight it.

To get back to the question you asked about following Mahler's instructions, I'm sure that he himself, when conducting his music, did not always follow his own instructions, which is right. Sometimes there are acoustical questions: something in the 2nd might work very well in the Musikverein but will not work in Avery Fisher Hall in New York – it just doesn't work. And many times I have done the same piece with different orchestras, and I always adjust to their different realities, to the acoustics. And so I find myself making changes, subtle changes – very rarely major changes – but they *are* changes. It is fascinating to me as a conductor that when I conduct my own music I find myself having to make changes – and Mahler did the same thing. Take his 5th – he not only made changes, but he re-orchestrated it, as if he hadn't written four symphonies before that, which were fantastically well orchestrated. So he was still learning on the job, though it's hard to believe. But he was so right; I compared the two orchestrations and he was right in every instance. It did need improving, but what I ask is why he didn't get it right the first time because his changes are very clear – they had to be made. It's just that it was a new world, and he just felt that certain things had to be changed and he was quite right. So it's a learning curve, and the sign of a good composer is one that is willing to learn and willing to change; bad composers never change anything and suffer the consequences. I don't want to imply that composers have to change their music – I don't think Bach changed a note; he didn't have time to change anything. I mean, with his 21 children and 2,000 compositions he was a busy man. He had to come up with a new prelude and fugue, or whatever, every week. And I don't think Mozart changed very much because he composed everything in his head anyway, and so he was simply taking dictation from himself, he just couldn't go fast enough. It was all there, he never stopped.

I just ask myself, "Had Mahler lived to be 100, what would he have written?" He would have gone past Schönberg undoubtedly, because he was already writing 12-tone rows. You wouldn't know it, but there is a 12-tone row in the woodwind if you look at the last movement of the G minor Symphony.

How would you describe Mahler's influence on the Viennese School?

Maazel: Oh, a great influence indeed. Yes, they all knew their Mahler. But then great composers go their own way. Look at Sibelius, he came so many years after Mahler and was totally uninfluenced, as was Benjamin Britten. They were geniuses, they had their own road to follow. Being influenced stylistically isn't a good idea; one shouldn't be influenced stylistically by any composer, but to be influenced by his vision or by his capacity to integrate so many elements, that's a very good idea. But any composer worth his salt writes his own music after his own fashion.

Why did it take so long for Mahler to be accepted?

Maazel: Well, because his music has a very personal quality. Mahler is unmistakeable – you hear three notes and you know: this is Gustav Mahler. It is *so* personal that there is a lot of jealousy surrounding it; most people want to hear a rehash of what they already know, they want to feel comfortable. They don't mind hearing just a little bit of pepper and salt there, something a little different, but basically it's a repeat of what they've already heard a thousand times. Mahler – and this was my problem as a young musician – came out of nowhere, in a way he was saying things that no one had ever said before, and very boldly, with great self-confidence. This is very shocking for a professional musician, or someone who is going to be a professional musician, so I can't imagine what it might mean for an average listener.

At that time, being Jewish or having a Jewish background was a factor, but not the main one, because after all, Mahler was given the position of music director of the Vienna Court Opera. He had many opportunities to perform, so that was just one other factor, but not the main one; it shouldn't be blown out of proportion. He was a genius and people are envious of geniuses.

You were in the same position as Mahler in the Vienna Opera; you had your own share of struggles. Did you sometimes think that you were facing the same difficulties and conflicts that Mahler did?

Maazel: I would never have had the incredible nerve to compare myself to Gustav Mahler. That would have been the height of arrogance. I never really took any of it personally, because by that time I was in my early 50s and I had already begun to learn what all of that was about. And it didn't take me very long to discover that we were basically talking about very, very few people.

I was working in an opera house with several hundred people and from the first day I was there to the last, I had nothing but love and friendship and support from everybody, the entire Vienna State Opera. I was always treated well and felt very good there, so I never compared myself to Gustav Mahler for any reason because my life was quite marvellous.

It was the rank and file of the press, and the Minister of Culture at the time, who insisted that I engage his wife and I refused to, so he said, "You will pay for this", and of course I did.

I paid for being an honest administrator, because in the contract for the Vienna *Operndirektor* [opera director] the autonomy of his position is guaranteed, and no one, not even the Minister of Culture, may tell him whom to engage or not to engage.

Mahler conducted the Vienna Philharmonic so many times; do you think he was influenced by their sound, and also by their repertoire, especially by Wagner?

Maazel: Well, it is interesting that he never wrote an opera; he conducted so many of them. There are many explanations for that, which have been offered by greater minds than my own, but I rather think that, simply because he was so involved in the world of opera, he felt that he had integrated that art form into the way he looked at music. Though he used vocal elements, and though he often thought theatrically, I think his decision was a wise one. I don't think he would have written the kind of opera that you would expect a genius to write. I think he felt too limited by his subject matter, because all the words that he chose, for example for his 3rd, they're words that create situations, contexts. These words are frame-forming, but in terms of action – A doing something to B because of what C said to D, and E is there waiting with a knife, and F is there with a gun – that wasn't for him; it's too specific.

And coming back to your question, therefore, his conducting the Vienna Philharmonic *must* have had an enormous influence on him, although, curiously enough, he was, like all pianists, I suppose, less interested in strings. Having said that, you will probably ask me about his Adagietto, or the last movement of the symphonies where the strings play such an important role, or for that matter the first movement of his *10th* – and he wrote for strings fantastically well. Still, his concept was more cosmic, and the Vienna Philharmonic has always been noted for its fantastic strings. So I don't think it was that particular aspect of the Vienna Philharmonic that influenced him, but their wonderful music-making, their intelligent way of phrasing, which they still have today – I think that probably had a major influence on him because Mahler is all phrasing.

What would you have asked Mahler?

Maazel: Probably what his favourite cigar was; he loved cigars. I don't know, I'm always very embarrassed to ask any composer any question because I am instinctively against verbalisations. I once asked Stravinsky about a note in *The Firebird*. I showed him the score and it was obviously a mistake, and he said, "Oh, don't worry, it doesn't make any difference." Strauss was always saying the same thing: "*Es ist mir wurscht – Fis, F, na, spielt keine Rolle*" [*I couldn't care less – F#, F, doesn't matter*]. You get these ridiculous answers because composers need to be asked questions anyway – I mean good composers. So I don't think I would have asked him anything, and I think I would have been very embarrassed to have him hear any of my interpretations of his music, as he was embarrassed when interpreting his own music.

Composers, great composers, are embarrassed by their music, as opposed to mediocre composers, who love their music. The more you love your own music, the worse you are as a composer. I mean, of course you're embarrassed, because it reveals too much about you. Everything you could want to know about Gustav Mahler is in his music. It's like looking right into his soul, and that would embarrass anybody. Who wants to walk down the street and be transparent? People could look right into your heart and your mind, and that's what you do when you listen to his music. So I have respect for his privacy; I would never have asked him anything.

What did Mahler want?

Maazel: Well, as I said, he was a composer; he had musical ideas, and he felt compelled to put them together, in the course of which his life experience as he grew older fed a lot of information into the notes so that the whole became much more important than the sum of the notes. After all, he underwent many changes between his late twenties and his late forties because by the time he reached his late forties, he knew that he had a coronary affliction and he knew he was going to die.

That is something that could be cured today with one shot of antibiotics. It leaked out from his tonsils, probably, into his heart and that was it. And that is very depressing, to be 49 and know that you have two more years of life. No one had loved life more than he did, but it would depress all of us, even then, when people didn't live as long as they do today. So he was a different person, and by that time his music had taken a darker turn.

Mahler was a remarkable human being and also a very sensitive person, very well-educated; his letters are masterpieces of German grandeur. Astonishing – a very intelligent, well-read person. I'm not very fond of Alma as a person. And the way she later put all her husbands together in one book is not my cup of tea, and I'm rather sceptical as to whether she copied his music for him as she claims: a pretty arrogant person, highly intelligent, but he was much too good for her.

Did you ever meet her?

Maazel: No. I would not have wanted to.

(Vienna, 10/02/2010)

Zubin Mehta

"I would love to ask him a thousand questions"

Do you remember the first time you heard Mahler's music?

Mehta: That was in Bombay. It was a recording of the 4th, conducted by Bruno Walter, and the singer was Désirée von Halban. As a youngster, perhaps this was a good start, because the 4th looks at the world through the eyes of a child. I was not a child, I was a teenager, but the music was immediately accessible.

What was the first Mahler symphony you heard performed in concert?

Mehta: I can't remember; it was possibly the *2nd Symphony*. I heard it conducted by Josef Krips. I was at the rehearsals, I didn't know the piece, and of course I always went to the rehearsals with the score; that's how I started learning the symphonies.

The first time I conducted a Mahler symphony here in Vienna it was the 1st, with the Vienna Philharmonic; Willi Boskovsky was the concertmaster. And my professor, Otto Rühm, with whom I studied bass, was first bass and he was very nervous about playing the solo under my direction. I had to really sit down with him and say, "Professor, please, I am a conductor, just treat me like anybody else." And he said, "No, no, but I know you so well and my colleagues are all listening to me." So it was quite an occasion.

There is one person who links you and Gustav Mahler; you already mentioned him – Bruno Walter. Can you tell me about your relationship with him and how you talked with him about Mahler?

Mehta: Yes. I visited him at his home in Beverly Hills a few times before he passed away. That was the great loss of my early life in Los Angeles. I was able to communicate so well with him because he knew I was from Vienna and he liked the way I spoke German, in a Viennese way, and he always smiled when I spoke. I asked him once, "Why are you smiling?" He said, "Well, because you are bringing Vienna back to me." Because in those days I couldn't speak High German, I only spoke Viennese.

But I went through the whole *1st Symphony* with him, and he was the one who told me about Jacques Callot's lithograph that Mahler saw and was so affected by that he composed the Funeral March in the third movement. But the Funeral March goes right into a very vulgar, Jewish dance, and he said, "Don't be shy, don't try to make this dance appealing; play it in a vulgar way."

I was doing Mahler's *1st* in Los Angeles in those days, and in the afternoon I would go with the musicians to Walter's recording session for Mahler's *Ninth*. And this is a story I always repeat because that was the first time I ever heard Mahler's. Nobody played it in Vienna in my youth. In fact, the first time I heard the *5th* was on Mahler's anniversary – 1960 – when a foreign orchestra played it here. Fritz Zaun conducted an East German orchestra. And then Bernstein came and did it for the first time with the Vienna Philharmonic, and that generation also played it for the first time.

In fact, it was so unknown to the Vienna Philharmonic that the first horn didn't know there was an *obbligato* part in the third movement; it's a separate part and he hadn't looked at it. But today, the Vienna Philharmonic plays all nine symphonies as standard repertoire and they know them so well, but the music did have to evolve.

I did the Adagio of Mahler's *10th* for the first time with them, and I remember when Claudio Abbado rehearsed the *2nd* in '65, it was also new for them. What was not new for them was the style. This was not something you taught them – they knew it, they just had to learn the notes. The sound, the style, had never left them.

Bruno Walter premiered the 9th in Vienna on 26 June 1912. I believe he spoke to Mahler about the 9th before his death ...

Mehta: Yes.

Did he tell you about that?

Mehta: No. I didn't know Mahler's *9th* at all, so I wouldn't have known what to discuss with him. But I was at all the recording sessions, and I had no score so I just listened. But the tragedy was that he wanted so much to record this symphony that he accepted all of Columbia Records' conditions – I don't know what financial conditions, maybe he did it for nothing, I don't know – and they had twelve first violins and four basses. In other words, Columbia Records said, "We will do it, but of course it will never sell. So if you want to do it, we will do it for you, but we cannot provide more musicians." Not only that, but these musicians were all from the Los Angeles Philharmonic, and they didn't know the 9th either! So they were sight-reading and recording at the same time. They were good musicians and he was very patient with them, but you know, when you read the reviews of this recording they say, this is the definitive recording and nobody can play it like that – but they were sight-reading! They did the best they could because they loved him.

Did Walter's style of conducting influence you when you conducted Mahler?

Mehta: Of course. I met Bruno Walter for the first time here in Vienna, in 1960, the Mahler year. He came and Elisabeth Schwarzkopf sang Mahler Lieder, and then, after the interval, the 4th Symphony was performed. And I was at the rehearsals, and I didn't dare to go and speak to him, so I just met him for a moment backstage in the conductors' room. I told him I was an ambitious young man and he wished me the best, that's all.

When he met me in Los Angeles later, he didn't remember me from Vienna, but when I told him my name and that I was guest-conducting the Los Angeles Philharmonic, he said, "Yes, you are the one who just conducted Brahms' 3rd in Vienna a few months ago." I said, "How do you know that?" And he said, "Because I read *Die Furche* – it's a newspaper – and I read your review. The review said that you conducted it much more convincingly than Herbert von Karajan." That amused him.

And so then I asked Walter if I could come and ask him a few questions, and he said, "Please come", so I took Mahler's 1st and we spoke for hours about it. He was wonderful.

What was his main advice about conducting Mahler?

Mehta: There was no main advice, he just analysed the score for me. We talked about the fact that Mahler was a young man when he composed it and that it almost caused a revolution when he first conducted it – because he didn't present it as a symphony, but as a tone poem. Then of course he worked on it for almost 10 years; he had already composed the 2nd and 3rd while he was still revising the 1st. It begins like a Haydn symphony, with an introduction and then the main Allegro.

The introduction is his youth, the countryside around him, listening to the birds, listening to little military fanfares in the distance; all that was different, nobody had done it before. And so Walter's explanation was that Mahler was controversial from the very first to the very last note he wrote. This controversy never left him, but he was so convinced of what he was doing that he never stopped; it came out of him, sincerely.

Did he tell you something about Mahler as an individual, his personality?

Mehta: Not too much, no. I went to him with a score; when we finished, I left; he spoke about the music.

Alma Mahler was almost his neighbour, but by that time she had moved to New York. I met Alma once, when I visited her a few years later, and she told me a lot during that one visit. She told me how he used to sit in the hut and compose and she would advise him, and she would fill in the orchestrations as he instructed her. And then of course she showed me Kokoschka's fans and Gropius' plans. She lived with all that genius around her. It was like a Viennese apartment: lace, curtains, dark inside. But she was very informative, she wouldn't stop talking about all of them.

What did she tell you about Mahler's personality?

Mehta: That he was a difficult person to live with; that he would come from the Opera for lunch and would want his soup on the table at a certain temperature, and if he didn't get it, he would be furious. Of course there were many details she didn't tell me about, such as her other boyfriends. But Mrs Schönberg, with whom I was very friendly in Los Angeles, told me that people only talk about her in connection with her lovers, and how she influenced them. She was the fountain they borrowed from: Mahler, Gropius, Werfel, etc. And she suffered with all of them because they were all neurotic – according to Mrs Schönberg – and not easy to live with. She didn't think, "No wonder Alma had lovers" – she didn't say that. But she said, "Believe me, she paid with each one emotionally, and spiritually, she was a great help to them all."

Let me tell you a story. Alma moved to Los Angeles, Werfel died a few years later and Bruno Walter was almost her neighbour, and somebody asked her: "Now that you have Bruno Walter here, do you think you will become very friendly with him?" She said, "Bruno Walter? No, he's a recreator, I've always been with creators." [*laughs*] This was her reply, but actually she didn't like it very much. I didn't hear it from Walter, but it was quite common knowledge that she didn't like him too much. I don't know what happened there – they were not very close.

Did she show you Mahler scores?

Mehta: Some autographs, some pages which she had. I can't remember which symphonies they were, but she had these pages and she had some of Gropius' plans, and Kokoschka's fans were framed on her walls. And I knew her daughter, Anna, who was a sculptress in Los Angeles. When I said to Alma, that I know Anna and Marina, and Marina is so beautiful, she said, "No, her popo [bottom] is too big and she should be careful!" It was almost as if this 80-year-old lady was jealous that I was praising her granddaughter.

Did Alma have a Viennese accent too?

Mehta: Yes, and a fine one at that.

How did you find Alma as a person? Was she neurotic?

Mehta: Not at all. I only met her that one time, and she took a liking to me and wouldn't let me go. I had planned the visit and my taxi was waiting. I didn't know how much time she would give me; I was on my way to the airport because I had to go to Paris and she said, "No, you sit down, I want to talk to you", so I missed my plane. Thankfully, I didn't have to be at a rehearsal in Paris immediately, so I took the next plane. But I stayed voluntarily. I thought I would meet her for 10 or 15 minutes and then go, but I stayed there for about two hours.

You succeeded Leonard Bernstein in New York; could you feel some kind of Mahler tradition that he had brought to the orchestra?

Mehta: Well, he approached Mahler as a composer and he was really convinced, through all the research that he did and all the performances he did – you probably know that he did all the symphonies with the New York Philharmonic – that he knew Mahler personally, and I understand that completely.

I invited Lenny twice to my performances, so that I could talk to him. He came to the 5th and didn't like it much, so we sat and talked. And he said, "What you are doing is trying to make it more beautiful than it is. If Mahler becomes vulgar, in other words when he brings the street music in, don't be afraid, play it as street music. Don't try to cover it and make it more beautiful."

And then he came to the 3rd and he liked that much more. He told me that he would take the finale much slower. But he criticised the 5th a lot, constructively, because we were friends, and I learnt a lot.

Bernstein is sometimes criticised nowadays for overpowering Mahler.

Mehta: But that's what his Mahler was, and, for instance, when he found out that I didn't do that, he was very critical. Yes, he was criticised a lot in New York for everything, when he was music director. When he came as a guest conductor he could do no wrong, then everything he did was holy, infallible.

You know, perception is very important. The perception that a critic from the New York Times had of Bernstein when he was music director was so negative that he was crucified for whatever he did. It was unfair, and Lenny took it very personally. But later on, when the staff of the New York Times had changed, he came as a guest conductor and it was a coronation every time.

There's a story about Klemperer, that he visited one of Bruno Walter's rehearsals…

Mehta: Yes, I was there. I was in the box, and Bruno Walter started the third movement with the bell-like pizzicatos in the cellos and basses, and Klemperer said quite loudly in German, "Are the pizzicatos not together, or is it my hearing?" You know, they were also neighbours in Los Angeles. I don't think they were very friendly towards each other. And then I was at his [i.e. Klemperer's] rehearsals of Mahler's 9th – although by then he was so physically impaired he couldn't control it – but it was okay in the end.

Would you say that Klemperer's approach was different from Walter's?

Mehta: Yes, probably. But it was those Jewish conductors who carried on the tradition because the German conductors didn't conduct Mahler: not Furtwängler, not Karajan, not Knappertsbusch, not Keilberth – nobody conducted Mahler. But Steinberg, Klemperer and Bruno Walter did, and then in the next generation, Bernstein. That's why it was unknown in Vienna because the Viennese conductors didn't have the Mahler tradition after the war.

Was that a kind of late post-war anti-Semitism?

Mehta: It was a tradition that was carried on. This has nothing to do with Mahler, but when Swarowsky, my teacher, wanted us to practise accompanying violin concertos – this was in '55 or '56 – he asked the violin professors to send a good pupil to play the Mendelssohn *Violin Concerto*, and nobody knew it. It was not taught. It might sound scandalous today and people might not believe it, but it's a fact; nobody was teaching Mendelssohn's *Violin Concerto* at the Vienna Akademie in '55 or '56. The finale is very difficult to accompany, that's why he said, "Send a pupil and we will practise" – nobody was playing it.

Would you say that the anti-Semitism which Mahler faced all his life influenced his work?

Mehta: Well, the Jewishness in Mahler's music is sometimes not recognised. Lenny told me that even when the Israel Philharmonic *sight-reads* a Mahler symphony, it sounds Jewish. Maybe this is an exaggeration, maybe it's their vibrato or something, but it's true. There are hidden Jewish influences and, of course, there are also Christian influences, no doubt about it; the end of the 2nd is more Christian than Jewish; considering the whole spirit of the resurrection. But Swarowsky told me that when Mahler entered the Vienna State Opera as a Christian – you know, he converted – he had his letter of resignation already written in his drawer, so that if something happened, he could present it. That's what he told me; I don't know whether it's true or not. He said the letter was always ready.

Mahler knew the Viennese society.

Mehta: Yes, and the stories of Alma being in the Musikverein when Mahler conducted, and the two personalities being so evident – no doubt it was a golden age for Vienna. It reminds me of the story about when Mahler left Vienna to go to New York, there was a group standing at the station; one of them was Gustav Klimt. And when the train departed, Klimt said, "Es ist vorbei", meaning that the good times were over. It's very touching that these people came to say goodbye to Mahler.

Anton Webern's music is very close to you. How do you see the relationship between Webern and Mahler? Are there roots that you can compare?

Mehta: Well, more between Webern and Brahms. You can see the strict discipline of Brahms already in Webern's *Passacaglia*; it's very similar to the fourth movement of Brahms' 4th in its construction. And Webern's organisation, as with the *Concerto for Nine Instruments*, where all the rows are either a minor 2nd or a major 6th – his whole way of composing is so disciplined. Webern doesn't bring folk elements into his music as much as Mahler did, but Berg has that.

Schönberg was a great admirer. Mahler had already died before *Gurre-Lieder* was performed, but they were close. The Alma–Zemlinsky connection was very important for all of them, so Alma is a focal point there.

Would you say that your technique of rehearsing Mahler has changed over the years?

Mehta: Yes, of course. Experience is everything, and that's why I didn't approach the 7th or the 9th too early in my life. I listened to performances, I looked at the scores, I put them aside, and I did the 9th much later. In fact, I once did all the Mahler symphonies in Los Angeles, except the 9th. I invited Giulini and said, "You know, I'm breaking my cycle because I want to come to your rehearsals", and he knew the 9th, and he did it beautifully. I would go to the rehearsals and we would talk about it. Of course thematically, I had remembered what I heard at Bruno Walter's recording sessions, but I didn't know the symphony then – I didn't even have a score.

Have you conducted musicians who played under Mahler's baton?

Mehta: No. I met older, second-generation musicians in Vienna. By the time I came in 1954, there was nobody in the Vienna Philharmonic who had played under Mahler. But they were the pupils of the people who had played under Mahler – it was the second generation. So I sometimes used to hear anti-Mahler stories from my professors that they had heard from their teachers. "Mahler didn't compose original music, he only copied from others", for example. One story was that when Mahler's secretary went to the library and brought him scores of other composers' works, they would say, "Ah, Mahler is composing again." You know, these are musicians' stories that made no sense.

That was one of the first things I heard, that Mahler never composed an original note, he only borrowed from others. And when Swarowsky heard that, he would say, "Okay, maybe he borrowed a little theme or motif, but what did he do with that motif? How did he develop it? This is what you have to recognise as Mahler's genius, even though he maybe took three notes from an opera." And because Mahler was an opera conductor, whether in Budapest or Hamburg, sometimes you *feel* the music he conducted coming into his music.

What influence did his experience as a Wagner conductor have on his work?

Mehta: Oh, I would say a lot. When you do the *Ring* after doing Mahler, as I did, you sometimes hear things and think you've heard them before. Just little harmonic progressions – it's not copying or anything – or tonalities in certain important places, where Mahler uses D flat major and G flat major, which Wagner also uses to portray certain emotions; that is important. *Götterdämmerung* [Twilight of the Gods] starts in E flat minor – it's a chord that's difficult to tune. If you just come in and play it, it's not going to be in tune, you have to work at it. Siegfried's death starts in E minor; these are all tonalities which are important for composers, and of course Mahler absorbed that.

But sometimes, in the third movement of the 6th, I hear a little harmonic progression which is pure Rachmaninoff, and we know that Rachmaninoff played with Mahler in New York. It's not copying, but a little progression does come into it. Now, I don't know if Rachmaninoff heard [Mahler] conduct the

6th and put it in his concerto, but there is a similarity – some little *Carmen* motives. You know, in the Third Act [*sings excerpt*], Carmen, the smugglers. It appears in the 3rd all the time. Maybe he was conducting *Carmen* in Hamburg in those days, I don't know – it's worth checking. When I am rehearsing, I tell the oboes, "Just think you are playing *Carmen*", because they ask whether they should play on the beat or before the beat. One could write a whole anthology about this. It's not too important, but it's what he does with it, how he develops it, and that is pure Mahler. You can recognise it immediately, something which happens with no other composer.

What did Mahler want?

Mehta: Inner peace, which he never had. Even as a child he didn't know inner peace. From his first conducting appearances he was always fighting with everybody, not because he was a fighter, but because he had to assert himself as a conductor, as an interpreter, as a composer. And the end of his marriage was very painful to him; for his wife to tell him that she loved another man, half an hour before he went on stage to conduct the world premiere of his 8th *Symphony* – you can imagine his anxiety. Of course I didn't ask Alma about that because we don't know what she went through.

Would you like to have known Mahler as a person?

Mehta: Yes, I would love to know him. I would love to ask him a thousand questions, and I would love him to criticise my work. I would love it.

What are the main questions you would want to ask him?

Mehta: Whether it's a Mozart symphony or a Mahler symphony, I would like to know if my *transitions* are logical, going from the development to the recapitulation. These musical bridges are very important. The logic with which a conductor, pianist, or quartet, interprets a bridge, either from the exposition to the development, or from the development – I'm talking simply, now – to the recapitulation. These bridges are really what make us logical musicians. These are the questions I would ask him. The same applies to a Mozart symphony – bridges are very important.

(Vienna, 05/10/2009)

Ingo Metzmacher

"Mahler is my point of reference"

Do you remember the first time you heard Mahler's music?

Metzmacher: I think I heard Mahler for the first time in the context of Ives, who always interested me; there's the story that when Mahler came back from New York he had an Ives score in his suitcase and wanted to bring him to Europe, and then unfortunately he died – there are connections between Ives and Mahler.

I had a book by Kurt Blaukopf, his famous book about Mahler, and what interested me most at the time was the description of when he went to the *Jahrmarkt* [*country fair*]. He describes at length how it felt for him to hear the different types of music around him as he went through the fairground. He could hear a waltz here, a polka there, a brass band there. He could hear it all at the same time, but the perspective changed as he walked, of course, because he was nearer to one source of music than another. And there is a quote in that book which I have been trying for years to find again, because I have never forgotten it. It said that he was very interested in that, in simultaneousness in music. And I think the perspective in his music, the way certain things come out and others go back in very quick succession, is part of this. That must also have interested him in Ives' music because Ives had the same idea and it featured strongly in his music.

Did the door to Mahler open immediately for you?

Metzmacher: Yes, it did. I mean, as a young conductor, you dream of conducting Mahler. I think the first symphony I conducted was the 5th, years later, and then I worked my way through the whole catalogue. I think it's different today; it's a little frightening because there's such an enormous amount of information and conflicting ideas and you need a long time to understand what's happening.

So the more you know, the more difficult it gets?

Metzmacher: I think so, yes.

There are two extreme ways of conducting Mahler: to bring your own emotion into the music, or to be very faithful to the text and to make it rather dry.

Metzmacher: You can't really make it dry. I think every conductor brings in his emotions anyway, and the question is always, how do they fit in with the emotions of the music? Is there a link? But basically, if you say the song is at the heart of Mahler's music – at least in the beginning, with the first four symphonies – my understanding of it is that it's more like singing inside, and so it shouldn't be too prominent. You know, they are folk songs arising from very simple, straightforward sentiments, passed down through the centuries. And I very much like this tone, even in the poems on their own; there is a simplicity about it. Mahler was criticised a lot for using very simple tunes, but that's what I like. And there again you can put it into context with Ives, who used very simple tunes in his music: structurally, they were very complex, but the tunes were simple. You could even say that of Nono – if you think of the *Internationale* and all that – that he sometimes uses very simple tunes; the structure remains very complicated, but at the heart of it the material used is the simple song. I think a simple song can contain much more true emotion than many other forms. I love Schubert, for example, and I think it is very connected to that.

Would you say that Mahler is a precursor of modern music?

Metzmacher: Yes, absolutely. When I was music director in Hamburg, I opened every season with a Mahler symphony, and I do that in Berlin, too, because for me, Mahler is the point of reference. My father was born in 1906 and I think he might have said that his point of reference was, I guess, Beethoven or Bach. And of course I know about the enormous importance of Bach and Beethoven, but I would always say that Mahler is my point of reference. To explain; when you are a child, you know your grandparents as you are growing up and this relationship spans the period of history that you can still *feel*, because you know the people. I believe one grandfather was born in 1892 and my great-grandfather was born in 1856, so he was older than Mahler. I feel that the music I *really* understand as part of my history starts with Mahler. I would also like to understand the music that came before this and I think I do, but I would say that it feels more like history in the sense that, as a person, I have no connection with it at all. So I would say that Mahler is the first composer whom I really feel directly connected to, and that's my point of reference. And that's also because, as you said, modern music really starts with Mahler; I would definitely say that. So everything comes from him.

You directed a festival in Berlin on the subject of 1909, that crucial year: Breakthrough 1909 *with the German Symphony Orchestra. How does Mahler relate to that?*

Metzmacher: Well, you know the last programme featured *Das Lied von der Erde* [*The Song of the Earth*]. The programme was in this order: first, *Das Lied von der Erde*, then the interval, and then [Schönberg's] *Erwartung* [*Expectation*]. They were written almost at the same time, so you can see Mahler looking back and Schönberg looking forwards. I would say it was a very important moment in musical history.

How do you see the influence of Mahler on the Viennese School, in terms of technique?

Metzmacher: I think the person who was influenced the most is Berg, in the way he wrote his chords, and in that sense, I associate Schönberg more with Brahms. I would say that Berg is Mahler's true successor, also because Berg wrote operas, which I think Mahler would have loved to do. I don't know why he didn't because he conducted so many. And as for Webern, I always feel as though he takes the concentrate, the distilled essence of Mahler in a little bottle – I mean every single motif, every little melody in Webern reminds me of Mahler.

And there is also someone else we should mention, who learned a lot of Mahler and whom I consider to be a very important link to the 20th century, and that is Hartmann. Especially in the slow movements, in the Adagios, there are many, many moments that I would call a Mahler moment, particularly in his *8th Symphony*. There is a wild second movement and then suddenly at the end the violins, completely alone, play this incredible line, very much up in the air, and it always makes me think of Mahler. It's a way of looking back, in a very painful way actually, because it was written in the 60s. I think that's interesting; there are secret lines in music history, and they are like rivers in that you never know where they will re-emerge and where they go on to, or if they will dry up. And I think Hartmann and, of course, also Henze after that, retained something from Mahler.

Not forgetting Rihm …

Metzmacher: Of course, absolutely. And Nono, although Nono is a solitary rock anyway [*laughs*].

Did you ever talk to Nono about Mahler?

Metzmacher: No. He spoke about Verdi, not about Mahler, but that may have been because unfortunately, I only knew him for a very short time, at the end of his life.

When I spoke to Boulez about Mahler, he said that when he has had enough of the 'bombastic Mahler' he enjoys going back to the refined Mahler. Is there a side of Mahler that you feel especially close to? You once said you hadn't approached the 8th Symphony so far.

Metzmacher: No, and I'm not sure if I ever will. It's interesting that Boulez said that because I think the most refined symphony is the 4th, because there are no trombones and it's very light. I always felt very close to the *Fourth* – it's the most lyrical of all. It's as if Mahler were taking a step back. I really think that the last movement of the 4th is a farewell, it's a kind of lullaby, and it vanishes into the low E in the harp at the end and it really, truly departs. *Morendo*: something is dying there, I feel that very strongly. And then comes the 5th with its big statements – but the 4th is very close to my heart.

When you look back on your history of conducting the Mahler symphonies, are there any tricks you discovered?

Metzmacher: As I wrote in my book, no. In a way, I feel that you have to be on the edge to really do it right. It's not the sort of music where you can watch yourself conducting; I think you really have to go into it, I would say it demands total commitment. Maybe all music does, but I think with Mahler it is especially the case. Although I would still say that because of the length of the pieces you must somehow keep a clear head, because it is extremely important to be judicious with the tempi. Otherwise you will find you lose the structure of the piece, and you will have a lot of emotions in a collapsing framework; it will not help you. So finding the right balance between the two is maybe one of the biggest challenges.

Is there a danger, as a conductor, in being too emotionally involved?

Metzmacher: Yes. You know the old saying that it doesn't really matter what you, as a conductor, feel in that moment – it's not about my feelings, it's about the music. So I have to bring out the emotion in the music, not *my* emotion, which is a very minor thing compared to what the music is doing. And sometimes I think the danger can be that we substitute our emotions for the emotion of the music, or we think that we are very emotional and that will come across – maybe it does, maybe it doesn't, but the most important thing is that the music must have the strength it needs. And as a conductor, you sometimes have to restrain yourself in order to achieve this. There is a wonderful passage about this in Busoni's book – you know the famous, short *Sketch of a New Aesthetic of Music* – a passage which I really like, where he speaks about exactly this point. I think that book is from 1906, it's from that time, so we're right in the heart of the matter here.

What did Mahler want?

Metzmacher: I think what's really outstanding is that each of his symphonies has its own universe; I would say that he tries to describe the world in every one of his symphonies – like a great novel would do, his music tries to describe the reality of the world. He is not interested in parts or aspects; he is always pursuing the big picture. Every symphony is a universe. And they are also very different from one another, come to think of it – there is perhaps only one other composer you can say that about, and that's Beethoven – they are really very different. With each symphony he is writing a new book, maybe about the same thing, but it's a new book. And that's fascinating, and to me it's as if they are stars in a galaxy.

It seems that there comes a point when we are stuck with these nine symphonies because as a human being, you are not able to write more. There is no way that you could create more than nine symphonies in your life because there is a limit to your ability, to your forces – to your fantasy, your creativity, your ability to create a new symphony in the sense that you are creating a universe. There's some truth in that, there must be: the magic number nine, I don't know where it comes from.

That's what Schönberg said; he remarked that there was a limit to one's growth. Is Mahler an example to you, as a conductor who fought for new music in his time and adamantly stuck to his position?

Metzmacher: Yes, he was always a big example to me, especially as an opera conductor, you know, as *Generalmusikdirektor*. It's amazing when you think of how many performances he conducted, when working in Hamburg and especially in Vienna. He was the first conductor to be interested in musical theatre. This is something I really admire, and that's a tradition I certainly try to live up to. Mahler was the first to work with certain stage directors and set designers because he understood the importance of creating comprehensive music theatre productions. Unfortunately, that's a tradition which, even today, has not taken hold completely because many conductors still think, "they do their theatre on stage, I do my music in the pit", which I think is a complete misunderstanding of opera. So I read a lot about what he did with that, especially when I was in Hamburg, and I strive to do it in his tradition. I think it's very, very important to understand the theatrical aspect of opera music and to bring it together with the action on stage. It's crucially important. Since Mahler never wrote an opera himself, people sometimes forget about that side of his life, but it was a very important part of it. After all, he only composed in the summer and the rest of the year he was fighting for music theatre, he was fighting for music in general in his concerts.

We should also mention that he re-orchestrated a lot of music, which nowadays you would be killed for doing, because we now want music to be as historically correct as possible: only that has authority. But Mahler didn't care, he just re-orchestrated the pieces because he thought they were better that way. It's amazing actually, and I think that's also a very important part of his life. I think people today would scream if they heard what he did with Beethoven and Schumann. So he really was an innovator on all fronts, he was a pioneer – obsessed, maybe.

You have said your experience with Nono's Prometeo *helped you when you were conducting Mahler; can you explain that?*

Metzmacher: I think *Prometeo* helped me in a lot of ways. Maybe there is this inner contradiction in Mahler's music; we know he was always reworking his pieces after he performed them: he changed instrumentation, he changed dynamics, he changed indications in the score. So in a way, his music was always a work in progress – in the tradition of Schubert and *The Wanderer*, let's say – and there is a link to Nono here because Nono is just a work in progress. You have to approach it in a new way each time, that's what he demands of you. And I think Mahler would actually have said that too, although he wrote everything so explicitly in his scores. Thinking about it now, you could say maybe he wanted to fight his own inability to make a final decision by constantly re-notating his scores, because he didn't want his doubts, or his new feelings about how it should be played and how the music should go, to be there for anyone who lived after him – maybe that is at the heart of it. Because he started this tradition of writing everything meticulously in the scores and that has very much influenced the music that came after him. Composers began to think, "I really have to mark it very precisely", whereas composers before him very often leave us in doubt about what they really wanted – in terms of tempo or whatever – and you struggle a lot with that. Mahler didn't do that, but maybe that was also the wrong idea.

Having met Nono, I know that he was only interested in things he wouldn't be able to write down in the score. He would come and talk to me about the sound and when I wanted to ask him things about it, I asked him in the usual terms – loud, soft, attack, articulation – everything that you can actually write down in the scores, he would say, "No, no, no, no, it's the quality of sound I dislike." And he didn't mean quality in the sense we use it today, meaning very polished and soft and round; he meant it in an older sense of the word: the characteristics of the sound. He was very interested in that and he challenged you to look for it, never to think you have done it and that you can keep it in a bottle now and just open it up whenever you do Nono; he challenged you to always look for it anew.

I think Mahler was probably similar in that way; but he did write everything in his scores, so maybe we shouldn't feel too sure about that. We should look behind it because perhaps he tried to hide the necessity of always looking for the right balance in the orchestra, the right sound, the right positioning in the hall, the right acoustics. Maybe he tried to hide all this behind a very meticulously notated score. And so today we say, "Okay, this is fine, I can do it, nobody can say anything." Of course, I will always try to do the *pianissimo*, but I think, knowing that he was doubting and changing things himself, we should keep that in mind.

When you come to the *10th* you realise that suddenly you feel lost because the markings are very sparse in the *Adagio* and you can only guess. Suddenly you are left with your own doubts and thoughts, but maybe one should learn from that – that one shouldn't feel too sure about the other pieces, either, just because he wrote everything into them.

(Salzburg, 05/08/2009)

Kent Nagano

"Mahler was a pioneer – not only a radical"

Do you remember the first time you heard Mahler's music?

Nagano: The first time I heard Gustav Mahler's music was indirectly through the television. I was a very young boy, it was in the early 1960s, and I heard the second movement of the *1st Symphony* explained, and then conducted, by Leonard Bernstein and the New York Philharmonic. It was on what has now become a very famous television series called The Young People's Concerts, and for many children like me, who lived in rural America, far away from the big cities, where we didn't have regular access to symphony orchestras and opera houses, it was a tremendous outreach programme. I must have been eight years old at the time.

Leonard Bernstein made Mahler popular; was he crucial for you, too?

Nagano: Of course; I studied with Leonard Bernstein, because by consensus we feel that he was an extraordinary artist with an extraordinary ability to communicate far, far beyond the walls of the concert hall.

At the same time, he performed in such a way that was very different from Bruno Walter, that somehow through his performances – and again I speak as someone who later had the privilege of working and studying with Bernstein – one has the feeling that there was almost a physical struggle taking place with the musical form on stage at the time. But my memories of Bernstein's performances are not only about the music, I also have images of him actually, physically conducting the pieces at the same time. So the performances themselves took on other dimensions, both for the conductor – the interpreter, his relationship with the music – and the music itself.

Which was the first Mahler symphony you conducted?

Nagano: It was the 9th, and in a sense it wasn't by choice: it was due to an unusual set of circumstances. I was the assistant to maestro Seiji Ozawa with the Boston Symphony Orchestra and due to a personal problem, maestro Ozawa was unable to complete the series of performances of the 9th. And after the premiere, or the first performance, he was called away from Boston. As the assistant then, I was given a chance to conduct the 9th: probably not in the way one should conduct the 9th for the first time, but thanks to the tremendous support of the great Boston Symphony Orchestra and the commitment, professionalism and profound artistry contained within the tradition of it all, the performance was a very special one.

When you started to conduct the music of Olivier Messaien, you had a dialogue with the composer, you could ask him questions. If Mahler were alive, what questions would you put to him?

Nagano: The fortunate aspect of Mahler's life is that, at least during my lifetime, there is a chance to be exposed to interpreters who still knew Mahler. Americans were able to host Bruno Walter, who was in a sense a protégé, or a student, or at the very least, an assistant of Mahler. And many films still exist, many extracts of Bruno Walter either performing Mahler, speaking about him, or rehearsing his music. And from this we can catch glimpses of what Mahler really thought of his own music.

Probably, if I could ask Mahler a question, it would be on a more personal level, i.e. how he enjoyed his time in the United States and in what way his time in America might have influenced his composition.

No questions about the scores? They are clear?

Nagano: Mahler was a very meticulous composer. Simply looking at his manuscripts, one sees the incredible detail he included. It's different from earlier forms, when style was an assumed part of performance, and knowledge of the regulations of performance practice was simply built into the composition process itself. That's why, in older music forms, simply writing allegro would be enough to suggest to performers how they would then include aspects of flexibility, aspects of breathing. It was simply assumed that, through the prevailing stylistic performance practices, a performer would bring these human aspects into the performance.

And we see in Mahler, in his notation of the music, that it is a very modern approach. There is so much virtuosity in the technique in which he writes in these flexible aspects: these ideas of simultaneous events taking place, yet at the same time carefully written out so that spontaneity can be repeated over and over again, through simply realising the score carefully. And there is a surviving recording of Bruno Walter rehearsing a Mahler symphony and one sees how carefully he serves the written text of the music, to make sure that this flexibility or spontaneity comes out in the end. This then includes within it an inherent danger that putting further emphasis on yet more flexibility in a Mahler score can sometimes result in a performance that is really not very appropriate.

How much did Mahler's life influence his music?

Nagano: It's almost impossible to answer that question because it's such a personal one. We do know that Mahler's generation was a particularly flowering and fruitful time for the evolution of European society, European civilisation. The second half of the 19th century was a very exciting time to be alive. Societies were expanding and reaping the benefits of the Industrial Revolution, and people had big dreams that went far beyond the boundaries of what came before. For example, Haussmann was redesigning Paris; there were dreams of world expositions to share technology; the Eiffel Tower was built; Antarctica was discovered. So, this feeling of reaching out and having a vast universal optic, rather than a simple regional one, was very exciting.

And, of course, when you think of the great symphonic forms, Mahler's took on these very large, universal tableaux: very, very different from the kinds of contained forms and structures that he had inherited.

We can't really tell if the world in which Mahler lived, or his environment, had an influence on *his* music; we can't say that for sure. Especially when I think of how Messaien explained his music. People would often say to Messaien: "You're a Catholic, you're a profound believer, does one have to be a believer to appreciate your music?" It's interesting to think about what Messaien would say. He would usually say two things: that the source of his inspiration was personal – that the inspiration came and allowed him to be creative and create works, but once those works were created, then it was up to the performers to recreate them with their own inspiration, with their own sense of creativity. And: "Would you ask this question of Johann Sebastian Bach?" And these two responses, I think, are not so disparate in terms of how the true creator, which is to say the composer, thinks. The source of the inspiration is mysterious; if it weren't mysterious then we would all be composers and great ones. There is a mystery behind it, but once that mystery allows a creation to take place, and a work exists, in a sense that piece then needs to be interpreted by the people who inherit it.

Some say, Das klagende Lied *[The Song of Lamentation] is his only work that could be staged. You conducted the world premiere of the three-act version. Can you tell us about this project and your reaction to seeing the full piece?*

Nagano: In this particular instance, as with many other composers, one can see through studying the scores that there are times when the most radical, or inventive, or imaginative explosion of expression comes with the very first version of a score.

Mahler's not alone in this. If one goes back to the first versions of Bruckner's symphonies, very often one can see wildly inventive ideas that were later softened somehow: through criticism; through advisers, through friends. But the danger with that is that if it's over-refined, then it loses its seeds of excitement as well. Here in the United States we call this 'designed by committee' [*laughs*], where a board of directors or some sort of consortium put their heads together and take an idea, and then keep working on it until there's nothing left of the original idea. And you see terrible creations coming from this.

With the final version of *Das klagende Lied*, I admit there were very, very interesting parts that I was never really inspired to perform. But looking over the score of the *Urfassung* [*original version*], I was confronted by these wild statements of bitonality, simultaneous rhythms taking place, controlled chaos, overwhelmingly dramatic statements that were upheld by an extraordinarily large orchestra.

To me, it was a thrilling and undeniable statement by the young Mahler that the future was now, that Mahler was a pioneer – not only a radical, but a pioneer. Sometimes radicals destroy more than they create, but pioneers lead discovery, and usually their discoveries leave a legacy behind to those who follow. And this feeling of simultaneousness and conflict, because of seemingly random forces coming together, are contained within this first version of *Das klagende Lied*.

And that, combined with the fact that when the work is complete you can understand the story, makes absolute sense. There is a consistency, and the listener can follow why and how these themes come, and one also sees the influences of past traditions upon the young Mahler at that time. And while one can accept the criticism that, yes, there are moments that could be described as crude or not fully refined, on the other hand, the burst of energy, of optimism and creativity, is something I think all people have almost a physical response towards.

Thinking years later – well not that many years later, a few decades later – of when Charles Ives was to put the basic constructs of his 4th *Symphony* into place, one also thinks of the great joy and energy that's released through apparent cacophony or chaos coming together. But in fact it's something carefully placed together in an art form. This was fascinating to me, and it was a great privilege to participate in this project, to bring the *Urfassung* to light.

What did Mahler want?

Nagano: We can't answer that, and it's very presumptuous of anyone who dares to try. It's sometimes even dangerous for friends to answer on behalf of other friends, or even a husband to answer on behalf of a wife, or for a sister to answer on behalf of a brother.

We can only look objectively at what's left behind, to maybe get an idea or a glimpse of what might have been: through the music that Mahler left behind; through his writings; fortunately there are many writings, many letters. We can see that Mahler wanted what all humans want, which was somehow a universe in which there were positive things to be felt. But we also see that Mahler's sensitivity was, I would say, extraordinarily great, that he was very aware – in spite of these wishes for a very, very positive universe, or a vast environment in which humanity could live – that there was a constant and inherent potential of risk, and with that risk a constant potential of danger.

And thinking of the turbulent times in which he lived – on the eve of the First World War; during a time when the tension in the conflict between the privileged class and the population who had nothing was mounting to a point where you could feel that an explosion was about to take place; where societal mores were changing. The family structure was breaking down, if you think of Mahler's own life, and being redefined into something strange and untraditional. When you think the social structures, or the sociological structures, from an anthropological viewpoint, were being completely redefined: the sense of the aristocracy for example, and how it had reached a point where it was decaying and crumbling.

One had a sense, and Mahler almost certainly had the sense, that something was going to happen, within his wish to have a very positive universe. But these wishes of humanity, I would say, are something we can feel very, very much for Mahler. He had the ability, as we all do, to dream of things, and he dreamt of many aspects that he probably knew would be impossible for him to experience and to achieve. And with that came this sensitivity towards the darker side as well as the very light and positive side.

That's why I said before that I think Mahler's music is an expression of life's reality. And in this way it made him a very important composer, in that he was able to express this life's reality at that time, and in a way accessible to us, who live today – facing the complications of the world that cannot be explained and somehow cannot be resolved – through his art, through his great music, expressions of humanity that somehow offer a context or perspective. So that, probably, was not something that he particularly wanted, but through his dreams – which he wrote about – we can perhaps have a feeling of where his extraordinary sensitivity came from.

You say he had the ability to dream, to have visions; he would have fitted in perfectly with the United States. Which aspects do you find interesting in his relations with the US?

Nagano: America, at that time, was much more isolated than it is today. It was a destination of immigrants. People came to America – and in this I'm not speaking about our indigenous Americans, I'm speaking about this very unusual and particular culture, the American culture – because we were historically populated by people who left their own lands in search of something else.

They were searching for a kind of freedom; somehow America could offer them a different kind of hope, a place where things could potentially be realised, whereas they couldn't be realised in other lands. This was the case with my family, and it was probably the case with most families who made their way to America. Nevertheless, in that particular time, the East Coast was receiving an enormous number of European immigrants. So what was established there had a certain familiarity, aspects that could be recognised: architectural aspects, certain customs. But at the same time we were already very, very American, that is to say foreign to any Europeans that would come.

It is in that sense that I would like to ask Mahler how it felt, then, to work in the opera house, how it felt to work within the symphonic medium, with repertoire that he knew so well, not only as a composer, but through the great repertoire that he was performing regularly in Vienna. And I'd like to see through his own eyes and ears what the differences were, coming over to this new world in search of a new start, a new freedom, where immigration and, therefore, this idea of a melting pot came about.

Yes, the past was important, but just as important was being able to have a new beginning. And with that, what was so attractive about America in those days was that one had the feeling that what lay in the future was just as important as what lay in the past. So you could, somehow or another, gradually let the past go and really focus on a new life in America. In my own case, for example, that's why I can't speak Japanese – or speak Japanese very badly – because my parents were also born in the US, and their Japanese skills are limited. And my grandparents, who came over in 1895 in search of a new life, but enthusiastically embraced the new world, themselves became English speakers.

So in a sense, heritage can be lost in a relatively short amount of time, focussing on this melting pot phenomenon; it was already in existence in Mahler's New York, when he came. It would be interesting to see what his experience was like.

He wrote that he was beginning to love the American people more and more, and that he felt more inner freedom than he ever had before. I find that stunning.

Nagano: That is really surprising. But that's one of the very special parts about what makes up this American culture that's nearly impossible to define, because it's so complicated and so new.

I've been working my way through Henry-Louis de La Grange's new translation of Mahler's last years, and I'm just coming up to the American years now. It's a great book – wonderful! It's fantastic. I was so thrilled, I had to call him up and tell him that it is a true masterpiece.

(Munich, 27/07/2009)

Andris Nelsons

"Mahler wanted to show the world: I have a problem!"

Do you remember the first time you heard Mahler's music?

Nelsons: The first time I *consciously* heard Mahler's music was his *1st Symphony*. It was strange because I was very much interested in nature sounds at the time, in music about nature. I had recordings of water sounds and bird songs and one day I asked somebody what music they could recommend I listen to if I liked that kind of music, just out of interest.

This person gave me a tape and said, "There is one composer …" He had forgotten the name, but it was Mahler's *1st Symphony*. The beginning, which is a chord in the strings, is also the sound of nature, absolutely … [*sings*]. This was the first Mahler that I heard; I was maybe 11 or 12 years old and I fell in love with his music.

When you started to conduct Mahler, which piece did you choose?

Nelsons: I had always wanted to be involved with Mahler's music since studying conducting, and of course I realised, and still realise, how difficult this music is … to convey it honestly to the audience; how much emotion, how much power, how much love, how much of everything is required to perform this music.

I remember the first Mahler symphony I conducted was the *2nd* – that was in Riga when I was chief conductor of the Opera House; I remember it being a tremendous experience. I still get goose bumps … [*sings* "Aufersteh'n, ja aufersteh'n …"].

There are obviously very different ways to approach Mahler.

Nelsons: When you see maestro Boulez or Bernstein or Mariss Jansons or Simon Rattle or Barenboim or Haitink, all these great, fantastic conductors, they all do it differently. You can't say this is right and this is wrong because it's all great, they all have personal relationships with Mahler. I think Mahler wants every artist and every conductor to have a personal relationship with his music, so you can never say "this is the right or wrong way"; I have always believed that.

There will always be somebody who will disagree with the way you do things and there will always be those who think differently, but this is absolutely normal, I think. It's a testament to the richness of the vision of his music.

But you know, Mahler was a great conductor and he gives enormous help in his scores.

On your individual approach to Mahler: who influenced you?

Nelsons: I would say that it's a combination of great personalities. I think one of the biggest was Bernstein. You watch him and it infects you. You might not accept some things, but it still infects you, it makes you think "this is music about life and death". Of course there are other great conductors, for instance Bruno Walter, who personally knew Mahler, and also the interpretations by the younger generation: Mariss Jansons, Simon Rattle, Daniel Barenboim. Then there was Karajan, who again did it absolutely differently. I think all these personalities have influenced me.

From a technical point of view, what is the biggest challenge when conducting Mahler?

Nelsons: As Mahler was a great conductor, he helps a lot, putting the markings in the score. He is really great at balancing … Let's say there is a place where everything sounds very loud and you conduct a big gesture, then everything can become a little too loud or you don't understand what happens, but he writes it in the score. For example, for the trumpets he writes forte piano, for the first violins he writes forte and for the cellos he writes mezzo piano – so he balances the orchestra himself.

It's a challenge to find the right balance when you're conducting, because if you don't manage to encourage the musicians to play the music the way it's written, then everything can become extremely loud and extremely thick.

On the other hand, the combination of chamber music, which is so present in all of his symphonies, and the huge, gigantic culminations, the explosions … that is also a technical challenge when you're conducting, to see and encourage the difference when there is a chamber music moment, where you shouldn't disturb the music – you should never disturb the music as a conductor [*laughs*] – and where you need to mobilise the orchestra and go for a dramatic culmination. Also, it's a challenge to find out where the culminations are and where the goal is and indeed, whether there is a goal, because sometimes he doesn't reach it, sometimes he is looking for answers, but he doesn't attain them and at the last moment, it just fades out.

For example?

Nelsons: There are a lot of culminations in all of his symphonies. For example, the last symphony of Mahler I conducted was the *8th*; we did it in Birmingham for the opening of the season. In the first movement in particular there are so many culminations. You have one climax, the fortissimo, another, a third, a fourth ... And if you think this is the goal, the first time, the second time, then you think "Oh my God, it isn't working."

I think Mahler doesn't want you to go to the extreme. I have found that out for myself. I think he wants you to almost succeed, but not yet, and only at the very end do you succeed. So you have a certain difficulty in balancing the culminations, both emotionally and technically ... it's the same with Rachmaninoff and Wagner ...

And in the *8th Symphony*, I remember a lot of moments when you almost make an explosion too early, although he doesn't want you to do that. The music provokes. The same is true for the last movement of the *5th Symphony*. You think "this is the finale", but not yet, he backs off again. You need to find the right moment.

There is one moment towards the very end when he writes crescendo – it really explodes – and you need to know for yourself that that's the explosion. If you don't divide it, it doesn't work, because even though it sounds almost the same dynamically, psychologically, if you are not clear in your mind which is the culmination or the most emphasised sentence in his music, you might get misled.

It's very easy to get confused, not to know what to do or where to go because his symphonies are so long. I find this is also one of the difficulties.

What would you have asked Mahler?

Nelsons: That's an interesting question, and actually, a very relevant one because I'm about to conduct his *5th* – this year I'm doing the *5th* and the *9th* – and I would ask him about the Adagietto, about the duration and what he actually meant with it.

There are so many discussions about this at the moment; some say that he performed it on the piano in just over seven minutes, but there is a recording with Bernstein that lasts 13 minutes, if I'm not mistaken. And there is this tradition of playing it very slowly and very romantically, which is beautiful and maybe the body and soul prefer it, but when you know that he performed it on the piano in under eight minutes, then you must question it. I am questioning myself about this, about the right way to perform it, particularly the

Adagietto; I want to find an answer. Either way, it would be something very personal, whether it was intended as a love song to Alma or whether it has nothing to do with that and actually refers to an even more intimate and sad inner world which is not about Alma, but is even more personal and deeper than love.

How do you see his personality and the influence of his difficult life on his work? Do you see a connection?

Nelsons: Obviously there is a connection. On the one hand, his life was very successful; he was a great conductor and the director of the Opera, and he was mostly also a successful composer. Not all the symphonies were accepted as great, but he was not like Bruckner, for example, or other composers. So from that point of view, you could say that he was a successful composer. He had Alma; although he had her and then almost didn't have her ... it was complicated.

But still, he had an emotional world and he had children. At the same time, of course, we know about his heart disease, his problems with Alma, the death of one of his children and about his struggles with the opera house – the administrative problems and so on. This was the difficult part.

On the other hand, in life, there have always been and will always be people who face such problems, but what matters is whether we accept the challenges. You know, life is difficult, there are nice moments and sad moments, but we accept it and we live with it. Brahms, for example – he accepted life; for him it was more about religion and about nature. But Mahler didn't accept life how it really is. He enjoyed life in moments when he was happy and then he wrote, for instance, the Adagietto, or the last movement of the 5th or the first movement of the 8th.

In these pieces he is laughing or even being sarcastic. But then there are days when he can be the saddest or most romantic person: for instance, the first movement of the 5th or the 6th or any of the funeral marches. In those works you can see that he was most unhappy, that he didn't accept life; he was asking questions: "Why are things like this? Why am I in a situation in which I am not happy? Why do I have these problems and how can I escape them? What is wrong with life, what is wrong with religion and our attitude towards life, what is wrong with the political world? Why can't everything be fine?" I think he basically didn't accept life for what it is and he was struggling. His personality was so colourful. I think there were many people who had similar problems, but they could accept life for what it is, they didn't complain so loudly.

But he was knocking and saying: "Listen, this is a problem!" I think he was a revolutionist; he would say: "We should be fighting!" He probably thought that people shouldn't accept things like an economic crisis; he would have wanted them to do something about it. I think if he lived now and if he were to write a symphony in the present economic climate, it would be a great work. Some people just accept that we are going through a financial crisis, that the economy is in trouble. But he wouldn't accept it, I think. This doesn't necessarily mean that his life was worse than other people's. But he just couldn't accept it. That's why he talked about it in his symphonies.

So his character was revolutionary?

Nelsons: Yes, in a way. There are some people who like to be melancholic or nostalgic and they enjoy that feeling. Like in Puccini's music; he always killed the characters he loved the most, for example, Tosca, Butterfly, Liu … he loved them, but he always let them die and he almost enjoyed killing them and squeezing out the tears with his music.

I think it's the same with Mahler, even if he did it subconsciously – he liked to talk about the things that were hurting him. It hurt, but he showed that and he wrote about it, which was a big strain on his heart. I think he wanted to share his problems; he wanted to show the world "I have a problem! I don't know the meaning of life!" [*sings dramatically*]

Brahms wouldn't say that, for example, but Mahler was not too shy to say it. He even enjoyed it somehow. The slow movement of the 4th, for instance, really squeezes out the nostalgia and the melancholy, in a good way. But listening to this music, you can almost have a heart attack because it's so beautiful and so moving. Or the last movement of the 3rd – it's touching and emotional in a fatal way; he knew that he was destroying his heart with this music: you feel unwell just listening to it.

Not in a bad sense, but really, you are exhausted, you can't sleep at night. Maybe this contributed to his heart problem. It wasn't the only reason for it, obviously, but, while other people can relax, he was living 100% with his emotions. This is just my opinion – I also like very much what I heard maestro Haitink say about this – that we are always talking a lot about composers and we analyse them, but actually we don't know anything, really. We can only guess and read about them, and we *need* to know about them and read about them. But in the end, the music goes beyond even the composers' personalities.

They have a gift from God which sometimes even they can't explain. The music is ineffable. These composers are geniuses and we will never know exactly what they felt and where their genius came from. We should just enjoy the music and perform it.

Mahler himself said that a mystery remained even for him as a composer …

Nelsons: Yes, that's also interesting. I think, in the end, it has to do with a higher spirit; it has to do with God. I think that Mahler was disappointed with certain religions and dogmas, but I think he was never disappointed in God. He was always searching for God, for example, in his *Resurrection Symphony* and the *8th*. He knew that there was something after death, but he couldn't find it in religion and the time in which he lived probably made it even more difficult for him. So he had this gift from God, which he himself realised was a mystery. I think this is the highest spirit of music, as we all feel it when we perform. At that moment, we all have something coming from God which helps us. When you watch these conductors performing, you can see that it comes from above.

What did Mahler want?

Nelsons: I think in his soul, very subconsciously, he wanted to be happy and he wanted to be loved and to love. He wanted to know the answers to a lot of questions – for instance: why do we live? He honestly wanted to know. But he never really found out, perhaps because he was searching so hard for the answers. He wanted to be happy, philosophically speaking; he wanted to find the solution in life, to be happy, to be loved, to find out what love is and what eternity means. I think he wanted to learn that, but he didn't. He would almost succeed, but then it would all collapse again.

Would you say Mahler's life was a tragic one?

Nelsons: I think for him personally, it was quite a tragic life, although it was not as tragic as for many other composers whose lives were much more so – Beethoven's, for instance. But because of Mahler's obsession with these questions, I think he was very unhappy inside … and he screams through his symphonies about this. That's my personal feeling. Screaming. Exclaiming. Like Shostakovich, you know.

I think that's why he moves us. His music is not abstract, it's a personal statement.

Nelsons: Yes, that's what he wanted: "Listen to me, I am suffering! Help me! Understand me!" Yes.

(Vienna, 22/10/2010)

Jonathan Nott

"Frozen for eternity in death"

Do you remember the first time you heard Mahler's music?

Nott: Yes. I actually came across Mahler when I was eight years old, singing in the boys choir in Worcester Cathedral; it was Mahler's 8th.

Was Mahler part of the repertoire when you discovered his symphonies in the UK?

Nott: I wouldn't say I discovered them – apart from the 8th – I just had much more experience of the 8th than anything else. I wasn't really a concert-goer.

I grew up in the Midlands, in Worcester; there were concerts, but it wasn't like being in Vienna or even London. There were very few opportunities to experience a Mahler symphony, therefore I think my first encounters were in mainland Europe – Frankfurt, where I ended up in the late 80s.

Would you say that Sir John Barbirolli played a major role in bringing Mahler to the UK?

Nott: Yes. I recently came across recordings of his work and discovered what he stands for. You know, at that time, I was terribly preoccupied with just trying to sing, with being in Cambridge and studying music. I didn't actually focus on what was really going on, or how someone like Barbirolli actually brought Mahler to England – that was something I discovered only after starting to learn about it many years after leaving England. But I can see now – in terms of actual performance – what's left, what I can hear from his performance of Mahler. He had a very individual voice, and must have been extremely powerful to bring that about.

Does knowing the struggles Mahler faced in his life help to understand his music?

Nott: Absolutely. I would even go as far as to say that I feel happiest with what I want to say and what I feel needs to be said every time I think of his struggles, because I've regarded his music as being autobiographical virtually the entire time. It's not usually the story or the autobiographical element that tends to be striking.

I don't believe the *9th Symphony* is about his difficult circumstances. I don't believe you need that. As far as I can see, what you do need is to believe that his idea of heaven was going up into the mountains and hearing the cowbells and seeing how different the world was and how different the air was. That is extremely helpful in the *6th*.

And then if you look at his relationship with Alma and try to work out what it could have been like, being the complicated relationship it appeared to be in so many ways, and then take this information and find out that the tragic element in the *6th* is actually the slow movement – and not necessarily the last movement. I now find that most of my musical decisions are somehow linked to what I have read about his life and they have become autobiographical – but not always in the way that it's been given to us, or perhaps the way he or somebody else has tried to give it to us. That's my personal feeling about this. So I can never eradicate him from the music.

Is there a conflict between polyphony and monumentality – and conducting Mahler?

Nott: I suppose not, because the polyphony side is no more complicated than most of the contemporary music scores that I am required to perform, and which I enjoy performing. This means that because I possibly came to Mahler's music after having performed music quite a lot later, sorting out 10 different lines in one go is sort of everyday business, really. Being able to actually feel that and transmit it to an audience, that's another matter. But the complexity is therefore challenging and inspiring, and the problem is simply balance within the apparatus. How do you achieve this if you have one melody that keeps changing from instrument to instrument and changing colour? How do you make sure that it's heard and noticed? So no, I don't have a problem with the polyphony.

The block element, i.e. what we've been talking about, is about making sense of what's written there. I mean, even little things like no ritardando or accelerando markings, but a change in tempo – is it unmusical to do one or is it exactly what he wants? And deciding what you can get out of the paper and what he really means, e.g.: "I think he meant this exactly like it says here, that we drive this into a brick wall and change …"

Once you've made that kind of decision, then some of the blocks that come in more or less take care of themselves. I find it much more difficult with the first upbeat, making sure I know where everything is on the arch to the end – which is more a question of time because they are still very, very long arches. They are still very long points of concentration for the performer, for the listener.

Did Mahler anticipate the catastrophes of the 20th century?

Nott: Yes, of course. The question is if we are going to believe that these catastrophes in the music are somehow in him – whether they are his own personal catastrophes that he saw far beyond his own life. And I quite like to believe that. I somehow feel that he was a very special guy. The music that has emerged a hundred years later is still so frightening; it has so much power that there must be something special about it.

In the same way, we have to think about life and death, and we have to experience life and death as artists and as music lovers. And I suppose that's the main reason for making music – to provide answers to the eternal questions that humankind will eventually ask. Music offers hope and answers to these unanswerable questions. So if you believe that, if you believe the music is great, you are dealing with something that is taking you away, that is somehow moving in a sphere that is not actually on this planet in which we happen to be living. The catastrophes in the music are so strong that I would hate it if that were simply him feeling like that, the whole time. I like to believe that such great art – that we are in the big circle of things – is part of it and therefore it's got to be saying something more than what we see on paper.

Why is the 9th so important to you?

Nott: There are certain elements of truth in the *9th* – the symphony has slightly less room for manoeuvre as an interpreter. It doesn't play itself – well of course it doesn't play itself – but it seems to me that he has such strong ideas about how to play it that I didn't feel like I was thrown into despair with no hope of ever finding a way to perform the music.

I had to work out that I wanted the second movement to disappear into catastrophe, to drive it to the point of both dance worlds. And the third – obviously – how to try and link this gruppetto that comes at the beginning. How do I make sure that you really know it was important enough so that the *Fourth*, the last movement, has something to say? How to create this feeling of putting on a coat of death – trying it on in the last movement, seeing what it's like.

Yes, the music is sort of frozen in those thirds that keep moving around like individual cells of life. Life that is ongoing. But the whole thing is frozen for eternity in death, if you see what I mean. So that element, of course, is there, but I didn't have to struggle to find a way through in the same way that I did with the 6*th*, the 2*nd* and the 4*th*. But on the other hand, I still come back. It's the 9*th* that I think about most when wandering around.

But isn't there a danger of being too involved emotionally – of forgetting about holding things together?

Nott: Well, that's why I say: if you let go of the reins, if you just rush your way through it – that's not what it's about. It has an inner pull between the intellectual and the emotional. It seems to come from a purely compositional structure and therefore you cannot completely let go. Anyway, as a conductor, I can never let go completely because somebody might need my help in the next bar.

*When I discovered Mahler's 6*th* with the Vienna Philharmonic under Bernstein, I was a music student, I understood nothing. But I was seized, distressed … the last movement – what is it trying to tell me? And ever since then I've been wanting to find out.*

Nott: I absolutely sympathise and I totally agree. It happened every single time. To the point where even two weeks before I had to do Mahler's 2*nd* *Symphony* for the first time, two or three years ago, I rang up the concert manager and said, "I just don't understand this piece; I understand every little bit, bit by bit, but I don't understand where I am supposed to be going here. I don't see … a *Totenfeier* [*funeral ceremony*] works by itself, and the scherzo is fantastic, but it's full of …" And again, the last movement of the 6*th* is fascinating, isn't it? You can't analyse it and say: "It's 'this'." It isn't 'this' – that's what's so clever. But he pulls you. And in order to be able to communicate to every member of the audience, the tension, the excitement is in the actual form itself.

Is there one symphony where you feel your approach has changed more than in others?

Nott: Yes, the 5*th*. Because the 5*th* was one that I did quite early on. I fell into the trap of taking the first movement too … not importantly, because it's an important movement – but too significantly. So the second was then left by itself. The last time I did it, I tried again – because you have this expectation, when the chorale comes in that key; what are you going to get in the last movement when you've eventually made sense of it. So I had to see the first and second movements together as one block and not indulge myself too much in the first movement. The whole symphony then took a completely new turn.

It depends when these symphonies get you in your life. I am now a different conductor to the one I was four years ago. I did the 5th six years ago, I think, and then I did it three years ago. And you change. You're a different person. You see things differently and you develop. Therefore you have to keep questioning things. I write in my scores ... "Surely this means this (July 2004)." "No, of course it doesn't – it means THIS, idiot! (2006)." "No, you fool!" ... I write these things in because I have to know what I was thinking about them. There's this question: where does this come from? These scores are all sorts of diaries of me basically talking to myself.

I'm a real colourer. I use a score up, throw it away and then start another score and keep going. You know those Ligeti pictures of how he composed – my scores look like that. I am blue, red, green, blue, purple ... written in there, scribbled out there. I then find I have a structural analysis of the piece, through the colours and through the things I've written in.

Is there a problem of balance in some symphonies?

Nott: No, I don't think so. All right, every now and again you somehow for some reason get a rather important line in, let's say, the violas, marked *piano*, a lot of people are marking fortissimo ... just every now and again I find there are certain lines that I don't quite understand. I think they are more important than he thought they were. But no more than in a Verdi opera. Sometimes I might say: "Get rid of that mezzo forte fortissimo for three and a half beats and then ..." the usual sort of stuff. But that's rare. He's done most of the work for you. Of course, the instruments are never quite the same; that makes a difference. Also, I nearly always try to have divided violins, and that makes a difference in balance. I think in Mahler it's just a structural necessity. I need to know that the Adagietto starts with the second violins and then goes with the first violins. And there are two different things and two different sides – they're just next to each other. I tend to put the basses on the right and the violas on the left – simply because I like horns on the left and horns next to basses on the left is no good; they just fight each other and complain. So that sometimes makes a difference in balance, but I don't think I've found it yet.

(Vienna, 10/06/2009)

Sakari Oramo

"Mahler controls chaos"

Do you remember the first time you heard Mahler's music?

Oramo: I have to confess that I can't remember. I went to concerts with my father quite often when I was young, especially when my mother was playing, she is a pianist. But Mahler's music – I suppose it could have been when Igor Markevitch was conducting in Helsinki. And I seem to remember that my mother played Bartók's *3rd Piano Concerto* with him, and then there was Mahler's *1st Symphony*. It could have been then.

How did the Finnish public feel about Mahler when you were growing up?

Oramo: Mahler didn't really become a known composer in Finland until the late 1960s or early 1970s. I was still too young to know about it, but my conducting teacher Jorma Panula performed a series of all the Mahler symphonies; most of them were Finnish premieres. I should mention, however, that Finnish conductors were already conducting Mahler, mainly in Sweden, way back in the 1920s and 1930s.

There was Armas Järnefelt, who, as far as I can remember, conducted the Swedish premieres of both the 5th and the 6th. There was Georg Schnéevoigt, who was a big name at that time, also of Finnish origin, who frequently conducted Mahler. But his music never really became established in Finland; Finnish conductors had better success with it when they performed it abroad.

And you personally: did the door to Mahler open immediately for you?

Oramo: No. I was very slow, actually. I remember feeling comfortable with the *1st Symphony* and maybe also some of the songs in the early part of my conducting career. But that was about all, really. And it wasn't until I had been in Birmingham for a few years that I began to find my way into Mahler's world – maybe through the 4th and later on with the 5th, and then the 2nd and 3rd as well.

If you analyse the difficulties you had in approaching Mahler, how would you describe them?

Oramo: Well, you have to bear in mind that German is a foreign language for us Finns. That makes things different for us than Germans and Central Europeans. It's not as natural. So I think it takes more time for us to find the music's natural impulse. Having grown up with the music of Sibelius and Nielsen – and, of course, a lot of German and French music – Mahler represents something that is foreign, from another world.

In what way? In the material he uses, or how he puts it together?

Oramo: Both, I think. The material he uses is quite often based on folk songs, on dances like the Ländler, even on ancient forms of music, as you can see with the hints of concerto grosso in some of his symphonies. Yet his music is also extremely expressionistic, forward-looking – I used to think that it was not held together organically. The revelation, for me, was in finding the organic nature of Mahler's music, the deeply imbedded interrelations of all the material he uses. The whole is more than just the sum of its parts.

Johannes Brahms thought that when Mahler was a young composer in a competition he simply lacked discipline. Did this pose a difficulty for you, too?

Oramo: Absolutely. I'm not a friend of discipline at all. It's more about the organic growth of the material than the external manipulation of it.

You conducted many concerts in the Mahler cycle here in Stockholm. Would you tell us about the audience's response and about the festival itself?

Oramo: I've never experienced anything like the festival before. There was a Mahler symphony on every programme and we had full houses every night.

What is the biggest challenge in performing Mahler?

Oramo: Bringing out the continuity in the music, I think. I absolutely want all the contrasts to be as clear to the listeners as possible, yet they mustn't be so prominent that they stop the overall flow of the music. I also think that in terms of handling the tempo, it's very important to be flexible and let the phrases breathe, rather than to be trapped in an inflexible pulse. I think there is always either a kind of forward arch or a backward relaxation in Mahler's music. If there is no direction, then I find it difficult to see where it's going, to see its point. But there is a direction almost all the time in everything Mahler wrote.

Is there a danger of overpowering his music?

Oramo: Yes, I think there is. I have experienced Mahler performances where I felt that people were trying to push the music too much in one direction. If one decides that a piece is, for instance, about a certain kind of emotion and, as a consequence, excludes all other emotions – kinds of texture – then one runs the risk of taking the music too far in one direction. In Mahler, all the levels must be present simultaneously. As Mahler once allegedly said when he was talking with Sibelius, "a symphony must contain the whole world, not just one slice of it."

Are there other Mahler conductors who have influenced you?

Oramo: Yes: mostly Klaus Tennstedt. I never experienced him live, I am a little too young for that, but I think he had the ability to make the music sound very free yet very organic. It sounded as if he were improvising. I find most of his recordings exceptional, although some are not so wonderfully played. But the sense of urgency and the interpretation are simply unique.

Mengelberg also influenced me, although less than Tennstedt. I adore Mengelberg's version of the Adagietto of the 5th. And his surviving recording of the 4th is just wonderful. However, he does exaggerate a lot.

But we should remember that that was customary at the time. And we know that Mahler and Mengelberg had personal contact, about 20 or 25 years before those recordings were made. And we also know that Mahler didn't agree with him on everything, which I am quite glad about. I find it's wonderful, his keenness, his micromanagement of the rubati, his sense of rhythmic wit – that is very different from what has become customary for Mahler, the smooth Viennese way of playing. So I would say that Tennstedt and Mengelberg are my most influential Mahler interpreters.

It's interesting that Mahler knew Bruno Walter and Klemperer as well; Klemperer was his assistant in his 2nd Symphony. Yet Walter's and Klemperer's approaches to Mahler's music are totally different.

Oramo: Complete opposites, absolutely. I think the smooth, slightly ironed-out playing style has partly come from Bruno Walter. I like many of his interpretations, but not particularly his Mahler. I find them lacking in excitement and interest. Maybe it has to do with the fact that he made many of his recordings in America. Yet there is, of course, the wonderful Vienna recording of the 9th, which is something else altogether; I find it very exciting and extremely profound.

Mahler was not such a favourite in Scandinavia because of Sibelius' popularity. They knew each other. How would you describe their differences?

Oramo: In a way, Sibelius always started from one cell of music and then let it grow, as if it were a tree. Everything belongs together, the branches grow out of the trunk, leaves come out of the branches, and perhaps blossoms grow out of the leaves – they are all connected. They are all nourished from a single source. And that's the difference. In Sibelius' music, you anticipate a symphonic unity – a little piece of something which you nurture into a wonderful, mature organism – very much like a tree.

Whereas in Mahler's music you have many disparate sources, all of them jockeying for position. You have this and that, this emotion and that bit of his national heritage, a bit of folk music and another bit of military march. And you kind of combine it all and stir until it becomes a wonderful melange. It's actually two different ways of approaching the material. I still remember when I read some Finnish newspaper reviews from the 1970s about Mahler's music. In one of them, Erik Tawaststjerna – he was a Sibelius biographer and a great source of inspiration for many musicians – wrote about how he was unable to understand the banality of some of Mahler's music. Although he recognised, for instance, the great mastery of the first movement and of the sixth movement, *Abschied* [Farewell], of *Das Lied von der Erde* [*The Song of the Earth*], he still couldn't come to grips with Mahler. He thought that the middle movements of *Das Lied* were nothing but banality. I can't understand that because I think it's extremely subtle. Plus, the union of music and text is just incredible. So Tawaststjerna reveals something about the differing cultural views of the time. More exposure, I think, has helped – although I do think that Mahler's symphonies are not played often enough, and certainly not well enough, in Helsinki.

Still?

Oramo: Still, yes.

It's stereotypical to say that Scandinavians are more introverted and that Mahler's music is demonstrative and perhaps sometimes even deliberately too demonstrative. Could that possibly be an explanation?

Oramo: Probably, but [in Scandinavia] we've got to learn to exaggerate more because Sibelius' music, and certainly Nielsen's, sometimes profits from that. If you look after the big, long arc, colouring some episodes and themes a little more will help to take them closer to Mahler's essence. And I think it wouldn't do any harm to address his music more while keeping Sibelius' organic growth in mind.

How do you see Mahler as a person?

Oramo: Very, very interesting. I'm not aware of many details, but I have read a fair amount, and I find him interesting because he was always so concerned about standards of music-making.

However, I just can't understand his eagerness to rewrite other people's music. Maybe it was something you just did in those days, but, as far as I know, he was working on an opera by Weber called *Die drei Pintos* [*The Three Pintos*] for a few months. The project, however, didn't work out, and apparently, Mahler wasted a lot of energy and time on such projects. My opinion on his re-orchestrating of Beethoven's *Ninth* is similar. I even heard stories about Mahler rewriting pages of Debussy's *La mer*, which is quite amazing, actually.

What I find really interesting is that when Mahler was still in Hamburg as *Generalmusikdirektor*, he invited Tchaikovsky to do either *Eugene Onegin* or *Pique Dame* [*The Queen of Spades*] – I'm not sure which, but it was one of those big operas. And apparently, Tchaikovsky couldn't manage to conduct it properly, so Mahler had to step in. I mean – what a wonderful idea – Mahler conducting Tchaikovsky!

He conducted Rachmaninoff in New York, the 3rd Piano Concerto, with the composer at the piano. And Rachmaninoff said afterwards that Mahler was the best conductor he ever had because he was attentive to every detail, was very serious with him, very serious with the music, although it's a totally different aesthetic.

Oramo: Yes, it is, completely. I'm sure he was a great interpreter. It's a pity there's no film or audio evidence of his music, other than the piano rolls, which are something, but not everything.

Where would Mahler have gone had he lived longer?

Oramo: That's a really interesting question. I think he would have probably taken a lot more notice of what Schönberg was doing, for example with his piano pieces, and what Alban Berg would do later. Maybe also of what Stravinsky was going to do. As he was interested in many things, he would have picked up elements from those people. He was still Mahler, although it's interesting to think about how such elements would have affected his own music. And, say,

Bartók – that would have been an incredibly interesting juxtaposition. But it was not meant to be.

What did Mahler want?

Oramo: That's difficult to answer. I don't know. He wanted to touch and to move people. Also, he wanted to bare his soul to the whole world, to be scrutinised. He was something of an exhibitionist, psychologically speaking, and also something of a priest; not a religious priest, but a priest of a modern lifestyle, or of a modern view of the human being.

Would you agree that Mahler somehow expressed the condition of the modern human being and that's why he became so popular?

Oramo: Absolutely. Although he was very well known as a conductor in his time, he wasn't so popular when he was actively composing. Yet nowadays, I would say he's one of the top five popular composers in classical music. Surely this means he has something very special to say about the human being, and especially about the modern human being. I think the greatest thing he gave humanity was the gift of opening the human soul with his music. That's why I think so many people can adapt themselves to Mahler's music nowadays – they can feel the power of the contrasts, of the extreme simplicity and beauty in some parts, and of the extreme complexity and even chaotic nature of other parts of his music.

What does that mean – a modern human being?

Oramo: If you imagine the Romantic ideal of the artist as someone being in complete control, then Mahler was losing control all the time. But of course he had control over losing control. He really controlled chaos.

And to which Mahler do you personally feel closest?

Oramo: It depends a bit on which piece I'm doing, but for me, the 4th is very special because it's more like chamber music, and it has a fantastic range of expression, from this nightmarish ride with sleighs ringing to the devil's violin, the vision of heaven, with all its cruelty and realism. I think it's really very modern. In that way, I feel very connected to it. But of course, I love all the pieces. Absolutely every note he has written.

How do you see his influence on the music of the 20ᵗʰ century, the Viennese School and later?

Oramo: His influence has been greater than anyone else's. That's for sure. If you talk about the Viennese School, of course, he was deified by Schönberg and his friends, and his pupils. You have, for instance, Anton Webern conducting Mahler's symphonies in Vienna in the 1920s, when the master himself had passed away. Yet you can't imagine a composer further removed from Mahler than Webern, at least regarding his later output. But I think Mahler's music showed the way, and it gave so many possibilities to future composers to take what they liked and to discard what they didn't like.

Mahler's sense of texture and his orchestration certainly influenced everyone – as well as his kind of intellectual and emotional approach, which, I think, still influences composers today.

His obsession with suffering and redemption as well?

Oramo: Yes, a lot of music is about suffering, nowadays. A lot of our best music is still about the same things: suffering, redemption, introspection, dealing with the obstacles one has to face in life.

But also the idea of composing music about music, that's also from Mahler. It's not about external things, not all of it; it's also about pure music. That's how, in my opinion, Mahler influenced Shostakovich. I think there is a big connection between the two composers. Shostakovich is always seen as a political composer, but I think his work is mostly music about music. It speaks the language of Stalinist Russia, but it's still first and foremost music, not politics.

(Stockholm, 07/05/2010)

Sir Antonio Pappano

"Mahler wanted to live, that's the whole point!"

Do you remember the first time you heard Mahler's music?

Pappano: My first encounter with Mahler's music was, of course, with the vocal music; the *Rückert-Lieder – Ich bin der Welt abhanden gekommen* [*I am lost to the world*] had a huge impact on me, but you know, strangely enough, the song that stays with me is *Liebst du um Schönheit* [*If you love for beauty*]. I know that song was originally not part of the group, but it's so specifically Mahlerian. Mahler's identity is absolutely unmistakable – in three notes. And this is what made such a huge impression on me; it couldn't be anybody else.

It's very popular to say that Mahler was influenced by this or that. He was a conductor, the greatest conductor of his generation, certainly for opera, and he had everything in his head, so of course his music can be a mishmash of all different things; but what you do with this mishmash, what you do with your influences and how you make them into something that is your own – he did that like nobody else. The Jewish thing, the barracks, the difficult home life, the fights between his mother and father, the deaths of his brothers and sisters, to live with that incredible talent inside you – all that is somehow in his music. It's an amazing compendium of feeling, commingling with the psychological research of Freud. Romantic music is not only about a romantic idea or a love triangle or a dramatic scene, it's about how it makes you feel, it's about identifying these feelings – and Mahler was particularly good at being very precise about *a feeling*. This is very interesting, I find.

That's an intriguing expression – to be precise about a feeling.

Pappano: Yes, we say feelings are sometimes very elusive and ephemeral, but he's very precise in *exactly* distilling a human feeling in his compositions – it's like a bell that we can all hear, somehow.

Did the door to Mahler open immediately for you?

Pappano: I didn't conduct for many years. When I was young, it was a long time before I really started conducting, and the notion of conducting Mahler was foreign to me. When I was younger, I was much more enamoured with the music of Bruckner, and those vast cathedrals somehow made a greater impression on me. All that fanfare in Mahler's music made me slightly nervous. But today I understand a little bit better what he was trying to say. When something is almost too honest, too truthful, sometimes it hurts, you know ... "Stay away!" [*laughs*] People identify with Mahler's music because it's very, very human. So it took me a while. My first experience conducting Mahler was *Das Lied von der Erde* [*The Song of the Earth*] in 1994. I had just conducted my first *Tristan* and I conducted *Das Lied von der Erde* right afterwards, and my goodness, that first song drove me crazy. Also, he was a composer who dared to write hardly any bass, especially in the first five songs. *Das Lied von der Erde* is based on, or comes under the sway of the influence of Chinese poetry, which is either extremely delicate or extremely biting. It grimaces in the first song, in the tenor songs especially. But there is very little bass, so the composition is all high in a way until we get to the last song, *Der Abschied* [*The Farewell*], when we finally hear the tam-tam and the contrabassoon. That really impressed me, I remember.

Mahler was the greatest opera conductor of his time. I, who conduct a lot of opera and therefore have very important relationships with singers, kind of inhabit the same world as Mahler. I am not the only one, of course; many of my colleagues conduct opera. But when you come from opera, perhaps you understand some things more easily. For instance, his love for words and the voice as the *ultimate* expression – when the orchestra can do no more, the word must come, the voice must come.

He was a great Wagner conductor. How do you see Wagner's influence on Mahler?

Pappano: Well, in his compositions, the influence is quite minimal. You could say that chromatically, sometimes, there is a similarity; maybe to *Tristan*. In *Tristan*, of course, at the end of Act 1, you have the fanfare and the horns, and the menace of the offstage horns in Act 2. But actually, Mahler's music is very unlike Wagner's. With a couple of exceptions – the beginning of Act 3 of *Tristan and Isolde* – that prelude made a big impression on Mahler, I think. How not only the chords, but the violins in thirds leave the orchestra and, like a fog, drift up very high into the ether, that grey sky; how the first and second violins ascend, somehow. I think that effect must have made a real impression on Mahler. And I think the third act prelude of *Parsifal* probably made a huge impact, judging by the Adagio of Mahler's 9th – I don't think the harmonies are the same, I don't think Mahler's harmonic world is the same, but there is something similar in the mystical and the reaching for something. But otherwise I don't see too much similarity.

You grew up in England. Was there a Mahler tradition created by Barbirolli, or who influenced you in these early years?

Pappano: Oh, I didn't have many influences at all. When I started conducting Mahler, I hadn't heard many Mahler concerts. I remember hearing the *2nd Symphony* with Sinopoli, I remember hearing recordings of the 9th and the 6th with Barbirolli, and, of course, Lenny and Kubelík and Gielen. But isn't it interesting that every one of those conductors has a different approach to Mahler? Not one of them is like the other, *at all*! That says a lot for the music. I think all of them will say they are faithful to the score. But their sound worlds and their approaches are different. Some bring the music back to the full romantic approach and others see it as the predecessor of the Viennese School and create almost a skeleton of the music, which I find very interesting. I don't think it's the whole story, and I think these tumultuous explosions in the brass need a string sound as a weight to support the rest of the orchestra, but I think all approaches are useful for different moments. I think one has to have tremendous flexibility for his music because I don't think the whole story is in one approach.

You mentioned Leonard Bernstein. He created the Mahler renaissance, he was responsible for it, but he was later criticised for being overly emotional. Would you say there is a change in the general way Mahler is conducted nowadays?

Pappano: I think maybe one of the problems with Lenny was his stage persona. I think it affected the way we listened. Because Lenny was a great musician, a wonderful pianist – and actually his work is very transparent. It's not all just … [*makes an explosive noise*] He is linear, he is very, very faithful to what's going on. Of course you see somebody up there suffering and doing the whole show for you. But that was Lenny, that was his personality, and it was more than viable. I think his approach was very, very honest. Again, I think Lenny was part of a history of Mahler conducting and it had to go through that, had to go to the extremes, to find out how far one can go and how far one can push this music. But I think it's important to find the balance, even in hysteria sometimes, to always have the architecture in mind, to create the big moments. It's very difficult to find the balance with Mahler's music because there are so many climaxes. To know which one is 'the one' is tough.

So one of the biggest challenges is to connect these emotions, to tell a story?

Pappano: Well, in a certain way. Whether it's a story that Mahler talked about, or … Look, all his symphonies are somehow about struggle, but so is the sonata form. I think Mahler made it more personal. The struggle and the resolution of the struggle and how it ends, this is what makes a symphonic argument. I don't think that's any different from Mozart or Haydn or Beethoven, it's just that he found a more modern way of showing this struggle, a much more extreme and much more daring way of really showing what lies beneath the surface.

Would you agree that he anticipated the catastrophes of the 20th century?

Pappano: Well, there are catastrophes in all of his pieces. But like I said before, he suffered so many personal catastrophes that that was a very big part of his life. It's as if he was destined to live through catastrophes. And one of the great things about the 6th, for instance, is that in the last movement, it's as if the hero is struggling against what is going to be death – let's call it that for simplicity's sake – and it's about how many times he doesn't give up, even when he is hit. But it's not only that; it's a constant rebirth after being slammed down by catastrophe after catastrophe. What catastrophe brings out of the man, that's what's interesting. Not that there is a catastrophe and not that there is a symphony about a catastrophe, it's about dealing with it. The issue is trying to get over it, conquer it and come out the other side. But sometimes you lose.

So Mahler is making a very personal statement?

Pappano: Oh, definitely. Of course. I think this idea of Nietzsche's *Superman*, I think it's *man* with Mahler, do you understand? It's us, it's you and me.

Do you think Mahler became so popular because he touched on these human conditions, especially conditions of modern times, of the 20th century?

Pappano: Yes, but I think the spectacular orchestral showcase in each symphony also makes him so popular. It's a spectacle in itself. The demands made on the orchestra, the grandeur, it's something unique, it's another dimension. I think this makes for good theatre. His symphonies are his little operas. He, the foremost conductor of opera *ever*, didn't write operas.

Why didn't he write operas?

Pappano: These are his operas. The idea of different themes, contrasting themes, different ideas, bringing ideas together, the clash of ideas, the conflict

… this is somehow better worked through with notes rather than words, intellectually as well. I mean words often work, but …

Looking back on your career – has your approach changed over the years? What is the biggest technical challenge for you when you perform Mahler?

Pappano: My Mahler experience is still quite young. I've conducted *Das Lied von der Erde*, the 9th, 1st and 6th *Symphonies*, and in a couple of weeks I will be conducting the 2nd for the first time – and I am very, very excited. Yet my approach hasn't really changed; rather it's still developing. The challenges are the dynamics. It's very easy to let things get louder and louder, and they do need to be very, very powerful, but I think it's very important to create a balance in the orchestra, and to create those moments of pianissimo and a real delicacy and chamber-music-like sonorities. And that's more difficult to do. To go from one extreme to the other in a short period of time, that's difficult to achieve. And to insist that the musicians learn to really appreciate that part of Mahler, the intimate, the grandiose, the ironic, the sardonic – and the loving and the caring, too. That's beautiful.

What did Mahler want?

Pappano: Mahler is very, very precise in his scores. I get the feeling that every conductor says, "Just do what's in the score and it's all there." I think, in a way, the idea is that a conductor should try to show the struggle to the audience. And they need to be honest about it, and when it comes to the arrival, the resurrection or death if need be, or the heroic victory at the end of Act 1 [*laughs and corrects himself*] at the end of Mahler's 1st, they need to have shown all the different sides of what it is to be human, to come out with a precise result at the end. I think that is what Mahler was looking for, in a sense: the idea of the human struggle and hopefully victory at the end of it or, if not, to die trying. And I think it's very important to keep that in mind.

So his message is a positive one?

Pappano: Oh, I think so – very much so. You know, all this talk about death: he didn't want to die! The man wanted to live, that's the whole point! *That's* the point of his symphonies; it's the love of life, not the love of death. It's why death is a part of our lives; yes, these are big questions, but it's life as something wonderful, my goodness! That's it, that's all.

(Vienna, 20/04/2010)

Josep Pons

"Mahler is more contemporary now than in 1910"

Do you remember the first time you heard Mahler's music?

Pons: It was at the Schola Cantorum in Montserrat. I studied at the monastery from age 10 to 14 and sang in the Schola Cantorum. This is a place with a very long tradition and a very good library, and also where I heard Mahler's music for the first time – recorded, not live.

Straight after I left Montserrat, a few friends gave me the complete symphonies, conducted by Bernard Haitink with Elly Ameling singing in the 4th. That was the soundtrack to my life, so to speak, when I was 14, 15, 16 years old. Later on, the first time I conducted Mahler's music was with a small group. A chamber version of *Das Lied von der Erde* [*The Song of the Earth*], *Lieder eines fahrenden Gesellen* [*Songs of a Wayfarer*] – those were my initial contacts with Mahler.

Was the door to Mahler open to you right from the beginning?

Pons: Yes. One's relationship with composers is always interesting: there are composers who fill you with energy and there are composers that suck the life out of you like a vampire. Some composers you understand right away while others you never really come to understand. In my case, I was 'quick' to understand both Mahler and Mozart. Mahler was someone I found to be very naturally accessible due to his harmonic world and that 'instrumental cleanliness' of his, as well as his 'clean lines' – and because many questions sprang to mind; things that are part of my personality, too.

How has Mahler been received in Spain?

Pons: Mahler was a late arrival in Spain, a country with its own peculiar history. After a turbulent 19th century and rich 17th and 18th centuries, the country was ruined by imperialistic ambitions. This made it different from Germany, France and even Italy in the 19th century. Spain carried on with Italian opera – only opera with Italian influences – and successful composers wrote operas or a new genre that arose in the 19th century, the *zarzuela*: a folk genre written in Spanish that deals with popular themes, similar to the Viennese or French operetta. There was very, very little life in the symphonic world in Spain in the 19th century. Just imagine, we had symphonies from the mid 19th century that still used basso continuo! Haydn had stopped using basso continuo halfway through his composing life! So we entered the symphonic world quite late. Beethoven's symphonies reached Spain very late; his *9th* premiered in Barcelona in 1900. That's interesting because in 1913 Wagner's *Parsifal* arrived – it was the first city it was played in after Bayreuth, when the rights expired – and by 1925 there was already a Schönberg Festival: in 25 years we went from Beethoven to Schönberg! In other words, it all accumulated very quickly. So in 1925 life started to 'normalise'. In 1936 Alban Berg's *Violin Concerto* had its world premiere in Barcelona.

But then the Spanish Civil War came and tore up all that progress. In other words, symphonic life didn't even start to normalise until the mid 20th century. It was much harder for German music to break through than it was for French; it was much easier to understand Ravel and Debussy – even Stravinsky is much easier to take on board – than Brahms. Brahms came late. We had to wait a few more years. In fact, we had to wait for the National Orchestra and Ataúlfo Argenta, i.e. until the 1950s, for German music to become normalised in Spain, for a certain 'sound' to be created, a 'German way of playing'.

Mahler's music also arrived late; we had to wait until the National Orchestra and the 1950s – with all the guest conductors – brought us Mahler for the first time. It was the National Orchestra that first played a complete Mahler cycle. Just imagine, we had to wait so long for a complete Mahler cycle – it wasn't until the 1960s or 1970s! And even later in Barcelona!

If Spain's history had been normal and the Civil War hadn't happened then it would possibly have been more normalised. After all, in 1925 a Schönberg Festival came to Barcelona at which Anton Webern conducted and *Pierrot lunaire* was played, along with Webern's arrangement of Schönberg's Op. 9; normal life might have continued, but it was torn apart.

What is the situation like today? Is there an audience for Mahler?

Pons: Fortunately, nowadays, the country has returned to normal. Musical life has become more normal, especially since the 1980s; Spain must be the European country to have grown the most in musical terms. Miraculously, more than 30 new auditoriums have sprung up and some 30 new orchestras, all in the last 25 years! At a time when orchestras were closing down in Europe, they were being set up in Spain.

What is the most important factor when conducting Mahler's music?

Pons: That's a very delicate issue. I think the key to Mahler is in the songs. Primarily *Des Knaben Wunderhorn* [*The Boy's Magic Horn*], but also the *Kindertotenlieder* [*Songs on the Death of Children*] and the *Rückert-Lieder* are about the Rhine, the fish in the Rhine, that's where the key lies. A song such as *Wo die schönen Trompeten blasen* [*Where the Fair Trumpets Sound*] contains everything there is in Mahler – the transparency of its lines, the colour of its instrumentation, contrasts of tempo, contrasts of theme, the inspiration. It clearly has every aspect of Mahler in three minutes. I think that's the key to the symphonies, too. This aspect of Mahler should be seen as 'essential'. It's a bit like with Brahms: you find the essential Brahms in his *Lieder*. I think for Mahler, it's fundamental to look at his songs, to put effort into understanding them. And they are really difficult! They are not complicated, but they are very complex, hugely complex!

Is there a danger of overpowering Mahler's music?

Pons: I think there is a great danger. Mahler is authentic, there is nothing fake about him as a composer. He is not a composer who tries to create sensationalist music; he is not the sum of lots of 'effects'. His music contains authentic values. And often there is the danger that the conductors may polarise Mahler between the grand climax and the pianissimo contrast with 'effect', they may treat it as an 'effect'. This is a great mistake. We are often sold Mahler 'in bulk': 'there are eight flutes!', 'eight horns!', 'Symphony of a Thousand!', 'a thousand!'. The grandeur of Symphony of a Thousand lies not in the number of people, not in 'the weight', but in the polyphonic richness of the first part (*Venit creatum spiritum*), in the great polyphonic world. However, the second part, the *Faust* part, is the world of *Lieder*, it returns to the world of *Lieder*, of songs: Where is the grandiosity in the entire second part? In the grandeur of the text! What was Mahler concerned with? Mahler was concerned with *Faust* not being a sensationalist work. He was trying to explain the eternal feminine, he was trying to bring out the meaning of *Faust*. That was his concern and it should be ours too. But it is tricky because we could do it as if it were a Cecil B. DeMille film.

Has anything changed over the years in the way you conduct Mahler?

Pons: Everything changes; you change as you get older. When you are very young you want to conduct every note, but as you get older you tend to let the music flow a bit more. Mahler sometimes has certain aspects that may seem very complicated in terms of verticality. It's ultimately music that, like all great music, should not be played by conducting a lot. Instead, you should coax the musicians into hearing it well. As I said regarding the world of song, I think Mahler's music aspires to be chamber music; it tends towards chamber music. In that way, it specifically contradicts that image of the 'great Mahler'. He does require a lot of instruments sometimes, but only to make a kind of chamber music. It's like a large chamber orchestra, which is also sprinkled with many solos and many passages that are like chamber music in themselves – but it's music that aspires to be chamber music. In order for chamber music to work, sometimes you don't need to conduct a lot, but rather help others listen, invite them to listen. I think that's how Mahler's music works best: as a kind of chamber music.

To what extent do Mahler's instructions for the conductor help when performing?

Pons: They help a lot, very much indeed. Mahler obviously had a composer's tools, but he also knew very well how to use a conductor's tools. A composer's way of thinking is very different from a conductor's. He [also] had a conductor's eye. He gave very wise advice, such as "beat in 4" or "beat in 3". It's not so much about following it strictly, because perhaps you would be more comfortable doing it in one instead of in three, but it gives you the key to the kind of character he wants, the tempo he wants, and what should be clearly heard in the orchestra. He provides many hints of that kind.

Why is Mahler so modern and so popular in the 21st century?

Pons: For that very reason, I think he was able to foresee what would happen and he is a perfect fit for us. Perhaps Mahler is more contemporary now than in 1910, or in 1910 he was speaking to us about what would happen. Of course, he chooses eternal values. So he doesn't stop being contemporary because his values are eternal. In any case, there are some technical aspects in his favour: the development of orchestras; the improvement of orchestras means that his music can be interpreted with far greater quality than one could have thought. And there are composers who think almost as if they were in the future, like Stravinsky. His music is now much more natural than forced, it's not as 'difficult' as it probably was in 1910. [In the same way,] Mahler has now been much more assimilated and is appreciated in a much more 'natural' way. He is also a composer who allows an orchestra to express its great size; he allows the orchestra to shine: individually, the soloists, in sections, the tutti. The way in which he permits this is also very 'idiomatic'; musicians love playing Mahler because he is idiomatic. Musicians can really express themselves with their instruments, whether woodwind, brass or strings – and that makes orchestras more willing to perform Mahler. He also lets conductors conduct. You have to get involved, and everyone chooses to do so, we all love conducting Mahler.

How would Mahler's music have evolved? Schönberg? Berg?

Pons: He was obviously part of that Vienna and it was his world. When he saw Schönberg's scores, he told Alma, "Well, [Schönberg] may possibly be right because he is young", but he didn't really understand them very well.

There is no doubt that Berg is closer to Mahler. The music Berg made afterwards is very close to Mahler's music. But where would Mahler have gone next? Mahler obviously never heard the great Stravinsky pieces because they were not yet written. What would have happened? What impression would Mahler have had if he had heard *Sacre* [*du Printemps* – *The Rite of Spring*]? I don't know; perhaps it would have been a great shock. There is also influence from Schönberg himself: when he saw *Verklärte Nacht* [*Transfigured Night*] he didn't understand very well where that music was going, but we can see a much more direct influence of Schönberg's world in the *10th Symphony*, or in the last movement of the *9th*. What was he moving towards? It's in D flat. What would Mahler have done with classic tonality? Would he have broken it? It's difficult. The last page of the *9th* is in D flat, but what is the connection? It's the same with life. He was an authentic composer – let's say music was his life – and in his last notes, which break up, creating more silence than notes, it's as if his contact with life – and tonality – were getting shorter. The echo of D flat appears, but then it drifts away from D flat and for a moment we no longer know what key we are in. The first movement of the *10th* is obviously in F sharp – F sharp major, when the orchestral tutti comes in – and we could be in B minor when the violas begin, and we could harmonise or add an accompaniment. But he doesn't add an accompaniment, the violas are bare, outlining B minor, but then they move on to very strange keys. And this is without harmonisation, but obviously we could construct a harmony overtop. You hear it as a line and it's very close to breaking tonality, very close to atonality.

What would he have done? Would he have taken the next step and eliminated tonality? The 15th chord – G-B-D-F#-A-C-E – in the *10th Symphony* sounds almost like a cluster. And what would he have done rhythmically? We don't know that either. Rhythmically, in the waltz or the polka, he always used 2/4 or 3/4, but in the *10th*, for example, the first Scherzo in the second movement is full of five-beat groups, full of amalgams. So he is searching for another world. What would have happened if he had heard *Sacre* three years later, what kind of a shock would he have had? It's difficult to know. Had he known the world of Anton Webern – because he knew the world of Schönberg – what would have happened? Again, it's difficult to know how he would have been influenced if he had heard those musicians.

What would you have asked Mahler?

Pons: [*laughs*] Well, you know, many things. But I think Mahler explains himself very clearly in his music and, to start with, I would be more interested in talking to Mahler not so much about things to do with his music, but rather what he thought about other composers. That would really interest me. I would love to talk to him about Beethoven, for example, Wagner, obviously, and Mozart, because he doesn't lie in his music. It's very clear what he wants and where he thinks we might deviate, he leaves a note saying, for example, "No rallentando here!" He explains himself: we have many letters in which he talks about his works and what he wants; we have a lot of documentation and can read a lot about Mahler – in addition to Alma Mahler's books – there are many documents about how he made his pieces and what he thought of them. But what I would like to know is what he thought about certain composers, including Puccini, another world, I would really like that – to be able to talk about that world he knew so much about because he had been there so often. For example, talking to Mahler about Fidelio would be a unique experience because it followed him throughout his life – even in his final years, in 1909, he was still conducting *Fidelio*. If I could speak to Mahler, I would ask him more about conducting than composition.

What about Wagner's influence on Mahler?

Pons: It's clearly immense; you can tell he knew Wagner in depth. Wagner was obviously huge, and capable, after Beethoven, of creating a new sound universe – and that has not been done very often in the history of music – and Mahler, like Schönberg, drinks from that sound universe, that's clear to see. But, at the same time, Mahler reconciles what were then two separate worlds – Wagner and Brahms. But I think Mahler had the ability to be transparent, which neither of those composers had – or not in the same way; he is often capable of great transparency, orchestral clarity, which had not been heard before then.

How do you construe Mahler's personality?

Pons: If I had to describe him in a few words, I would say he was an extremely honest composer, extremely committed and also, at some point, tortured, but I see him as an honest composer or artist. He doesn't seem to be an artist who made concessions. In that sense, I would see him as being like Beethoven; he makes no concessions, he seeks a truth in art and is committed to the truth. There are other very great people. Goethe is huge, as is Wagner, obviously, who made theatre. But while Wagner was a very great composer, he had other intentions; Wagner not only wanted people to like his music – he wanted to persuade people. There is almost a kind of propaganda in it. In Mahler's case, I think he is extremely honest with his art and committed to it. He says what he wants to say; he shows it to you like Beethoven.

What did Mahler want?

Pons: It's very close to what I've just said; I think he had an honest ideal of searching for the truth: through music and through his way of being. He was searching for a truth.

(Barcelona, 26/09/2010)

Sir Simon Rattle

"Mahler is the reason why I'm a conductor today"

Do you remember the first time you heard Mahler's music?

Rattle: I'm not sure. I grew up in Liverpool when they were doing what was actually the first European Mahler cycle with the same orchestra and conductor. It's extraordinary when you think about it – this was the mid 60s, but no one in Europe had played all the symphonies with the same conductor. It had only been done in Utah, by the Utah Symphony Orchestra. And one forgets how off-centre Mahler was at the time. Berthold Goldschmidt had only just performed Mahler's *3rd* for the first time in Britain; that was in 1962. I still have a magnificent tape of that. So, Sir Charles Groves and the Liverpool Philharmonic did two a year for five-and-a-half years, because they also did *Das Lied von der Erde* [*The Song of the Earth*] and the early version of the completed *10th*. I can remember, because I was studying: violin with one player in the orchestra, percussion with another, and they said, "Ah! We're on our twice-yearly struggle with Mahler."

So I remember hearing all kinds of bits, and actually, the *10th* must have been one of the very first I heard. Of course, the thing that completely knocked me sideways when I was 11 or 12 was hearing the *2nd Symphony*, live, and that's the reason why I'm a conductor today. But we were all in our early teens, or kind of music students, or crazy about it, and we were going in and hearing these pieces for the first time and being simply swept off our feet.

For us, it was as if we had found our music. And this is exactly as Mahler said it would be. And then, of course, I bought whatever records I could afford. My father was travelling in America; he brought me back this extraordinary performance of Bruno Walter conducting the *5th Symphony*, the fastest performance on record, almost, of any piece. We were the generation who were given it, and had no doubts about it: we were blessed. And I remember reading famous books about the symphonies, saying: well, of course only the *1st* and *4th Symphonies* by Mahler are of any interest at all, the others are just monstrosities. It's weird – I'm old enough to remember when he was almost a joke.

Mahler?

Rattle: Yes.

In Britain?

Rattle: Exactly.

Even in Britain?

Rattle: Yes. I also remember when I first met the Berlin Philharmonic. I can clearly remember all the members of the Berlin Philharmonic saying to me: "Well, of course, Strauss is the much greater composer", as a matter of course. Nowadays, maybe we tend to undervalue Strauss. Fashion is a strange thing.

What was the role of Sir John Barbirolli at the time? Did he influence you?

Rattle: Here we have a really cultural point. When you ask if Barbirolli influenced me, you have to understand that I come from Liverpool, and Manchester – as far as anyone from Liverpool is concerned – doesn't exist. We are two warring cities. Now I'm being deeply ironic, but of course, if you are talking about religion, by which I mean football, it's no joke. They are so close together yet, if you lived in either city, you had almost nothing to do with the other. It's like Glasgow and Edinburgh, in Scotland. And it's fascinating. We knew things were going on in Manchester, but we paid no heed to them.

Yes, probably I could have taken the train over there and also heard extraordinary things. Sometimes the Hallé Orchestra would come … But when Barbirolli was still alive and working, I was very young. I remember hearing him conduct Bruckner's *8th* in Liverpool, but I think I was 15 when he died. So, in a way, I missed this. What I found completely fascinating was, wherever I went, as a younger conductor, first to Berlin or to Boston, everybody wanted to talk to me about Barbirolli. The older people in the Berlin Philharmonic adored him, everybody had stories about him, everybody loved him. And, in a strange way, he gave the Berlin Philharmonic Mahler.

It's very interesting how Bernstein gave it to the Vienna Philharmonic. And then Karajan – Karajan followed, although [Mahler's] music was never naturally close to him. And these testaments … of what Barbirolli did in Berlin … are still very powerful, because it's so much from the heart.

And it was all thanks to a music critic, Neville Cardus – the great – who was also the cricket correspondent and the music critic of the Manchester Guardian, and one of the most cultured men in Britain. He introduced Mahler to Barbirolli and he said, "John, it's your music. You must do it." And he went on, and on, and on … and so Barbirolli took it up. That's a wonderful story and people now don't know it.

You started conducting Mahler's 2nd in December 1973. With a student orchestra …

Rattle: The very first we did was the 4th. The 2nd was much more official, when I realised who was playing in the orchestra, and who was singing in the chorus. The idea of having Felicity Lott singing in the chorus – it looked as if they were all students together – Felicity Lott, David Rendall … these people. Why wasn't Felicity singing the soprano solo, I asked myself. But the Arditti Quartet, Christopher Warren-Green, the leader [concertmaster] of the Philharmonia. Chris was 17, he was at the back of the seconds. Anybody I could persuade, cajole, bribe, threaten to come and play – I don't know how we did it. We must have been out of our minds. Mahler was considered too strange and too difficult for music students. And we were just angry. We wanted to play this music. So we all got together to learn it. And then – it's not something you ever forget.

Based on your experience, what recommendations would you give to young students making a first attempt at conducting Mahler? Where are the dangers?

Rattle: It's so funny because I just spread this time from when Mahler was almost unplayed, to now, when Mahler is played almost far too much. And, of course, there's the huge shape of Mahler; but there is a terrible danger of generality in this music.

First of all, you have to believe what he says. And if you have an instinct for the music, particularly the scores he conducted, there is the extraordinary point where you think: "Oh God, this feels good", or "I could move into larger beats now, because it seems to be flowing." And at that point, you look at the score and he says "stay in four". You think: I should move this on, and right at that moment he says, *"nicht eilen"*. He also knew his own instincts as a conductor. Because there had probably never before been a great composer who was such a great conductor – maybe Wagner, we don't know – who conducted so much of other people's music, who was so curious. I mean, just look at the programmes he was playing in the last years in New York: Elgar, Debussy, d'Indy, all these things … [the] Rachmaninoff *3rd Concerto*, with Rachmaninoff playing. He knew the *Dream of Gerontius*, he had the score – he had programmed Elgar's *2nd Symphony*. In fact, since he used the same copyist as Charles Ives, people even think Ives is not out of the question. He knew, of course, that he would have been fascinated by all this. I mean, he was one of the most open-minded musicians that has ever been.

First of all, believe him. Secondly, when you believe him, think about what it means … A few great old men like Berthold Goldschmidt, who was the first conductor of the *3rd Symphony* in Britain and conducted the first performance of the completed *10th*. He was Kleiber's assistant for the first performance of *Wozzeck* in 1925, in Berlin. He said so many interesting things to me … For instance: "Simon, will you please remember what the phrase 'Ohne Hast' [without haste] means in a time when there were no automobiles?"

Berthold said, "When we were growing up in the late teens and 20s, those of us who were composers went to hear performances of Mahler wherever they were. But there was only one performance a year of a Mahler symphony in Europe, so we travelled." He remembers when the oboists stopped playing the glissando in the *3rd Symphony* in the fifth movement, when the oboes changed, when the extra key came and it was considered too high. He was the person who said, "Look, when Mahler writes the word glissando on the trombone, he uses the same word that he uses for the oboe. And I used to hear this, and people stopped doing this."

What is a *Naturlaut*? It makes a huge difference if it is played as he says. But I remember I was given so much heat for doing this, for instance. And it was simply an elderly composer's memory of how it used to be. Berthold explaining to me, taking me patiently through all the different versions of the beginning of the *4th Symphony*. Saying what the tempo relationship was. From the very first version, where there was no rubato of any type, where everything was in one tempo. From the first tempo being faster and the second slower, and then changing that … All the different versions. So you have to be very careful how you read it. But I would say, what is incredibly important first of all is the mosaic, the detail – first putting this in place and then looking at the wider picture. Not simply playing it as … in the way people often mistakenly play Tchaikovsky. And not playing it as familiar romantic music, but absolutely as its own creature.

Again Berthold, in the *1st Symphony*, the finale, said, "Simon, when he says molto rubato, all of you forget the fact that everybody played everything molto rubato. That if he says rubato at that point, this means something extraordinary." Because Mahler, a conductor of his generation, is staggered at how very stiff people are and how little freedom they would give the music – how little ebb and flow. As he said, the ebb and flow that was natural, was the ebb and flow of great Wagner conductors, which never changed. But in Mahler, the instructions are so very, very precise that one can think that that is all the instructions mean. And so you come back to this Harnoncourt thing; it's not only what it says, it's what it means.

When you say Mahler was immediately your world – you discovered, this is somehow 'my composer', and he made you become a conductor: Where was the difference in terms of other composers? Why did Mahler capture you with such intensity?

Rattle: Who knows what love at first sight is? At slightly different times in my life, both Mahler and Haydn simply … they came to live with me. Whether that means you conduct it well or not – that's another matter, that's not the same thing. But they came to live in my house. Whatever it is – these were people for whom I felt I didn't need a translation. That really doesn't necessarily affect what comes out, but it does mean a slightly different feeling. [It] can be dangerous maybe, [because] then you feel you have more licence to kill – in the music. And I think it was a generational thing, too, with Mahler, because there was the feeling of new ground being broken.

Would you agree that Mahler, especially in the last pages of the 9th Symphony, somehow opens the door to everything that came later in the 20th century?

Rattle: Oh, I think Mahler always did. The *10th Symphony* even more so. [In the] first movement of the *10th* there is *Lulu*, in the second movement of the *10th* there is Hindemith. In the last movement Mahler was going in a completely different direction – strangely, a direction of more simplicity. He was only 51.

At 51, Janáček was writing *Jenůfa* – his first mature score. You can imagine what might have been. The only composer for whom there are no minor works is Mahler. What he did write was of immense importance. But of course, he opened up new worlds.

Wozzeck is really made up of Mahler's *9th* and *Salome* and *Elektra*, and all in this different way, these very opposite people were finding a new world. And obviously Mahler was embracing it and, rather fast, Strauss moved away from it. But they were finding a new world. And when you think of all the people who went to hear *Salome* at the first performance – and the arguments on the train coming back … It's wonderful that Mahler was so concerned and said: "How can this be a wonderful piece and a popular success at the same time?" And he fought with himself about it. Then there's Mahler's wonderful naivety … that he was so staggered that people loathed the first symphony.

Because he was absolutely convinced that this would be a huge success and he could retire from conducting the next day and make his living as a composer. He was simply not expecting it because of course the music was so natural to him. It's so without artifice, he thought if he just showed himself to the world, they would understand. Some things take time.

Why did it take so long?

Rattle: Why does music always take so long? Why did Weber walk out of the first performance of Beethoven's *7th*, saying: "This man is ripe for the madhouse, he's no longer writing music?" I mean, Weber. Some things take time.

Did Mahler anticipate the catastrophes of the 20th century?

Rattle: I'm very divided about that. Part of me feels that's a dangerously sentimental thing to say about the kind of catastrophes we had in the 20th century. But part of me also feels that it's impossible not to listen to the *Resurrection Symphony* without thinking of it as a prefiguration – whatever it meant. But composers don't always know what they are writing, and what it will mean. We have to remember that Mahler really felt that the most undilutedly joyful music he had ever written was the finale of the *7th Symphony*, which sounds to all of us like people marching towards hell. It's one of the strangest, and the most miserable and wildest C majors you can possibly imagine.

So who knows? All great composers have such a degree of depth that we cannot help feeling they are prophets as well. Whether this is true or not – who knows? But it's a sign of the importance we attach to the really great composers, that we can't help feeling that they had some foreknowledge.

Is there a connection between his life and his art?

Rattle: For someone who was trying to write the whole world into his pieces, there has to be a connection. On the other hand, when you think of his schedule as a conductor, what he did in such a short time … Nobody, not even a crazy workaholic like Valery Gergiev could touch the sheer amount he was doing. And yet, in the holidays, he was able to write these things.

And, of course, you also hear the operas. In the *7th Symphony* you really do hear *Seraglio*, you really do hear *Boris Godunov*. You hear all the things he was studying. When you hear the *8th Symphony*, you have to realise immediately that he'd seen Elgar. These are fascinating things. Of course it's there. But I have the feeling that when he actually composed, he did it almost in a rage. And sometimes he describes that, in his little house, seeing the great God Pan looking at him. He's obviously indivisible from his music but … here we are, almost today as we speak, I can touch Schumann – the 2nd, of course.

In a way, Schumann is the great link, because there, too, you have a man unsparingly picturing himself – not as some kind of hero, but in all his frailty and weakness, his sickness and generosity, his humour. And there in the fineness of both composers is a huge connection. Because, of course, although Mahler takes things to enormous proportions, it always starts from fineness and the blade of grass. It's always such a mistake to put Bruckner and Mahler together. Or Haydn and Mozart, Debussy and Ravel, Schumann and Brahms …

Wherever Mahler went, he was an outsider, a kind of alien. But I feel he chose this lifestyle – perhaps to have more inner freedom?

Rattle: You really think a Jewish person in his time had an option? To be on the inside? It would be very naive of us to think that. I think, of course, he embraced it. But I don't think he always had a choice. Who knows what the conversion to Catholicism actually meant? Open verdict.

For many listeners, Mahler seems to be a contemporary composer because he touches our life, our problems, our daily living conditions, like nobody else from his period.

Rattle: If you go just outside the Concertgebouw, you can still sit in the place where he had coffee every morning, this little restaurant around the corner. And they still say: "This was the corner where he sat."

A few years ago, I toured the Beethoven Symphony cycle with the Vienna Philharmonic. We were in Japan and we were looking for an encore. I thought how wonderful it would be to do the *Fidelio* overture. And they said, "But that's really funny because we haven't played the *Fidelio* overture without the opera in anyone's living memory." Because actually, the Vienna Philharmonic don't normally play overtures in their concerts. But I thought … well, they're exaggerating. And I looked at the part and it was very, very old material. And God help me if the rehearsal numbers and extra dynamics were not in Mahler's handwriting. He'd marked them in himself. And it looked as though nobody else had used the material since that time. But his writing, of course, is unmistakable.

He himself?

Rattle: He himself. Before the days of assistant conductors. And when I was last here with the Vienna Philharmonic and doing *Tristan*, Peter Poltun, the librarian, said, "I thought you might like to have this for a couple of weeks."

And I said, "What is it?", and he said, "Just look at it." Mahler's conducting score of *Tristan*, with all his markings, with all his ironic comments. What he had seen other conductors do, sardonic comments about Strauss conducting it, one 4/4 bar he marked "Strauss? – in 5?"

Every dynamic he had made, what choices he had made … and it was like having Mahler in the room. So, here we are, in this city … These people, they still walk here.

Do you think the sound of the Vienna Philharmonic influenced his orchestration, his sound imagination?

Rattle: Of course. And the qualities of the Musikverein, in particular. The balances for his symphonies, the way he writes dynamics are for the Musikverein. Where the strings are louder than they are in other halls. And when you come here you realise that immediately. But of course, it's enormously tied up with that character of pine, too, even if they hated it at that time.

What did Mahler want?

Rattle: You know, sometimes we forget that composers are human beings like the rest of us. I don't think there was an overriding plan. I think that's the exception. Wagner is the exception. And even he changed his ideas, his plans, and his philosophies throughout the course of his life.

I think Mahler wanted a life and creativity in its entirety. I don't think he was a calculating musician, or a calculating person. Strauss filled that corner very nicely. And they were polar opposites. The story of Strauss going in after the first performance of the *6th Symphony* and saying: "But why is everybody looking so sad? It was a big success!", and simply not understanding the import of the music. Shows you what you were talking about.

Would you distinguish between a refined and a 'bombastic' Mahler?

Rattle: No, there is only one Mahler. He takes in everything. And the fact is that Mahler has an irony about himself. He said about the 3rd *Symphony*: "I know I've always had an addiction to triviality, but in this piece I've really gone too far. You might think you're in a barnyard or a tavern, half the time." He had an irony about himself. Include everything. They are all part of the same.

What would you have asked Mahler?

Rattle: Well, I think Bruno Walter was the luckiest conductor who ever lived. This is my answer to that question. Because he just got to imbibe it. Straight there. Of course, everybody's dream would have been to be there and take it in, without asking questions. If you had asked me that question 30 years ago, I would have told you 10 questions I would have asked immediately. I'm a little older and wiser now and know that's not how you gain knowledge.

(Vienna, 27/01/2011)

Esa-Pekka Salonen

"Mahler embraced everything that exists"

Do you remember the first time you heard Mahler's music?

Salonen: It might have been the 5th *Symphony*. My teacher, Jorma Panula, was the first Finnish conductor to conduct a complete Mahler cycle – that is, all the Mahler symphonies – in Finland in the 70s. I did hear every piece in the cycle during that time, but I cannot remember what the first one was. I do, however, remember feeling slightly bewildered. I was very familiar with Bruckner at the time, and I was very taken by the simplicity and clarity of form in Bruckner.

When did you first conduct Mahler?

Salonen: The first Mahler symphony I ever conducted was the 3rd, and that was in 1983. I was 25 at the time, and I stepped in at very short notice for Michael Tilson Thomas with the Philharmonia in London. I had to learn the symphony very quickly; so I did and I conducted it. And that basically launched my conducting career – it was one of those events. Since then, I've done all of them, except the 5th – it just happened that way, actually.

So you started with Mahler's longest symphony?

Salonen: [*laughs*] Yes; everything else felt easy after that.

And you really have to organise it because the first movement is so breathtakingly long. What was your strategy?

Salonen: I can't remember what I thought really, because I think it was a very instinctive process at the time. The problem, the challenge, and of course the fascination of the first movement of Mahler's 3rd lies in the vast scope. You have this sonata form that is really straining at all of its seams; stuffing is leaking out of it until the form is scarcely there at all. And I would say that the only element of sonata form that remains is the recapitulation. Everything else is already practically forgotten. And there is a double exposition as well, which complicates matters somewhat. So the problem is that if you stop for too long to smell the flowers along the road – although it's very tempting – you lose sight of the goal, and you lose the flow of the music. There are lots of beautiful corners there, I know that. But I think that when I conduct Mahler's 3rd now, I really try to make the first movement as cohesive as possible, rather than kind of letting everything grow freely.

You did it here at the Salzburg Festival last year with the Vienna Philharmonic. It is now more than 20 years since you started conducting Mahler; do you generally approach Mahler's symphonies differently now?

Salonen: I think the more I conduct Mahler and the older I get, the simpler things become; I do less, basically. I no longer invent very much rubato in his music. I try to make it sound organic, which is sometimes a problem in Mahler because it is not always organically put together. But when it sounds simple, natural, and organic, and not twisted or artificial, then I think it works for me.

I'm fascinated by the richness of the music and the wide scope of material, and I'm fascinated by the sudden twists and turns of the mood and the expression and all that; but I'm not particularly looking for the neurotic quality in the music. It is there – absolutely – but I don't think that's the point. I think it is music that works on so many different levels, and it's also very uneven: the worst moments in Mahler's symphonies are truly terrible, I think, and the best moments are unbelievable. And somehow all this coexists, and it's like the world: we have the good guys and the bad guys; we have the geniuses and the idiots; we have the holy men and the prostitutes. That kind of richness of material is quite unique in all music, including rock and pop. I don't think anybody else came anywhere close to that kind of world-encompassing attitude, embracing everything that exists.

Could you give an example of one of Mahler's worst moments?

Salonen: Well, in the first movement of the *3rd Symphony* for instance, there's this sort of C major phrase in the middle of the march that sounds like the American navy arriving at one of their military bases. There are some unbelievably banal, painfully banal moments. Some of the first *Nachtmusik* [*Night Music*] movement in the *7th* is also like that; sometimes it's hard to believe that he put that in – not the whole movement, but some phrases.

How would you identify the neurotic aspect in his music that you mentioned before?

Salonen: I think it's in the sudden shifts and jumps between different moods and expressions. I think that's typically neurotic behaviour. And also, from the *6th Symphony* onwards, the thematic material is quite often very elusive: the themes are complicated. Think of the march theme in the Finale of the *6th*; it's really complicated, and kind of jumpy and nervous. But I think it has more to do with the way it moves from one expression to another, sometimes without transition, just flipping over, and I think that's typically neurotic.

Some conductors have told me that in the last movement of the 6th*, Mahler had somehow anticipated the catastrophes of the 20th century. Would you go so far as to say that Mahler was a kind of prophet on the eve of the First World War?*

Salonen: I don't think so – I think for Mahler the struggle was personal. I think he always felt displaced wherever he was, and kind of homeless in a way. Of course the irony of the *6th Symphony* is that it was composed during the happiest time of his life. He had started at the State Opera and it was all going very well, he was very successful and he had the most prominent conducting position in all of Europe, or the world; he was married to this young, beautiful, smart woman; and he had two loving children. And you would think that this would be the moment to write the apotheosis of love and such things, but no – he decides to dig into the very dark realms of the human mind. But I think it's always personal; I don't think that he is particularly commenting on political events. The catastrophe is but a personal catastrophe, rather than a global one.

Speaking of premonitions – this is slightly off-topic – Strindberg's last play, *The Great Highway*, quite literally and precisely predicts the first atom bomb in Hiroshima. The Wanderer in *The Great Highway* meets a blind Japanese man, who explains that he saw a light which was brighter than the sun, and it blinded him, and he has been blind ever since. The Wanderer asks him where he comes from and he says, "I come from Hiroshima." This was Strindberg's last play. *That* is clairvoyance, but in Mahler's case I think it was more personal.

What did the composer Salonen learn from Mahler?

Salonen: Well, one obvious thing is the orchestration. If you look at Mahler's techniques of orchestration and how he develops over the span of the nine symphonies, it's really interesting because again, less is more. It really becomes rather like chamber music at times, and the *7th Symphony*, for example, contains moments which are like that. And somehow you can tell that the entirety of his orchestral music was trying to move towards maximum clarity and simplicity. Of course, conductors do have problems to solve in the late Mahler pieces, which he didn't conduct himself: the *9th* has balance issues that need to be sorted out because of course he never heard it; *Das Lied von der Erde* [*The Song of the Earth*] obviously needs rewriting here and there, in terms of the balance between the tenor and the orchestra, especially in the first song; and of course with the *10th*, even the *Adagio* is not a finished score.

Yes, I've learnt lots of things about orchestration, and also about the idea of the material being in a constant state of flux and the principle of continuous variation. Also, the kind of harmonic thinking that is so characteristic; it's the harmony that makes the Mahler identity in a way, in the same way that the lack of harmony in Berlioz creates the Berlioz identity. If you play the chords of a Berlioz piece on the piano, you think, "God, this is really clumsy and bad and amateurish, like a child has written this music", but when you hear it in context, played by an orchestra, you realise that this is a unique genius.

But Mahler is quite the opposite – the chords themselves are unbelievably expressive and his sense of harmony is so highly developed. And it's really fascinating because in his later output it hovers very close to the last frontier of tonality, then crosses firmly to the other side, then comes back again, and it's this sort of no-man's-land where he is working. And you know, it doesn't take a huge push to move from that kind of harmony to organised atonal harmony, so the distance between that and Berg is very short. And then, of course, moving from early Berg to mature Berg, we then have the principle of organising the atonal material into 12-tone systems, and that distance really is very short, too.

If Mahler had lived 30 years longer, what would his influence on the Viennese School have been?

Salonen: That's an interesting question because Mahler was on his way towards quitting tonality, but I don't think he ever even considered abandoning tonality altogether – there was always the tonal reference. So the moments where he leaves tonality become incredibly exciting and expressive, because of the fact that the reference is still there, and I don't think that he would ever have left that tonal thinking completely. If you think of somebody who had a very long career and experienced all these changes in thinking, like Stravinsky, well, he went into 12-tone composition in the late 50s, but if you actually listen to those pieces carefully, it's not atonal music, it's pure Stravinskian music. His harmonic principles are still there; he uses a 12-tone technique, but it's still him, the reference to tonality has not completely disappeared. So that is a big difference from, say, late Schönberg, where the tonal reference is no more. Berg never left the tonal reference. Even in his most atonal pieces – like some of the movements of the *Lyric Suite* and some moments in the *Kammerkonzert* [*Chamber Concerto*] – you can tell that the tonal reference is always there, whereas late Webern is completely free from any tonal principle, and the same applies to Schönberg.

When we look at Mahler's scores, everything is so clear and detailed, with the dynamics and everything else: in this sense, did he open the door to modern music?

Salonen: I think he was one of the pioneers of the notion of trying to write foolproof music; of trying to notate everything so precisely and clearly that not even an idiot could ruin it. I mean, even if you compare him to people like Brahms and Bruckner, if you look at a Brahms score, there's not a lot of information there; he marks things very sparingly, and then if he writes something remarkable, it really stands out and you know it's important. But Brahms was still able or willing to trust the instinct of the musicians of his time, whereas I think Mahler's experience was that people just didn't get it, that people made lots of wrong decisions and treated his music in a way that he had not intended, so he ended up notating everything incredibly clearly.

And there, of course, you have the start of the process which then becomes inflated in later works: if you look at some scores by Berg – for instance the *Drei Orchesterstücke* [*Three Pieces for Orchestra*] – there is so much information for every note that it in fact loses its impact, because every note has some kind of story to tell. So from the musicians' point of view, you then have to make a reduction when you perform this music – you have to reduce it to something that you can actually process, and at the same time physically manage. And it was not only the Viennese of course: Debussy did this as well, and there is a rumour that on the day of his death he still spent the morning at the Durand offices adding some articulation markings into *La mer*. I don't know whether this story is true or not. But of course this process then leads to the kind of hyper-notation in Brian Ferneyhough and James Dillon, and the composers of the super-complex school, where it is unthinkable to write one note without at least three or four or five different markings. And I think in this respect, Mahler was the predecessor of that kind of school of composing.

We spoke earlier about the fact that you plan to conduct Das klagende Lied [The Song of Lamentation] *in the first version. Can you tell me what fascinates you about the piece?*

Salonen: Das klagende Lied is an amazing piece and I'm very pleased that the original version is finally available. I've conducted it a couple of times, and the whole piece is a miracle because all of Mahler is there. His basic pool of material is already there, and the modes are there, and the whole of his subject matter, like the use of the voice, and everything else – it's all there as a prototype. Of course the piece has some dramaturgical problems: it goes on a bit here and there, and it doesn't form a proper dramatic shape because there is no new combination, and also the phrases are very short. It really is like a child's piece in the sense that he does one thing, then the next thing, then this other thing, then goes back to something else, but nothing is ever allowed to develop into anything. It's very moving, very touching, but sometimes it's also annoying because it's as though you can tell that this was a teenager with a short attention span. The sound is amazing too – from the first bar you can tell that it's Mahler.

You once said that the 9th is probably the symphony to which you feel closest.

Salonen: There is a sort of feeling of summation in that piece; everything becomes like an archetype of an aspect of Mahler. The first movement is an archetype of Mahler's extended sonata form; and the *Scherzo* is like an archetype of the Mahler *Scherzo* – everything he had done is reflected in that music to some extent. The *Burleske* is a completely manic exercise in counterpoint – relentless, like a homage to Bach I suppose, and the great masters of counterpoint; and then the *Adagio* contains all *Adagios*. There is this kind of summary that feels like the end of life. It's strange to think that Mahler wrote his last music when he was my age, and I don't feel particularly old at this point. I've always just been very moved by Mahler's *Ninth*, but I also discovered lots of new things in Mahler's 6th recently, when I conducted it a few times. So it's music that you never get tired of because there is so much there.

Is there a danger of overpowering Mahler?

Salonen: There is so much emotion in the music already, and to tell your story as well as Mahler's story in this music is … well it's Mahler's story – it's his story, not mine. Often, the Mahler performances by my colleagues that I have really truly enjoyed have been rather simple, including some very masterful performances, like those of Haitink, Pierre Boulez, and so on. And then the

Mahler performances that I've *really* hated have been ones where I got the feeling that there are two stories being told at the same time: there is Mahler's story and then there is the story of the guy who is conducting, who is also wallowing in it. And I don't think it's right, but that's just a matter of personal taste.

What did Mahler want?

Salonen: What does a great person want? I think the ultimate impetus to create is the need to reach out to people, and with music you can say things that you can't with words or with any other means of communication. It's a unique way of communicating something to other people. I can't think of any other reason. I mean, of course one is always fascinated by music itself as a phenomenon, and I think in many cases the creative process, in the long term, also seeks to understand the mysteries of creation and the mysteries of music: Where does it come from? What makes it work? Why does music affect us so much? But I think the simple answer is that [Mahler] wanted to share something with other people, and in this respect, he was very powerful.

(Salzburg, 08/08/2009)

Michael Tilson Thomas

"Jump! Cut! Bang!"

Do you remember the first time you heard Mahler's music?

Tilson Thomas: I remember very clearly the moment when Mahler's music reached out and grabbed me; I was 13 years old. I was waiting at the house of my parents' friends for some reason or another; they were very busy people and they said, "Would you like to listen to some music? For example, do you know Mahler's *Das Lied von der Erde*?" – which of course I didn't.

And they said, "Why don't you listen to the last movement – it's about 20 minutes long and your parents should be here by then." And they put on this section, and really I divide my life between before I heard that recording – which was Ferrier and Walter – and after I heard it. The music made a *stunning* impression on me; it was as if it gave voice to all kinds of feelings that I had, that were part of my family, that were part of the whole connection that my family had to life in small villages in the Ukraine, and the presence of Jewish music – both secular and sacred – in those villages, and the pull of those different cultures. But when this part [*sings excerpt*] came in, it went right into my heart. I couldn't believe that such symphonic music existed, and I never got over it.

What came then?

Tilson Thomas: Well, I began to look into his symphonies – just with some scores and recordings, familiarising myself with them. I got a piano score of *Das Lied von der Erde* and began to play it, and that led me to some of the other songs. But of course, as a very young conductor, you don't really have many opportunities to conduct Mahler symphonies, so I maybe just accompanied some songs a few times.

But I had another experience with Mahler at Tanglewood. Bernstein was conducting the *2*nd *Symphony* and I was still a kind of fellowship student at the Berkshire Music Center, as it was called then. It was around 12.30 on a Sunday afternoon and I got a call saying the assistant conductor of the Boston Symphony is sick, and someone has to conduct the offstage music in Bernstein's performance of Mahler's *2nd Symphony*. You have been assigned to do this, and would you please go over there and talk to him. I had heard Mahler's *2nd Symphony* a number of times – Walter's recording, probably – but I hadn't studied it. Moreover, my responsibilities that summer were only to do with the contemporary music festival that was happening there; I hadn't been at any of the rehearsals – nothing.

And I went over to see Bernstein, and of course he came at the last moment – I was waiting and waiting for him to show up – and he said, "Oh yes, nice to meet you. I have a question for you, I need your advice." And I said, "What, you need my advice?" And he said, "Yes; everyone thinks of me in terms of Mahler's *2nd*, like Mr Mahler the *2nd* – people think I wrote the thing for heaven's sake, but I've always conducted it with the score. I've never done it by heart in my entire life, but today I'm thinking of doing it by heart for the first time. What do you think of the idea?" And so I said, "What do I think of the idea? You must be joking!" But he was serious.

Well, the thing with those Mahler symphonies is that you go along and there's no problem, but then you always come to one of those transitions in the *2nd Symphony*, and you can't remember: are there two bars of 3/2 and then a general pause, and then something starts? Or are there only two bars of 2/2, then silence, and then something? And so you can really get mixed up. So he said, "Well, I thought what I'd do is just conduct less and less, and finally I'd just stop and the music would stop, and then I'd go on." And I said, "Okay, I'll remember that." And that's what he did in the performance; I was watching backstage through a little spyhole to see what he did.

Did you discuss Mahler with Bernstein later?

Tilson Thomas: *Much* later, but in the meantime, I did suddenly, at the last moment, have an opportunity to conduct a Mahler symphony, when I was 24 years old. The very first one I did was the 9th, which everyone thought was completely crazy, but actually I think it was the symphony that spoke to me the most. Those were the two pieces that were the most natural for me at that point: *Das Lied von der Erde* and the *9th Symphony*. And I did the piece and then I began to do many more of them. Bernstein came to many of my early performances of those pieces and sometimes he would talk about, say, tempo relationships – like "that was exactly the right tempo relationship, that was good" or "you need to figure out this one" – but he wouldn't really tell me anything, he would just encourage me to find my own way with the piece.

Besides, Bernstein could see that I was on a particular track with the music, i.e. that I was going back to my first appreciation of it, to really investigate the possibilities of making it sound idiomatic. So, although it's part of a big structure, at particular moments the sound of a particular kind of music, a particular kind of ensemble comes through. It could be street music, cabaret music, religious music, salon music, military music, or whatever; but I really wanted to bring the exact character of this music sharply into focus, so that the piece would be more like Mahler describes.

He said, "I'm making my own worlds." This is the kind of thing that a filmmaker would say – you know, it's like this big film and there are these different levels of activities. If it was a big Tarkovsky movie or something like that, you might have a scene where a large army is invading, and an enormous storm is taking place, and these big events are happening; and then on the side there's this poor little old pedlar of pretzels or something, and he's going along pushing his cart and saying, "Pretzels! Pretzels! Buy my pretzels!" And the cart has a broken wheel, and he has three unmarried daughters, so he has to make a lot of money selling these pretzels. A director wouldn't even use an actor for a part like that; he would probably go out – someone like Fellini or Tarkovsky – and find a real person on the street to come in and just do it.

And I think that's part of the challenge of these big Mahler pieces, that there are moments when things really need to have a rough character, coming from one of these other genres. It's a challenge for orchestral players to do that because they have been trained to play everything as beautifully and perfectly and nobly as possible, and here Mahler is asking them from time to time to do something which is completely grotesque, and way beyond the boundaries of what good taste is supposed to be.

That is exactly what irritated performers in Mahler's time so much, and it still does irritate them. They say, "There are too many instructions, there are all these sforzandos and accents, and this and that, and markings like *grell* [= harsh, garish] or whatever. And he's just asking for too much – he's forcing us to do all of these things, many of which go against the way we would really like to play." But of course Mahler really wants the symphony, his 'world', to represent worlds that he actually knew in his life. And his version of those worlds is in the music, and that is the challenge, to make that as vivid as possible while at the same time allowing the big shape, which is so powerful in this music, to emerge.

Would you say that Bernstein's style of emotionalising the music influenced you?

Tilson Thomas: In some pieces, yes. For example, it was a shock for me to hear his performance of the 6*th* with the New York Philharmonic, which I think suited the nature of the orchestra and the nature of his energy in the early days; it was *so* powerful, so on the edge. And then later, he went through a process of discovering the lyrical side of the music much more. But you know, Bernstein did not believe in musical absolutes so much; it was more like you were on a particular journey with the music – everybody is – and different things emerge from that. He once said to me, when I asked him what he thought about something in one performance – in a much ruder way than this: "When *you* have totally made up your mind, you will think it won't make any difference to you what I think."

Does Mahler's music require a special technique of conducting?

Tilson Thomas: Yes; I mean, as he goes on, he gets more and more interested in very slow tempi, so some of the most difficult things are in the later pieces. For example, in the last movement of *Das Lied von der Erde*, at the end of the *Abschied* [*Farewell*], you have this rubato of twos and threes and fours, and some pizzicato and some tenuto cantando, and somehow this all has to work. It can't sound like it's in a *tempo Gefängnis* [*prison*], it has to have a kind of flow and freedom within this organised rubato. And of course this had a strong influence on Berg, particularly – there are so many situations in Berg where you have minim [half note] equals 38 or whatever, and all sorts of things are going on – and subdividing this music doesn't really work, you just have to be able to get this big, very slow pulse, while people are playing all sorts of different things. And the idea of the pulse does get slower.

The first movement of the *10th* is one of the hardest things to learn in Mahler – for me, anyway – because there is no pulse really, just this sort of floating feel, although there is a pulse sometimes in the middle section. But a lot of it is like … I don't know … like expressionistic Palestrina or something, it's just these moving lines, and you have to develop your sense of where the cadences are and where the rubati are. The quality of the sound is not easy to absorb; it's much easier to absorb [some] other lines, like this [*sings excerpt*].

Some conductors have told me that when they started to conduct Mahler they overpowered it, but their personal approach changed and developed. Would you say something similar?

Tilson Thomas: Well, I've always been very faithful to what the score actually asks for – of course that can mean many things – but particularly in the tempo relationships between one section and another. I mostly found that when I did things which I felt were more exciting or gutsier or gave me a chance to inhabit my 'maestro-dom', I ultimately came to regret [it]. As I understood more, I felt that they obscured some points which were better or stronger, and that he really knew what he was doing and knew very well what he was asking for.

In all of Mahler's music I can think of a few places which just don't add up, no matter what. One of these is the end of the song *Um Mitternacht* [*At Midnight*]; no matter how hard you try to figure out a relationship, you have to really work at it. Another one, which I think works much better once you've decided that's the way it is – is the last movement of the 7th, which I so love. But I struggle and, my God, I've seen many of my colleagues struggle to figure out some way that this relates to this, relates to that, and I think that really imprisons the music. I think the idea of that movement is very much 'discontinuity'. It's like it anticipates techniques in film or in sound editing, of just, Jump! Cut! Bang! [*sings excerpt*]. The more discontinuous it is, the better it works, I think, and actually you discover that orchestras can learn and remember an exact place in tempo and in musical gesture, and they can just play it like that, going from one to another, in a very exciting, if dangerous, way.

So that was probably one of the difficulties for audiences that made it hard for them to accept Mahler.

Tilson Thomas: Well, the audiences were confounded by how long it was, how it seemed to be so many different things. They could accept that one part was very beautiful, but then what about this other part that was so noisy or confrontational, and they couldn't [figure] it out. Maybe this was one reason why the 4th *Symphony* was the Mahler piece that was liked the most by musicians and more traditional audience members, for a very, very long time.

And then maybe *Das Lied von der Erde* joined it, but it took longer with some of the other pieces, like the 2nd *Symphony*. People were disturbed by the number of different things the music contained. Maybe they were also disturbed – and this was something that Mahler himself recognised – by his obsession with presenting music, and then presenting it again as a parody, in a way that went against what the mood of the music had been the first time. People couldn't figure out why somebody would be doing that – there was no space in the music for them to relax, which was very much what audiences wanted to be able to do.

You probably know that as a conductor, Mahler was criticised by the press in Vienna. They said, "He's trying to show us his [own] ideals, he's trying to show us the moment of creative crisis when the composer" – Beethoven or whoever – "wrote this piece." And the critic who wrote this article says, "That's completely wrong. For example, in my living room at home I have a beautiful little niche in the wall and I'm going to commission a sculptor to create a beautiful marble statue of a young woman to go in this niche. And I understand that when the sculptor is doing this, making a statue can turn into a major crisis; you can hammer too hard and the stone can break, and [he] can have a major crisis of fear and think, 'Do I dare do this?' – and all the tension that goes into making this statue – but I'm completely uninterested in that. I just want to sit in my living room and have a beautiful statue, and it's there and it's smooth and it's decorative and it makes me feel good. That's the way I feel about these great musical masterpieces, so I don't want to be taken to this moment of crisis in which the piece was written." So this was a very daring thing that Mahler was doing, just from the standpoint of modern, interpretative impulse.

What did Mahler want?

Tilson Thomas: I think that Mahler was one of those composers in the early 20th century who succeeded in making us appreciate the value of many different kinds of music and music-making. He made us appreciate the sincerity of people who, at whatever level, are making music. Mahler managed to find a way to put this music together in a world, a single view of the world, and to understand that there is a kind of shared spirit that all of this music-making witnesses. I've often said this in relation to other composers, like Ives for example, and to some extent Debussy. There is a wonderful poem by Walt Whitman – actually it's not a poem, it's something he was sketching, a poem about music. And he says in that poem, all the different songs in the world – the song the blacksmith sings, the song the mother sings, the song the soldier sings, the song the Chinaman sings – all these different songs pull in different directions, and seem to be in conflict with one another; yet, from another perspective, perhaps all of them merge into one great song of mankind. And there's something of this in Mahler's perspective. Perhaps also his feeling [is] that the music is made and will come to an end, but that the feelings we have when the music is over – what we can take from the music into our lives and hearts – is maybe his most important message. He wants us to understand the way he feels about things, the way life tastes to him.

(Munich, 03/07/2010)

Franz Welser-Möst

"Mahler was like an earthquake for me"

Do you remember the first time you heard Mahler's music?

Welser-Möst: Yes, I do. It was the *1ˢᵗ Symphony*; I must have been 10 or 11 years old. It was the student orchestra of the Wiener Musikhochschule [Vienna Academy of Music], at that time with Karl Österreicher. So that was quite some time ago.

At that age, everything was sort of new and I was not immediately drawn to Mahler in particular. The next experience with Mahler that I remember was the 5ᵗʰ with Sir Georg Solti and that was like an earthquake for me. That I remember very well. I think I was about 15. And from that moment on I took a real interest in Mahler's music.

When did you first conduct Mahler?

Welser-Möst: I was 23; it was Mahler's *1ˢᵗ* with my wonderful Jeunesse Orchestra in Linz.

When you compare your understanding of Mahler then and now, has it changed?

Welser-Möst: Completely. But I have to say, that probably applies to every composer. You get drawn more towards the so-called easier symphonies, the first five: the 2ⁿᵈ was especially appealing to me back then, along with the 4ᵗʰ. Later on, the 4ᵗʰ was also one of my first recordings – in 1989 with the London Philharmonic and Felicity Lott. But I admit, as time passed, I became increasingly attracted to the more complex, or so-called more difficult symphonies, especially the 7ᵗʰ. I would say the 7ᵗʰ and the 9th are my favourites.

As a conductor, what is the main thing you have to deal with when performing Mahler?

Welser-Möst: It's simply not only the range of emotions, but also the range of expressions. Take the 7ᵗʰ, for instance; the *Nachtmusik* [*Night Music*] with the guitar and the mandolin draws your attention completely to its chamber music quality. On the other hand, you have typical Mahlerian outbursts in the first and last movements.

The 7th is also quite special because its architecture is very tricky, very difficult for a conductor. The problem is similar in the 8th.

The first movement can be so overpowering that it can make the first 20 minutes of the second movement very problematic – although I think here, as so often, the problem might actually lie somewhere else. If you put too much into the first movement of the 8th – which is so easy to do – and you are simply concerned with balancing it, you get lost. Because, especially with the brass and the choruses, if they don't play or sing a real legato in fortissimo, it will always be too loud, wherever it occurs. And that is the key issue, especially in the first movement of the 8th – if you really keep it under control, it pays off in the second movement.

Is there a danger of overdoing it when conducting Mahler in general?

Welser-Möst: Yes. I think that danger is always there in music anyway, but especially in Mahler. And as a conductor, you can wallow in it – which is very easy to do with his type of music. But I think that, especially from the 6th onwards, it detracts from the modernism of his music and the finesse of the orchestration – such as the second *Nachtmusik* in the 7th. Or take *Das Lied von der Erde* [*The Song of the Earth*]; if you overpower the first movement, you're done for because there's nowhere to go from there. The emotional architecture is as carefully planned as the formal structure. You have to support both, otherwise you just sort of muddle along from one very emotional moment to the next. And ultimately, the audience finds it boring. You must pay attention to the arch and the structure.

Why did it take so long for Mahler to become established in the repertoire?

Welser-Möst: I think there are several reasons. One is Mahler's modernist aspect. Secondly, all of the arts are always connected to their time – and our time when we are perceiving them. The 1930s and 1940s were not good times for Jewish composers, Mahler included. The expression 'out of sight, out of mind' might hold, but I still know many people – some of them from when I was growing up here in Austria, the previous generation – who said that Mahler is in bad taste. To put it clumsily, the onstage ego trips were not in vogue.

And now look at how our society has developed since the Second World War. And how, especially since the 60s, self-indulgent ego trips have become more and more important. That also relates to what you said before about self-indulgent interpretations of his music – the ego trips you can easily take in Mahler's music, since Mahler's music has become attractive and appealing again. For me, it is highly interesting to look at Leonard Bernstein, who no doubt was a big egomaniac as well as a wonderful genius and a brilliant conductor – and of course I have only admiration and respect for him.

But you know, he really showed us the egomaniacal side of Mahler's music. And I think it took other people like Karajan, who didn't touch Mahler's music till very, very late [to counterbalance that]. But actually Bernstein's recording of Mahler's 9th, the live recording, is extremely touching and beautiful. And I think that sort of connects with what Bruno Walter saw in Mahler's music. And as with every work of genius, there are many different ways to look at it because it is so rich and so vast. And so I think you cannot pigeonhole Mahler's music any one way. That's impossible.

How do you deal with Mahler's obsession with suffering and redemption?

Welser-Möst: Sometimes, actually, I feel a little taken aback by it. I think it can be overdone and there is always that trap for me. But at the same time, if you take it in a less personal sense and a more universal sense, then I find it extremely touching – but not via self-indulgent interpretation. That's what's difficult for me.

Why is the 9th Symphony so important to you?

Welser-Möst: I am always very taken by composers when they speak about the last things in life – when approaching death. Take Schubert, Mozart, or Wagner with his Parsifal, take Bruckner's 9th or the last piano sonatas by Beethoven, the string quartets and so on … where it becomes, in a certain sense, less materialistic and less real in a way. And that is why Mahler's 9th, especially the last movement, and especially the last page, are very interesting to me. And the same applies to the last few pages of *Das Lied von der Erde* – the material is very economical. Composers can only do that late in life – I mean, use very little to say much more than with all the bombast of previous pieces.

Some say Mahler was a kind of prophet, that he anticipated the catastrophes of the 20th century and the conditions of modern human living.

Welser-Möst: I fundamentally have problems with that because it imprisons the arts and connects them too much with a specific time. If that were true, in a hundred years, we wouldn't be playing Mahler anymore because we wouldn't have to, because he was only talking about our time. That is, philosophically, a very risky thing to say. I think we should agree that great art has the element of timelessness within itself, it carries what in certain ideologies or philosophies you would call the eternal spark. So I rather look at the bigger picture than at the one I think is too politically influenced.

And from a spiritual point of view, what would be Mahler's message?

Welser-Möst: I think the message is the same as with all great art; that there is more than just what we touch and feel day in, day out; that there is something we call spirit. And I think he touched that in a very individual way. And that makes him unique and very special.

You now have the same position Mahler once held at the Vienna State Opera. Have you read his letters?

Welser-Möst: Oh yes. You know, what is really interesting to me is not the complaints about the house as it is – I think it hasn't changed that much since his time. If you look at it from a positive angle, there is no other city in the world where the opera house is the topic of such clashes and intrigues and politics and all that – which means it is very important. And so I really value it very highly that people can still wrangle over something like an opera house. That is unique.

What interests me is what Mahler did artistically. If you look at his first year – I think I am right in saying he conducted basically every production of every piece they did at that time. He wanted to judge it from the conductor's podium, not just by sitting in the audience or watching rehearsals. That is amazing. I couldn't do that. I mean, that is beyond human what he did there. And he influenced music theatre, opera as such, in such a big way, with Alfred Roller, not only as a composer, but also as the director of one of the most important opera houses in the world. He basically achieved more than almost anyone else.

What would you have asked Mahler?

Welser-Möst: My questions to Mahler would mainly concern the Vienna Opera House. I would have liked to be able to ask him how he saw his duties as opera director; what he thought needed reforming and which goals he aimed to achieve, or rather which goals he managed to achieve; and how he managed to combine his artistic ethos with his daily administrative tasks?

How do you see his personality?

Welser-Möst: From my point of view, Gustav Mahler seems to have had a troubled personality, both privately and professionally.

Would he have written music in a different way if he had had more time to compose?

Welser-Möst: That is speculating, of course, but I would say yes. All great artists are influenced by their surroundings. And when you look at ... well, say, the holiday composer ... and you look at his *3rd Symphony*, for instance; he was at Lake Attersee – I actually have a house there, too, and having experienced the nature there for a while now, it speaks to me in a very special way – I don't think he could have written the same piece during a grey November in Vienna; I think surroundings do influence composers and what they do influences them. So I would agree. He would sometimes have written different music.

Did the sound of the Vienna Philharmonic Orchestra influence him?

Welser-Möst: Absolutely. I think the specifics of the Viennese horn, the string sound, which has been famous for many decades, and the Viennese oboe, which is very important because in Mahler's music – like Bruckner's – certain solos are really low and are easier to play on the Viennese oboe than on the French oboe. So yes, I think these sound specifics influenced him in a big way.

What did Mahler want?

Welser-Möst: His driving force was an incredible urge to express himself, just as with many artists at the *fin de siècle* in Vienna.

(Vienna, 18/05/2009)

David Zinman

"Mahler is a universe in itself"

Do you remember the first time you heard Mahler's music?

Zinman: Yes I do, but I didn't know it was Mahler at the time. It was in New York City when I was about 13 years old, and I was taken to a rehearsal of the New York Philharmonic there which Mitropoulos was conducting.

After that, I heard some Mahler on the radio, conducted by Bruno Walter. I just thought, yes, this is great music. Then of course the most important time for me was when I finally left America and went to England, where I heard Horenstein conduct the *3rd Symphony* and Solti conducting the *4th*, and many conductors were beginning to play more and more Mahler – this was in '60 and '61. Then I moved to Holland, where there is a great Mahler tradition of course, and I got to hear all the symphonies conducted by Haitink, who was very young. And I also conducted some Mahler myself; the first time I conducted the Royal Concertgebouw Orchestra, I put some of the *Rückert-Lieder* on the programme. And once, when I replaced Haitink in a concert, I did all of *Des Knaben Wunderhorn* [*The Boy's Magic Horn*] with Jessye Norman. So I was becoming more and more steeped in Mahler, and when I got my own orchestra – the Rochester Philharmonic – I started to do all the symphonies, and then when I went to Baltimore, I did all the symphonies there as well, sometimes twice. And now here in Zurich I am doing them all again.

Can you explain what it was in Mahler's music that captivated you?

Zinman: Well, at first you are attracted to it in the same way that you are attracted to the music of Berlioz – its bizarre qualities. But then I began more and more to see the human qualities of it; how it really expresses human emotion, human thought, humanity's striving for utopia.

In my opinion, the most impressive parts of Mahler are the calm and the contemplative moments, rather than the frenetic activity elsewhere. For me, it is music you can listen to over and over again, and find more and more and more in it. Like Beethoven's music, it struggles and it speaks about questions that are very deep and important to humanity. Not only does it take into account the search for God and for the meaning of existence, but it deals with the frivolities of human life and what human life is, with all its warts and blemishes and so on; that's all there in the music.

Is there a danger of overpowering him?

Zinman: Yes, I think there is. I think the thing is that if you only see him as a neurotic, you're missing a lot of what Mahler is about, because he was also a very pure soul, and if you read about his conducting, you can see what kind of a musician he was. He was a very exact musician, a very precise musician, and he was extremely interested in making sure that he was not overpowering anyone. Sometimes you have to be overpowering, but those contrasts must be there and they must be layered in various ways; there is so much more to it than just those elements. A piece like the *9th Symphony*, which I'm doing tonight, has so many contrasts in it and so many layers and so many levels, and the most desperate feeling of crying out, and yet it has the most calm, beautiful moments. I think that all these 'valleys' and 'peaks' in the music need to be very carefully judged; you can't just go for climax after climax.

What's very interesting to me about Mahler interpretations is that you can hear 10 performances of any one of his symphonies and they will be completely different from one another, whereas you hear 10 performances of a Beethoven Symphony and they're all the same. Mahler wrote down precise instructions for everything that he wanted, and Beethoven wrote nothing, yet they all end up playing it the same, and the Mahler performances are completely varied and different: various ideas of tempi, various ideas of balance, various ideas of expression, and so on. It really lets you get into that world. So when Boulez conducts Mahler, or Horenstein, or Bruno Walter, or Mitropoulos, or Abbado, or Karajan, or whoever – they're all imposing their own very strong point of view on the music. But I also believe that the details in a Mahler score are very, very important, and if those can be fully realised, I think you get a very clear picture of what the music is about.

You mentioned that you had heard recordings of Bruno Walter. Is there a Klemperer influence as well?

Zinman: I heard Klemperer when I was living in London. I heard him do the *Resurrection Symphony*, and that was monumental. I can't say that I knew enough Mahler then to really appreciate what he did, but I've heard some recordings since. In my opinion, it's a Klemperer-Mahler, whether it's Mahler-Mahler or not. I'll tell you an interesting story; I was a pupil of the French conductor Pierre Monteux, and when I was studying with him I once asked him, "Did you ever meet Mahler?" He said, "Yes, I met Mahler, but I don't like his music." I asked what he was like, and he said, "Well, when Mahler came to Paris I was the first viola in the orchestra; he had come to do his *2nd Symphony*. I was the assistant conductor of the orchestra, so I was hired to prepare the chorus and orchestra for him. So I prepared the *2nd Symphony*, and he came and he conducted it, and I didn't like it, but he was a great conductor." And I said, "But what was he like?" and he said, "Well, he was a little like George Szell, very precise, very strong, very small gestures." This was towards the end of Mahler's life of course. But Monteux said he was a very exact person, and he said the reason he didn't like him was because Mahler hadn't thanked him for preparing the chorus, so it was a very sad day in a way. And of course he wasn't French, and the French tended to stand together. Monteux was not a Mahler person, but I became one in spite of that.

I heard that you once described the Mahler symphonies as chapters of one huge novel.

Zinman: Yes, well it's a story that starts with this youthful idea of Jean Paul, the 'Titan', and so on. Each symphony takes elements from another one and transforms them. So the *2nd* deals with the idea of suddenly starting to struggle with these ideas: What does life mean? What are we given in life? Is there something after life? So the *2nd Symphony* is all about that, that there will be a resurrection after death. The *3rd Symphony* is about what nature and life give us, what flowers tell us, what love tells us, what God tells us, what children tell us, and all of these things. The *4th Symphony* is another view of trying to get to God, but perhaps through the eyes of a child. The *5th* is a less religious idea, but still contains the notion of death and conquering it; and then of course the *6th* is all about death, and the horrible idea that there is nothing after death, and essentially the fear of death. The *7th* to me is a bit about war, and meeting the prince of darkness and all of these things, and then going into the light. The *8th* is of course the apotheosis of Goethe's idea of the 'eternal feminine', approaching God that way. And *Das Lied von der Erde* [*The Song of the Earth*] is about moving towards eternity again, and finally, the *9th* is a farewell and departure and what life means: the beauty of life and the tragedy of life. And then the *10th* goes further still with these ideas; I think it's just another episode in the same story.

Where can you see Mahler's modernism?

Zinman: Well, you see it in Alban Berg immediately; you see how strongly he had been affected by, let's say Mahler's *9th Symphony*. Of course he was writing after Mahler's death, but the influence is tremendous because *Wozzeck* and *Lulu* could not have been written without Mahler's *9th*. Mahler's modernism is a way of thinking on various levels, it's very Freudian in the way that voices come and go, and ideas are sublimated, brought out, and layered – and this is what modern music does. It's very close to Ives in a certain way, when Ives tried to bring all of nature into an idea, and the same kind of banality occurs in Ives as occurs in Mahler. So in a way it's very reactionary music, but it's also very modern and forward-looking. Schönberg and Berg and Webern deeply appreciated what Mahler was doing.

There is this story that Mahler took Ives' 3rd Symphony back to Europe…

Zinman: I don't know if that's true, but I read that he saw a score of Ives' *3rd Symphony* at his publisher's, or maybe the *2nd Symphony*, I don't know. And maybe he brought it back because he wanted to play it with the New York Philharmonic in their next season, but he died. I don't think anyone can verify it.

Christian Thielemann recently said that you cannot educate an orchestra with Mahler's 1st Symphony.

Zinman: Why not? You can educate an orchestra with Brahms, and with Beethoven, and with Schubert, and with Mendelssohn, and with Bruckner – and Mahler, too. For us, playing *1st* to *10th* in order has been a tremendous education, and the orchestra has improved every time, and now they have a deep understanding of what they're doing and how to do it, and they know that they grasp how to do it. I don't understand what Thielemann means at all.

So Mahler gives an orchestra the chance to improve in terms of flexibility, balance…

Zinman: Yes. It's chamber music; they have to hear, they have to listen to what's going on. There is so much subtlety in it. He had a desperate need for clarity, and you can see in all of his versions of the *5th* that he was trying to make it work as far as balance is concerned. And you can see that even in the scores he hadn't played yet, in the *9th*, for instance, there is this obsessive idea of what balance is. And of course Berg got that from Mahler – he is even more obsessive with his instructions and in his ideas about layering sound, and so on.

That's a different view, but I also think it's a conductor's view. Some composers just leave things to the conductor and the orchestra; Mahler couldn't just leave it, and probably he was right in that.

Have you talked to people in New York who heard him conduct?

Zinman: I never spoke to them personally, but I have that record of people discussing him as a conductor, and his music: people from the New York Philharmonic who I assume are all dead now – but there is still that tradition in that orchestra of course. But when I first went to Holland, there were still some people in the Royal Concertgebouw Orchestra who had played with Mahler, and they had many Mengelberg scores. Mengelberg had annotated them with what Mahler said about this, and what Mahler said about that, and what this means, and so on. They still had the parts they had used with Mahler, and you could see the changes and additions that had been made.

I think it's very hard to talk about different versions because with the 9*th*, for instance, we don't know how perfect that is, and what he would have changed. There is one part which is just four harp notes, and in the old edition they are D A F-sharp A, and in the new edition it's D A D A. That change was probably there in his manuscript, but I think the F-sharp is better because the phrase rises through the octaves, but if you don't have that the first time, then it's not a sequence. So you have to make little judgements about that, and people fight about it, they quarrel about every little note in Mahler. I think it's a good thing because it focuses your mind on the detail – like talk of whether the order of sequence in the 6*th* is right or wrong: if you do it one way, you're wrong, if you do it another way, you're wrong, if you do two hammer blows, you're wrong, if you do three hammer blows, you're wrong. He actually considered having four hammer blows, but nobody talks about that. Many musicologists quarrel with one another over these things, and maybe this gives meaning to their lives. But people say to me, why did you do that? And I say, well, I had to make a choice one way or the other, and for one person that choice is wrong, and for another person that choice is right. It's quite hard in that way; we don't know some things, we don't know if Mahler always played the 6*th* *Symphony* with the Andante second because perhaps he thought it was too powerful to have *boom boom boom boom*. But then again, Alma wrote a letter saying it should be the other way around – but how believable is Alma? One always has to make the choice oneself.

Is it true that as a young man you had a picture ...

Zinman: Yes, it's very strange. I remember that in my bedroom there was an engraving over my bed that my mother had gotten from somewhere, and she had framed it and put it there. It was *The Huntsman's Funeral* by Jacques Callot, the one referred to in the *1st Symphony*. And I never knew that until I studied Mahler. She liked it because there were little rabbits playing instruments; she didn't know anything about Mahler.

What do you admire most about Mahler?

Zinman: He's uncompromising; he doesn't give in. He's not *geschmeidig* [pliable]; his is a personality that remains true to itself, always striving for purity and perfection. That's what I admire about it.

What did Mahler want?

Zinman: He wanted to be a great poet, and to be Beethoven in a way, to be a kind of super Beethoven. He wanted to describe all of life; he wanted his music to be a universe in itself.

(Zurich, 25/09/2009)

Conductors' biographies

Claudio Abbado, b. 1933 in Milan. Debut 1965, Salzburg Festival. Principal conductor, La Scala, 1980–1986. Music director, London Symphony Orchestra, 1983–1986. Music director, Vienna State Opera, 1986–1991. Founded *Wien modern*, 1988. Principal conductor, Berlin Philharmonic, 1989–2002. Artistic director, Lucerne Festival Orchestra, since 2003.

Daniel Barenboim, b. 1942 in Beunos Aires. Principal conductor, Orchestre de Paris, 1975. Principal conductor, Chicago Symphony Orchestra, 1991–2006. Artistic director and general music director, State Opera Unter den Linden, Berlin, since 1992. Founded West-Eastern Divan Orchestra with Edward Said, 1999. Music director, La Scala, Milan, since 2011.

Herbert Blomstedt, b. 1927 in Springfield, USA. Principal conductor, Saxony Staatskapelle, Dresden, 1975–1985. Music director, San Francisco Symphony Orchestra, 1985–1995. Principal conductor, Gewandhaus Orchestra, Leipzig, 1998–2005. Regular appearances with the Berlin Philharmonic, Concertgebouw Orkest and Bavarian Radio Symphony Orchestra, among others.

Pierre Boulez, b. 1925 in Montbrison (France). Principal conductor, BBC Symphony Orchestra, 1971–1975. Principal conductor, New York Philharmonic, 1971–1977. Founder and director, Ensemble intercontemporain (Paris) from 1976. Conductor, *Ring des Nibelungen*, Bayreuth, 1976–1980 (Patrice Chéreau, director). Regular appearances with Vienna and Berlin Philharmonic, Chicago Symphony Orchestra, Cleveland Orchestra, among others.

Riccardo Chailly, b. 1953 in Milan. Principal conductor, Berlin Radio Symphony Orchestra, 1982–1989. Principal conductor, Concertgebouw Orkest, 1988–2004. General music director, Leipzig Opera, 2005–2008. Principal conductor, Gewandhaus Orchestra, Leipzig, since 2005.

Christoph von Dohnányi, b. 1929 in Berlin. General music director, Lübeck, 1957. Principal conductor, West German Radio Orchestra, Cologne, 1964–1969. General music director, 1968, director, Frankfurt Opera, from 1972. General manager, Hamburg State Opera, 1977–1984. Principal conductor, Cleveland Orchestra, 1984–2002. Principal conductor, Orchestre de Paris, 1998–2000. Principal conductor, North German Radio Orchestra, 2004–2011.

Gustavo Dudamel, b. 1981 in Barquisimeto, Venezuela. Symbolic figure of a national educational programme, now a household term under the name *El Sistema*. First experiences as conductor with the Simón Bolívar Youth Orchestra. Principal conductor, Göteborg Symphony Orchestra, since 2007/2008. Principal conductor, Los Angeles Philharmonic Orchestra, since 2009.

Christoph Eschenbach, b. 1940 in Breslau (Poland). Director, Houston Symphony Orchestra 1988–1999. Music director, Ravinia Festival, 1995–2003. Principal conductor, North German Radio Symphony Orchestra, 1998–2004. Artistic director, Schleswig-Holstein Music Festival, 199–2002. Music director, Philadelphia Orchestra, 2003–2008. Music director, Orchestre de Paris, 2000–2010. Artistic director, National Symphony Orchestra, Washington, D.C., since 2010.

Daniele Gatti, b. 1961 in Milan. Music director, Accademia Nazionale di Santa Cecilia Orchestra, Rome, 1992–1997. Principal guest conductor, Royal Opera House, Covent Garden, 1994–1997. Music director, Royal Philharmonic Orchestra, 1996–2009. Music director, Bologna Opera House, Orchestra del Teatro Communale di Bologna, 1997-2007. Music director, Orchestre National de France since 2008. Principal conductor, Zurich Opera, since 2009.

Valery Gergiev, b. 1953 in Moscow. Director, Armenian State Orchestra, 1981–1985. Artistic director, Kirov Opera, 1988. Principal conductor, Rotterdam Philharmonic, 1995–2008. General manager, Mariyinsky Theatre, St. Petersburg, since 1996. Principal conductor, London Symphony Orchestra, since January 2007.

Michael Gielen, b. 1927 in Dresden. Music director, Stockholm Royal Opera, 1960–1965. Music director, Frankfurt Opera, 1977–1987. First conductor, BBC Symphony Orchestra, London, 1978–1981. Director, Cincinnati Symphony Orchestra, 1980–1986. Principal conductor, Southwest Radio Symphony Orchestra, Baden-Baden and Freiburg, 1986–1999.

Alan Gilbert, b. 1967 in New York. Assistant conductor under Christoph von Dohnányi, Cleveland Orchestra, 1995–1997. Principal conductor, Royal Philharmonic, Stockholm, 2000–2008. Music director, Santa Fe Opera, 2003–2006. First guest conductor, North German Radio Symphony Orchestra, since 2004. Principal conductor, New York Philharmonic, since 2009.

Bernard Haitink, born 1929 in Amsterdam. Principal conductor, Concertgebouw Orkest, 1961–1988. Principal conductor, London Philharmonic Orchestra, 1967–1979. Musical director, Glyndebourne Opera Festival, 1978–1988. Musical director, Royal Opera House, Covent Garden, 1987–1998. Principal conductor, Staatskapelle Dresden, 2002–2004. Appointed first conductor, Chicago Symphony Orchestra, 2006.

Manfred Honeck, b. 1958 in Nenzing (Austria). First *Kapellmeister*, Zurich Opera, 1991–1996. Music director, Norwegian National Opera, Oslo, 1997/1998. Principal conductor, Mid German Radio Symphony Orchestra, Leipzig, 1996–1999. Principal conductor, Swedish Radio Orchestra, Stockholm, 2000–2006. General Music Director, Stuttgart Opera, 2007–2011. First guest conductor, Czech Philharmonic, since 2008. Music director, Pittsburgh Symphony Orchestra, since 2008.

Mariss Jansons, b. 1943 in Riga (Latvia). Principal conductor, Oslo Philharmonic, 1979–2000. Principal conductor, Pittsburgh Symphony Orchestra, 1996–2004. Principal conductor, Bavarian Radio Symphony Orchestra, since 2003. Principal conductor, Concertgebouw Orkest, Amsterdam, since 2004.

Lorin Maazel, b. 1930 in Neuilly-sur-Seine (France). General music director, Deutsche Oper, Berlin, 1965–1971. Principal conductor, Cleveland Orchestra, 1972–1982. Music director, Vienna State Opera, 1982–1984. Principal conductor, Pittsburgh Symphony Orchestra, 1988–1996. Principal conductor, Bavarian Radio Symphony Orchestra, 1993–2002. Principal conductor, New York Philharmonic, 2002–2009. Principal conductor, Munich Philharmonic, as of 2012/2013.

Zubin Mehta, b. 1936 in Bombay. Music director, Los Angeles Philharmonic, 1962–1978. Principal conductor, Israel Philharmonic, 1977 (music director for life as of 1981). Principal conductor, New York Philharmonic, 1978–1991. Principal conductor, Maggio Musice, Florence, since 1985. General music director, Bavarian State Opera, 1998–2006. Regular appearances with the Berlin and Vienna Philharmonic, among others.

Ingo Metzmacher, b. 1957 in Hanover. General music director, Hamburg State Opera, 1997–2005. Principal conductor, Netherlands Opera, Amsterdam, 2005–2008. Principal conductor, German Symphony Orchestra Berlin, 2007–2010. Has conducted operas at the Salzburg Festival; *Al gran sole carico d'amore* (Luigi Nono, 2009), *Dionysos* (Wolfgang Rihm, 2010), *Die Soldaten* (Bernd Alois Zimmermann, 2012).

Kent Nagano, b. 1951 in Berkeley, California. Music director, Opéra National de Lyon, 1989–1998. Artistic director, German Symphony Orchestra, Berlin, 2000–2006. Music director, Hallé Orchestra, 1991–2000. General music director, Bavarian State Opera and music director, Orchestre symphonique de Montréal, since 2006.

Andris Nelsons, b. 1978 in Riga, Latvia. Principal conductor, Latvian National Opera, Riga, 2003. Principal conductor, Northwest German Radio Orchestra, Herford, 2006–2009. Principal conductor, City of Birmingham Symphony Orchestra, since 2008. Bayreuth debut with *Lohengrin* (Hans Neuenfels, director), 2010. Regular appearances with the Vienna and Berlin Philharmonic, Boston Symphony Orchestra and the Concertgebouw Orkest.

Jonathan Nott, b. 1962 in Solihull, England. Principal conductor, Lucerne Symphony Orchestra and Lucerne Theatre, 1997–2002. Principal conductor, Ensemble InterContemporain, 2000–2003. Principal conductor, Bamberg Symphony – Bavarian State Philharmonic, since 2000. Has toured Asia extensively with them (e.g. China, Japan).

Sakari Oramo, b. 1965 in Helsinki. First conducting appearance, Finnish Radio Symphony Orchestra, 1993. Principal conductor, City of Birmingham Symphony Orchestra, 1998–2008. Principal conductor and artistic director, Royal Swedish Symphony Orchestra, since 2008. Appointed principal conductor, BBC Symphony Orchestra, as of summer 2013. Debut with the Vienna Philharmonic February 2012.

Sir Antonio Pappano, b. 1959 in Epping (England). Assistant to Daniel Barenboim and Michael Gielen in Frankfurt. First conducted at Norske Opera, 1987; Music director, Théâtre de la Monnaie, Brussels, 1992–2002. Music director, Royal Opera, Covent Garden, since 2002. Principal conductor, Accademia Nazionale di Santa Cecilia Orchestra, Rome, since 2005.

Josep Pons, b. 1957 in Berguedà, Spain. Founded Llure Theatre Chamber Orchestra, 1985. Music director, Olympic Games, Barcelona, 1992. Principal conductor, Orquesta Ciudad de Grenada, 1994–2004. Principal conductor, National Orchestra of Spain, 2003–2012. Music director, Grand Teatro del Liceu, Barcelona, as of September 2012.

Sir Simon Rattle, b. 1955 in Liverpool. Youngest conductor at Glyndebourne Opera Festival, 1977. Principal conductor, City of Birmingham Symphony Orchestra, 1980–1998. Principal conductor, Berlin Philharmonic, since 2002. Artistic director, Baden-Baden Easter Festival. Regular appearances with the Vienna Philharmonic and the Orchestra of the Age of Enlightenment, among others.

Esa-Pekka Salonen, b. 1958 in Helsinki. First guest conductor, Philharmonia Orchestra, London, 1985–1994. Principal conductor, Swedish Radio Symphony Orchestra, 1985–1995. Artistic director, Baltic Sea Festival, Stockholm, since 2003. Principal conductor, Los Angeles Philharmonic, 1992–2009. Principal conductor, Philharmonia Orchestra, London, since 2008.

Michael Tilson Thomas, b. 1944 in Los Angeles. Winner of Koussevitzky Prize, Tanglewood, 1969. Principal conductor, Buffalo Symphony Orchestra, 1973–1979. Regular appearances with Boston Symphony Orchestra, London Symphony Orchestra, Los Angeles Philharmonic. Principal conductor, San Francisco Symphony Orchestra, since 1994.

Franz Welser-Möst, b. 1960 in Linz. Principal conductor, London Philharmonic Orchestra, 1990–1996. Music director, Zurich Opera, 1995–2002, general music director there 2005–2008. Principal conductor, Cleveland Orchestra, since 2002. General music director, Vienna State Opera, since 2010.

David Zinman, b. 1936 in New York. Assistant to Pierre Monteux in Maine, 1958–1963. Principal conductor, Rochester Philharmonic, 1974–1985. Principal conductor, Rotterdam Philharmonic, 1979–1982. Principal conductor, Baltimore Symphony Orchestra, 1985–1998. Principal conductor, Zurich Tonhalle Orchestra, since 1995.

Gustav Mahler (1860–1911)

1860	Born on 7 July, 2nd of 14 children, to Bernhard Mahler, Jewish merchant and his wife Marie in the Bohemian village of Kalischt (Kalist) near the Bohemian-Moravian border. Family moves in December to Iglau (Jihlava) in Moravia. Mahler evinces special musical talent even as a young child.
1866	First piano lessons
1870	First appearance as a pianist in Iglau
1870–75	Secondary school in Iglau and partially in Prague
1875–78	Student at Vienna Conservatoire. Fellow students include Hugo Wolf and Hans Rott. Encounter with Anton Bruckner. First compositions (incl. Piano Quartet)
1878–80	Writes and composes *Das klagende Lied*
1880	First engagement as conductor, summer theatre in Hall (Upper Austria)
1880–83	First *Lieder und Gesänge aus der Jugendzeit*
1881	Vienna Gesellschaft der Musikfreunde rejects *Das klagende Lied* for Beethoven Prize
1881–82	Conductor, Laibach (Ljubljana) Theatre
1883	Conductor, Olmütz Theatre – chorus master of an Italian opera troupe, Carltheater, Vienna – work on a *Northern Symphony* and the fairy-rale opera *Rübezahl*
1883–85	2nd conductor, Kassel Court Theatre – Lieder eines fahrenden Gesellen
1884–88	*Symphony No. 1* (world premiere 1889, Budapest)
1885–86	2nd conductor, Deutsches Landestheater, Prague
1886–88	2nd conductor (with Arthur Mikisch), Neues Stadttheater, Leipzig
1887	Arrangement of Weber's opera fragment *Die drei Pintos*
1886–90	First part of Lieder aus des Knaben Wunderhorn
1887–94	*Symphony No. 2* (world premiere 1895, Berlin)
1888–91	Director, Royal Hungarian Opera, Budapest
1888–92	2nd and 3rd volumes of *Lieder und Gesänge aus der Jugendzeit*
1888	Mahler's father dies
1889	Deaths of Mahler's mother and his sister Leopoldine
1891–97	First conductor, Stadttheater Hamburg. Meets Hans von Bülow, conducts the Hamburg Musikfreunde concerts after Bülow's death (1884). Acquaintance with Bruno Walter.

1892	Conductor of an opera season with German singers and German repertoire at Drury Lane Theatre, London
1892–98	Second part of Lieder from *Des Knaben Wunderhorn*
1893–96	Vacations at Attersee (Austria), works on his 2nd and 3rd symphonies in his "composing cottage"
1895–96	*Symphony No. 3* (world premiere 1902 in Krefeld)
1897	Conversion to Catholicism. Appointed conductor at Vienna Court Opera in May (debut: *Lohengrin*). Appointed Director in October.
1897–1907	Artistic Director, Vienna Court Opera: closest associates are Bruno Walter and stage designer Alfred Roller. Ensemble includes Anna von Mildenburg, Marie Gutheil-Schoder, Selma Kurz and Leo Slezak
1898–1901	Conductor, Vienna Philharmonic subscription concert series
1898	Reworking of *Das klagende Lied* (omitting *Waldmärchen*) premiered 1901 in Vienna
1899	Acquires a property in Maiernigg am Wörthersee
1899–1900	*Symphony No. 4* (world premiere Munich 1901)
1899–1902	*Sieben Lieder aus letzter Zeit*
1901–02	*Symphony No. 5* (world premiere Cologne 1904)
1901–04	*Kindertotenlieder* (world premiere Vienna 1905)
1902	(March) Marries Alma Maria Schindler (1879-1964) – children: Maria Anna (1902-07) and Anna Justina (1904-88)
1903–04	*Symphony No. 6* (world premiere Essen 1906)
1904–05	*Symphony No. 7* (world premiere Prague 1910)
1906–07	*Symphony No. 8* (world premiere Munich 1910 under Mahler's baton)
1907	Death of Mahler's daughter Maria Anna. Mahler diagnosed with severe heart disease.
1907–11	Tours in the U.S.A. conducing concerts and operas (Metropolitan Opera, Boston, Philadelphia, etc.), guest appearances throughout Europe: work during the summers at the composing cottage at Alt-Schluderbach bei Toblach (until 1910)
1908–09	*Das Lied von der Erde* (world premiere Munich 1911, Bruno Walter) *Symphony No. 9* (world premiere Vienna 1912, Bruno Walter)
1909–10	Arrangements of Bach suites, symphonies of Beethoven and Schumann: work on *Symphony No. 10* (world premiere of two movements arranged by Ernst Krenek Vienna 1924)
1910	Consultation with Sigmund Freud, Leiden
1911	Returns, ill, to Vienna from New York: dies in Vienna on 18 May of septic angina

Index of names

A

Abbado, Claudio **14ff.**, 65f., 79, 118, 236, 241
Adorno, Theodor W. 42, 46
Ameling, Elly 195
Arrau, Claudio 23
Ataúlfo Argenta 196, 249

B

Bach, Johann Sebastian 28, 31, 82, 104, 133, 136, 152, 161, 218, 248
Backhaus, Wilhelm 23
Barbirolli, Sir John 22, 24, 67, 133, 175, 191, 204f.
Barenboim, Daniel **20ff.**, 40, 43, 46, 69, 167f., 241, 245
Bartók, Béla 69, 86, 126, 181, 185
Beethoven, Ludwig van 7, 21f., 24f., 27f., 31, 33f., 65, 71ff., 79ff., 86, 90, 96, 98, 117, 121, 123, 126, 133, 152, 155f., 156, 172, 185, 192, 208f., 226, 231, 235f., 238, 240, 247f.
Behn, Hermann 9
Beinum, Eduard van 111
Benjamin Britten 136
Berg, Alban 41f., 44f., 54, 75f., 82f., 89, 95, 98, 107, 133, 147, 153, 185, 216f., 224, 238
Berio, Luciano 53
Berkan, Wilhelm 9
Berlioz, Hector 62, 216, 235
Bernstein, Leonard 8, 22ff., 27, 32, 39ff., 51, 67, 72ff., 85, 93, 95f., 105, 112, 118ff., 123, 127, 134, 142, 145f., 159, 167ff., 178, 191, 204, 221ff., 231

Birtwistle, Harrison 26
Blaukopf, Kurt 151
Blomstedt, Herbert **30ff.**, 241
Boskovsky, Willi 141
Boulez, Pierre 7, 25f., **38ff.**, 81f., 102, 105, 154, 167, 218, 236, 241
Brahms, Johannes 22, 25, 31, 72, 82f., 117, 123, 127, 143, 147, 153, 170f., 182, 209, 217, 238
Bruckner, Anton 8f., 15, 22, 25, 31, 33ff., 45, 74f., 109, 112ff., 117, 119f., 123, 127, 162, 170, 190, 204, 209, 213, 217, 231, 233, 238, 247, 249
Bülow, Hans von 86, 247
Busoni, Ferruccio 58, 155, 249

C

Callot, Jacques 142, 240
Cardus, Neville 204
Carter, Elliott 26
Celibidache, Sergiu 63
Chailly, Riccardo **48ff.**, 241
Chopin, Frédéric 21, 42, 79
Cooke, Deryck 113

D

Debussy, Claude 23, 44f., 86, 185, 196, 205, 209, 217, 226, 249
DeMille, Cecil B. 197
Dillon, James 217
Dobrowen, Issay 31
Dohnányi, Christoph von **56ff.**, 242f.
Dostoyevsky, Fyodor 98

249

Dreyfus, Alfred 44
Dudamel, Gustavo **64ff.**, 242
Durand, Auguste 217
Dvořák, Antonín 24

E
Einstein, Alfred 7
Eisler, Hanns 44
Elgar, Edward 205, 208
Eschenbach, Christoph **70ff.**, 242

F
Fellini, Federico 223
Ferneyhough, Brian 217
Ferrier, Kathleen 15, 221
Fischer-Dieskau, Dietrich 21, 25
Fischer, Edwin 23
Fournier-Facio, Gastón 55
Freud, Sigmund 21, 72, 189, 238, 248
Fried, Oskar 51
Furtwängler, Wilhelm 22, 24, 29, 97f., 146

G
Gatti, Daniele **78ff.**, 242
Gergiev, Valery **84ff.**, 208, 242
Gielen, Michael **92ff.**, 191, 243, 245
Gieseking, Walter 23
Gilbert, Alan **100ff.**, 243
Giulini, Carlo Maria 15, 27, 147
Goethe, Johann Wolfgang von 37, 201, 237
Goldschmidt, Berthold 203, 206
Gropius, Walter 144
Groves, Sir Charles 203
Gründgens, Gustaf 71
Gutheil-Schoder, Marie 248

H
Haitink, Bernard 50, **108ff.**, 167, 171, 195, 218, 235, 243
Halban, Désirée von 141
Harnoncourt, Nikolaus 207
Hartmann, Karl Amadeus 153
Haussmann, Georges-Eugène 161
Haydn, Joseph 22, 31, 88, 94, 117, 119, 143, 192, 196, 207, 209
Heifetz, Jascha 27
Henze, Hans Werner 153
Hertzka, Emil 10f.
Hindemith, Paul 58, 86, 207
Hitler, Adolf 27, 29, 44, 71, 89
Honeck, Manfred **116ff.**, 243
Horenstein, Jascha 24, 235f.

I
Ives, Charles 47, 99, 151f., 162, 205, 226, 238

J
Janáček, Leoš 207
Jansons, Mariss **124ff.**, 167f., 243
Järnefelt, Armas 181

K
Karajan, Herbert von 22, 85, 114, 117, 143, 146, 168, 204, 231, 236
Keilberth, Joseph 146
Kempff, Wilhelm 23
Kleiber, Erich 86, 111
Klemperer, Otto 23f., 27f., 51, 80, 86, 88, 96, 146, 183, 236
Kletzki, Paul 24, 39, 93
Klimt, Gustav 147
Knappertsbusch, Hans 146
Kokoschka, Oskar 144

Kolisch, Rudolf 60
Kondrashin, Kirill 85, 125
Krenek, Ernst 248
Krips, Josef 141
Kubelík, Rafael 24, 80, 85, 111, 123
Kullmann, Charles 109
Kurz, Selma 248

L

La Grange, Henry-Louis de 165
Leinsdorf, Erich 85, 102
Levine, James 102
Lott, Felicity 205, 229

M

Maazel, Lorin 105, 118, **132ff.**, 244
Mahler, Alma 12, 46, 52, 67, 81, 94f., 98, 139, 144f., 147, 149, 170, 176, 239, 248
Mahler, Anna Justina 126, 144f., 145, 248
Mahler, Bernhard 247
Mahler, Leopoldine 247
Mahler, Marina 145
Mehta, Zubin 7, 41, 49, 85, **140ff.**, 244
Mendelssohn Bartholdy, Felix 97, 146, 238
Mengelberg, Willem 50ff., 66, 73, 86, 109ff., 183, 239
Mertin, Josef 127
Messiaen, Olivier 47
Metzmacher, Ingo **150ff.**, 244
Michelangeli, Arturo Benedetti 23
Mildenburg, Anna von 126
Mitropoulos, Dimitri 40, 93, 235f.
Monteux, Pierre 237, 246

Mozart, Wolfgang Amadeus 15, 22, 29, 31, 65, 79f., 90, 117, 121, 127, 133, 136, 149, 192, 209, 231
Mravinsky, Yevgeny 85, 127, 130
Mussolini, Benito 27
Mussorgsky, Modest 44

N

Nagano, Kent **158ff.**, 244
Napoleon 27
Nelsons, Andris **166ff.**, 244
Neruda, Pablo 68
Nielsen, Carl 182, 184
Nietzsche, Friedrich 44, 192
Nikisch, Arthur 86
Nono, Luigi 152ff., 244
Norman, Jessye 235
Nostradamus 129
Nott, Jonathan **174ff.**, 245

O

Oramo, Sakari **180ff.**, 245
Österreicher, Karl 127, 229
Ozawa, Seiji 49, 159

P

Palestrina, Giovanni Pierluigi da 224
Panula, Jorma 181, 213
Pappano, Sir Antonio **188ff.**, 245
Patzak, Julius 93
Paul, Jean 237
Polnauer, Josef 94
Poltun, Peter 209
Pons, Josep **194ff.**, 245
Prawy, Marcel 90
Pré, Jacqueline du 27, 67
Proust, Marcel 63
Puccini, Giacomo 52f., 171

R

Rabinovich, Nicolai 125, 127
Rachmaninoff, Sergei 148, 169, 185, 205
Rattle, Simon 167f., **202ff.**, 245
Ratz, Erwin 11, 93f.
Ravel, Maurice 44, 196, 209
Rendall, David 205
Richter, Hans 86
Rihm, Wolfgang 153, 244
Rimsky-Korsakov, Nikolai Andreyevich 86
Roller, Alfred 232, 248
Rosbaud, Hans 39, 111
Rossini, Gioachino 51, 79
Rostropovich, Slawa [Mstislav] 125
Rott, Hans 247
Rudolph, Ernst 12
Rühm, Otto 141

S

Salonen, Esa-Pekka **212ff.**, 245
Schlingensief, Christoph 23
Schnabel, Arthur 23
Schnéevoigt, Georg 181
Schönberg. Arnold 8, 22, 37, 42ff., 52, 54, 75, 86, 89, 95, 98f., 107, 136, 144, 147, 153, 155, 185, 187, 217, 238
Schönberg, Mathilde 144
Schopenhauer, Arthur 60
Schubert, Franz 71, 74, 117, 119, 123, 152, 156, 231, 238
Schultz, Klaus 62
Schumann, Robert 22, 25, 74, 98, 117, 156, 209, 248
Schwarzkopf, Elisabeth 143
Shostakovich, Dmitri 45, 71, 74, 87, 89, 125f., 129f., 172, 187

Sibelius, Jean 31f., 37, 136, 182ff.
Sinopoli, Giuseppe 191
Slezak, Leo 248
Sollertinsky, Ivan 86
Solti, Sir Georg 41, 85, 229, 235
Stalin, Joseph 29, 89, 125, 129
Steinberg, William 146
Steuermann, Eduard 93
Strauß, Johann 118f., 122
Strauss, Richard 45f., 53, 58, 77, 86, 118f., 122, 138, 204, 207, 210
Stravinsky, Igor 37, 44, 79, 86, 138, 185, 196, 198f., 216
Strindberg, August 98, 215
Stritzko, Josef 10
Swarowsky, Hans 16, 127, 146ff.
Szell, George 237

T

Tarkovsky, Andrei Arsenyevich 223
Tawaststjerna, Erik W. 184
Tchaikovsky, Pyotr Ilyich 7, 80, 86, 90, 128, 185, 206
Tennstedt, Klaus 85, 183
Thielemann, Christian 63, 238, 249
Thorborg, Kerstin 109
Tilson Thomas, Michael 213, **220ff.**, 246
Tolstoy, Leo 130
Toscanini, Arturo 27, 80, 98, 103

V

Varèse, Edgar 47

W

Wagner, Richard 8, 22, 35, 41, 44, 45, 61, 80, 86, 90, 97, 103, 122, 137, 148, 169, 190, 196, 200, 205f., 210, 231

Walter, Bruno 23f., 40, 50, 73, 79,
    86, 93, 96, 109, 111, 133, 141ff., 146,
    148, 159f., 168, 183, 203, 211, 221f.,
    231, 235f., 247f.
Wand, Günter 63
Warren-Green, Christopher 205
Webern, Anton 42, 81, 89, 98, 107,
    133, 147, 153, 187, 196, 200, 217,
    238
Weinberger, Josef 9, 11
Welser-Möst, Franz **228ff.**, 246
Werfel, Franz 12, 144
Whitman, Walt 226
Wolf, Hugo 247
Wöss, Josef Venantius von 11

Z
Zaun, Fritz 142
Zemlinsky, Alexander von 86, 147
Zinman, David **234ff.**, 246

Gustav Mahler
(1860–1911)

Study Scores
www.universaledition.com/studyscores

"I make every concession from a human perspective, but none at all as an artist; if you are afraid of losing, then you have already lost."

Gustav Mahler

Conductors' Scores
www.universaledition.com/conductors-scores